BACK to the FUTURE
END TIMES PROPHECY, FROM GENESIS TO REVELATION

Patti Malpass

Back to the Future
End Times Prophecy, from Genesis to Revelation
©2012 Patti W. Malpass
Revised 2016

Published by
CreateSpace, a DBA of On-Demand Publishing, LLC.

Cover design by Michal Rudolph
Michal Rudolph Designs

ALL RIGHTS RESERVED.
No part of this publication may be
reproduced, stored in a retrieval system,
or transmitted, in any form or by any
means – electronic, mechanical,
photocopying, recording or otherwise –
without prior written permission.

Additional copies can be ordered online at Amazon.com
Requests for information should be addressed to:
Patti Malpass
btf.endtimes@gmail.com

Scripture references are primarily from the
New American Standard Bible.

Consideration has been made
to footnote sources whenever necessary.
In the case of any unintentional omission,
future editions will include appropriate notations.

PREFACE

I first remember seeing a chart of end times in a Bible Study Fellowship lecture sometime around 1985. Fascinated, I began reading both scriptures and books related to prophecy. I taught my first class on end times around 1999. It was a lecture-formatted class taken by high school students in the youth group at Colonial Baptist Church. After teaching it several times, I approached my dear friend Anne Winters about co-developing a Bible Study that we would teach as part of Colonial's Women's Ministry. She, too, had become very interested in the subject of prophecy.

Over the course of a summer, we created a 7-lesson study, called Until the Day Dawns, which we taught two different times as a semester class. The material was very well received by the ladies, but the feedback indicated that it was too much information to comprehend in such a short time. Our Bible Studies director, Gwen Brodd, who is also a dear friend, asked me if we would consider teaching the study as a year-long class!

About that time, Anne's oldest daughter, Kristi, received the terrible news that she had breast cancer. Kristi was eight months pregnant with her third son. She fought valiantly, but died four months after giving birth. Needless to say, it was a very hard time for everyone, during which Anne was a faithful and loving mom and grandmother. The family was also a faithful witness to the community during this time. Kristi's funeral was a worship and praise service to God, as we celebrated Kristi's earthly and eternal life. Many hearts were touched, and several people were added to the kingdom as a result.

I tell you this to explain why I took over the writing, expanding the study to be an eighteen-week class. This took me about a year, as prior lessons were expanded and new lessons were added. Back to the Future - End *Times Prophecy from Genesis to Revelation* is the result of that effort. To God be the glory!

It is my desire that this study will impact your life greatly as we wait for the return of our Lord and Savior, Jesus Christ. I pray first of all that you will realize the certainty of your future. As a Christian, we can rest in the troubled times of today, knowing that we will escape the trials of the Tribulation and that we will spend eternity in the Presence of God and in fellowship with His Son.

It is clear, however that the unbeliever alive at the time of the Rapture will undergo the terror of the Tribulation, and that ultimately, unbelievers from all of history will be experience eternal punishment in the Lake of Fire. Realizing the certainty of the unbeliever's future should cause us to increase our efforts to witness to friends, family, and those with whom we come into contact. We should make every effort to allow God's Truth to "snatch" them out of the grips of Satan.

In closing, I would like to give you some advice. Do not be discouraged when you feel overwhelmed with all the information. We cannot possibly understand every detail of prophecy. Our finite mind cannot grasp all of our infinite God's love and plans. Also, do not expect to understand or remember everything on your first pass - or even your second! Every time I have rewritten a section or teach the class, I learn something more. One day we will see perfectly, but for now, simply allow the Holy Spirit to enlighten and teach you through God's Holy Word. Another thing I have learned is that, while some areas of prophecy are crystal clear, there are other areas on which we cannot be dogmatic. Many devout and intelligent scholars, who have studied God's word much longer than we have, interpret some passages of scripture differently. Ultimately we have to rest in God's Sovereignty and His love, knowing that whatever happens, we serve a mighty God who is just and righteous and holy and true. Our Heavenly Father will lovingly take care of us beyond our wildest dreams.

I pray nothing but blessing for you as you join me in going "*Back to the Future!*"

In His grip,

Patti H. Malpass

ACKNOWLEDGMENTS

All praise and thanks and honor and glory go to the God my Father and to Jesus Christ, my Savior and my Lord. Thank you for creating me, redeeming me from the power of sin, and setting me free from the penalty of death. Thank you for giving me Your Holy Spirit, Who teaches, convicts, and guides me in Your Truth. Thank you for your sanctifying work in my life. I can't wait to spend eternity in Your Presence.

I am forever indebted to my dear family, friends, and colleagues who have prayed for me and guided me as this study has unfolded over the past 12 some years.

First and foremost, I wish to thank my wonderful husband, Mike, who patiently watched me research and type on my computer morning, noon, and night - both at home and on vacations. He also answered my *many* questions from, "What time is it?" to "What do you think this verse means?" Mike has been my best friend during our thirty two years of marriage. He has faithfully been the spiritual leader of our family.

I also wish to thank my two daughters and their husbands, Allison and Seth Lynch and Kristen and Nate Ennis, my son, David, and my mom, Mrs. Myrtle Westmoreland, who all encouraged me greatly. Their constant love and support gives me great joy and strength.

This project could not have been started or completed without Anne Winters, my dear and longtime friend. She contributed research and writing to the original seven lessons that we first taught as a Women's Bible Study. Anne was the one who encouraged me to attend my first Bible study years ago. Her love for the Lord, through the good as well as the hard times has been an example and an inspiration to me.

During the writing process, there were "spiritual giants" whom I turned to for doctrinal teaching and understanding: Dr. John Milheim, *former Dean of Shepherd's Theological Seminary* and Dr. Doug Bookman, *Director of Student Recruitment and Professor of New Testament at Shepherd's Theological Seminary* were both gracious to meet with me and discuss some of the more challenging passages of scripture. Rev. Mark Robinson, *Director of Jewish Awareness Ministries,* also answered many of my questions and gave me tremendous insight into many of the Old Testament scriptures. I am so grateful for each of these men.

I also wish to express my gratitude to Dr. Stephen Davey, pastor Colonial Baptist Church, Cary, NC, my pastor for twenty-four years. As God would have it, Stephen preached an entire series on the book of Revelation during the time I was writing this study. I sat on the edge of my seat for two years as he expounded the Scriptures, making sure my writing was consistent with his teaching.

A special thank you goes to Linda Walters, someone who has become a good friend during the last year. Linda very graciously volunteered to edit the entire eighteen lessons at no charge. She spent many hours combing through the text and marking it with her colored pens. Her humble, loving, and giving spirit truly reflects the love of Christ.

I would also like to mention Michal Rudolph, whom I have known since she was in our high-school youth group years ago, who designed the cover for this study. How delighted I was to be able to work with someone who is so dear to me.

I would be amiss not to mention the many other friends and family members who have prayed for me during these years of research and writing. Thank you for diligently lifting me up and taking me before the Throne of Grace. Through your prayers, I have received the strength and confidence to keep on "keeping on."

Back to the Future
End Times Prophecy, from Genesis to Revelation
Table of Contents

Lesson 1 — Why Study Prophecy?
- Day 1 — God Considers It *Important*
- Day 2 — Prophecy Reveals the Lord in *His Exalted State*
- Day 3 — Prophecy Enables Us to *Recognize the Times*
- Day 4 — Prophecy Gives Us an *Eternal Perspective*
- Day 5 — Prophecy Gives Hope, *Purifies the Believer*

Lesson 2 — Jesus, The Promised Messiah
- Day 1 — The Messiah Promised
- Day 2 — The "Godly Seed" from Adam to Abraham
- Day 3 — The "Godly Seed" from Abraham to the King David
- Day 4 — Jesus - Heir to the Throne of David
- Day 5 — Jesus' Family Tree

Lesson 3 — Israel and Her Promises
- Day 1 — The Abrahamic Covenant - Part I
- Day 2 — The Abrahamic Covenant - Part II
- Day 3 — The Land Covenant - *amplifies the "land" promises*
- Day 4 — The Davidic Covenant - *amplifies "seed" promises*
- Day 5 — The New Covenant - *amplifies "blessing" promises*

Lesson 4 — Israel: Her Fate and Her Future
- Day 1 — The Kingdom Divided and Exiled
- Day 2 — God's Revelation of the Future - The Gentile Program
- Day 3 — God's Revelation of the Future - Program for Israel
- Days 4 & 5 — Review of Lessons 2 - 4

Lesson 5 — The Church
- Day 1 — Anticipation of the Church
- Day 2 — Beginnings of the Church
- Day 3 — Destiny of the Church
- Day 4 — New Covenant of the Church
- Day 5 — Distinctions of the Church

Lesson 6 — The Rapture
- Day 1 — Christ's Second Coming
- Day 2 — Christ's Return for the Church
- Day 3 — The Glorified Body - Equipped for Eternity
- Day 4 — The Rapture is Next!
- Day 5 — The Rapture is Imminent!

Lesson 7 — The Judgment Seat of Christ
- Day 1 — What is the Judgment Seat of Christ?
- Day 2 — Paul's Three Analogies of the Judgment Seat of Christ
- Day 3 — What Will Be Judged?
- Days 4 & 5 — Rewards Given

Lesson 8 — Jesus' Letters to the Seven Churches
- Day 1 — The Revelation of Jesus Christ
- Day 2 — The Churches at Ephesus and Smyrna
- Day 3 — The Church at Pergamum
- Day 4 — The Churches at Thyatira and Sardis
- Day 5 — Philadelphia & Laodicea

Lesson 9 — This Present Age
- Day 1 — The Inferred Gap between Christ's 1st and 2nd Comings
- Day 2 — The Mystery Kingdom - During this Age
- Day 3 — Revealed Mysteries - Character of This Age
- Day 4 — Kingdom Parables - Course of This Age
- Day 5 — Increased Apostasy Marks the End of the Age (Jude)

Back to the Future
End Times Prophecy, from Genesis to Revelation
Table of Contents

Lesson 10 — Tribulation: Introduction
- Day 1   God's Divine Plan: The Tribulation
- Day 2   Purposes of the Tribulation
- Day 3   The Timing for the Tribulation
- Day 4   Scene in Heaven - Part I
- Day 5   Scene in Heaven - Part II

Lesson 11 — Tribulation: Six Seals
- Day 1   The First Seal
- Day 2   Seals Two, Three, and Four
- Day 3   The Seals Continue
- Day 4   The 144,000
- Day 5   The Great Multitude (*Tribulation Saints*)

Lesson 12 — Tribulation: First Half
- Day 1   The Antichrist
- Day 2   Religion during the 1st Half
- Day 3   The Fate of the Harlot
- Day 4   Gog / Magog
- Day 5   As the First Half Comes to a Close

Lesson 13 — Tribulation: 7 trumpets / 7 thunders
- Day 1   The Seventh Seal Begins the Seven Trumpet Judgments
- Day 2   First Four Trumpet Judgments
- Day 3   Fifth Trumpet Judgment - The First Woe
- Day 4   Sixth Trumpet Judgment - The Second Woe
- Day 5   Seven Thunders; Seventh Trumpet

Lesson 14 — Tribulation: Second Half Evil
- Day 1   The Woman, the Dragon, and the Son
- Day 2   Another War in Heaven
- Day 3   Woman Persecuted by Dragon, Protected by God
- Day 4   Beast out of the Sea
- Day 5   Beast out of the Earth

Lesson 15 — Tribulation: Last Days
- Day 1   God's Special Witnesses at the End
- Day 2   Three Angels and a Voice from Heaven
- Day 3   Final Reaping on Earth; Three More Angels
- Day 4   The Seven Bowl Judgments
- Day 5   Political, Commercial Babylon Destroyed

Lesson 16 — The Return of Christ
- Day 1   Concurrent Scenes on Earth and Heaven
- Day 2   National Salvation of Israel
- Day 3   Christ's Glorious Appearing, Return to Earth
- Day 4   Earth's Armies Destroyed by Christ
- Day 5   Events Associated with Christ's Return

Lesson 17 — The Millennial Kingdom: Christ's Reign on Earth
- Day 1   Introduction to the Kingdom
- Day 2   Government during the Kingdom
- Day 3   Changes during the Kingdom
- Day 4   Spiritual Life during the Kingdom
- Day 5   King of the Kingdom

Lesson 18 — Eternity
- Day 1   At the Close of the Millennium
- Day 2   New Heavens and Earth
- Day 3   Descent of the New Jerusalem
- Day 4   Life in the Eternal City
- Day 5   We've Come Full Circle - Now What?

Charts and Appendices

"Back to the Future"
End Times Prophecy, from Genesis to Revelation
Lesson 1 – Why Study Prophecy?

*** DAY 1: God Considers It *Important*

1. Using a dictionary, state the meaning of "eschatology"?

2. Looking at Revelation 1:3 and 22:7, answer the following:
   a. How does God describe those who study Biblical prophecy concerning the end times?

   b. What must we do with what we learn, and why?

3. What two warnings concerning prophecy does God give in Rev. 22:18-21?

4. What promise is found in II Timothy 4:8 for those who "long for His appearing"?

5. Read II Peter 1:19-21 and answer the following:
   a. What does Peter say would be well for us to do?

   b. To what does Peter liken prophecy?

   c. To where does "dark place'" refer (Eph. 6:12)?

   d. When will "that day" be (Luke 1:78; Eph. 5:14; Mal. 4:2)?

   e. Who is the "Morning Star" (Rev. 22:16)?

   f. Where does prophecy *not* come from?

   g. What is its origin (also II Tim. 3:16; II Sam. 23:2)?

ON A PERSONAL NOTE . . .
- Read John 14:29 and Amos 3:7. For what reasons do you think God chooses to reveal His plans to us?

- Why do you want to learn more about God's plans? Is there a particular area of prophecy that you wish to learn more about, and why?

- How can knowing prophecy bring light to your life?

"Back to the Future"
End Times Prophecy, from Genesis to Revelation
Lesson 1 – Why Study Prophecy?

REVIEW:

The word "eschatology" comes from the Greek words *eschatos* ("last things") and *logia* ("discourse"). Eschatology refers to the doctrine of the last or final things. For a Christian, this doctrine is based solely upon the Scriptures and includes topics such as life after death, the Rapture and Judgment Seat of Christ, the Marriage Supper of the Lamb, the Tribulation, the second coming of Christ, the Millennial Kingdom, the End of the World, the resurrection of the dead, the Great White Throne Judgment, Heaven, Hell, and the renewal of creation for eternity.

God never leaves His servants in darkness as to His plans and His work. Amos 3:7 says, "Surely the Sovereign LORD does nothing without revealing His plan to His servants the prophets." Over one-third of the Bible is either directly or indirectly related to prophecy, containing over 10,000 prophecies. God obviously thinks it is important for us to study prophecy.

Over 300 prophecies concerning the Messiah were fulfilled by Jesus when He came to earth the first time. Josh McDowell says that if you just took eight of these prophecies, the odds of a person coincidentally fulfilling all eight would be one in ten to the 17th power (1×10^{17}). To help us picture what this means, he gives this illustration: "Suppose you took the state of Texas and spread silver dollars two feet deep across the whole state, then marked just one of them and buried it somewhere in the state. Then, if you chose one person, blindfolded him, and told him to pick just one silver dollar, his chances of getting the marked one on his first try would be one in ten to the 17th power!" (Josh McDowell, *Evidence That Demands a Verdict*, Vol. 1, pp. 144, 167)

Fulfilled prophecy is one of the most powerful proofs that the Bible truly is the Word of God. Because no human author could be 100% accurate and all of the prophecies of Christ's first coming were fulfilled to the smallest detail, we can be confident that the Bible itself is God's revelation to man (2 Peter 1:21). We can also be confident that what God reveals to us concerning the last days will also be fulfilled to the minutest detail. Jesus himself, referring to prophecy, said in Mt. 5:17-18, "I tell you the truth, until heaven and earth disappear, not the smallest letter, not the least stroke of a pen, will by any means disappear from the Law until everything is accomplished."

God promises that we who study prophecy and "take it to heart" will be blessed (Rev. 1:3), but warns that we must be careful not to add to or take away anything from His words (Rev. 22:18). II Timothy 4:8 promises a Crown of Righteousness to all who have longed for His appearing.

In II Peter 1:19-21, we are told to "pay attention to the words of the prophets, as a light shining in a dark place." God's prophetic Word is like an oil-burning lamp (Ps.119:105) shining in today's darkened world (Eph. 6:12). But when the day dawns (Rom. 13:12) and Jesus Christ returns, we will have the true Light to illumine our hearts forever. (Walvoord and Zuck, *The Bible Knowledge Commentary*, New Testament Edition, pp. 868-869)

As we study, remember that Jesus Christ is the unifying theme of the entire Bible:

The Old Testament proclaims, *"Jesus is coming!"*
In Jesus' time, the message was, *"Jesus is come!"*
And both the Old and New Testament shout, *"Jesus is coming again!"*

"Back to the Future"
End Times Prophecy, from Genesis to Revelation
Lesson 1 – Why Study Prophecy?

*** DAY 2: Prophecy Reveals the Lord in *His Exalted State*

1. Read Ephesians 1:20-23 and Philippians 2:9-11.
   a. Where is Jesus now?

   b. What is His position at this time? What name has He been given?

   c. What is the current relationship between Christ and the Church?

   d. What will everyone someday do?

2. Read Revelation 5:1-14.
   a. Describe the scene. In John's glimpse of God's throne room, where is Jesus?

   b. What two names are attributed to Jesus?

   c. What is the main praise of the four living creatures and the 24 elders?

   d. What do the many angels ascribe to Jesus? Who else joins them?

   e. What is the response of the four living creatures; of the elders?

3. Look at Revelation 17:14 and 19:16.
   a. What title is given to Jesus?

   b. What does *kurios*, the Greek word for Lord, mean?

4. Read Revelation 20:4-6 and Zechariah 9:10.
   a. When Jesus returns, what will be the scope of His Kingdom on earth?

   b. How long will His Kingdom on this earth last?

5. Looking at Revelation 22:3, who will rule from the throne (singular) of the new heaven and new earth?

ON A PERSONAL NOTE . . .
- Who is Jesus in your life?

- Has there been a point in your life when you have confessed Jesus as your Lord and Savior? Describe that time.

"Back to the Future"
End Times Prophecy, from Genesis to Revelation
Lesson 1 – Why Study Prophecy?

- Where is Jesus in the throne room of your heart? What *someone* or *something* is pushing Him aside? What *rearranging* do you need to do?

- Write your own "song of praise" to Him now.

- Prayerfully identify areas of your life that need to be brought under Christ's rule and Lordship. What is keeping you from placing them at His feet? What changes do you need to make in these areas?

"Back to the Future"
End Times Prophecy, from Genesis to Revelation
Lesson 1 – Why Study Prophecy?

REVIEW:

Jesus is no longer the Babe in the manger. He is no longer the Suffering Servant. He is no longer on the cross. He is no longer in the grave. Having overcome sin and death, the Risen Messiah presents Himself as sinful man's way back into a restored relationship with God forever. He is the Savior of the World, that "whosoever believes in Him shall not perish but have everlasting life" (John 3:16). And for those of us who have confessed Jesus Christ as our Lord and Savior, He is the King and Master of our lives. If you have not taken this important step, do not continue with this study until you refer to the Appendix One: *The Best Decision of Your Life*.

Currently Jesus is seated in heaven at the right hand of God the Father, far above "all rule and authority, power and dominion" (Eph. 1:21) – both now and forever. God has given Him a name that is above all names, and all Creation has been placed under His feet. Furthermore, Christ is the appointed head over the Church, the fellowship of believers. The Bible promises that one day everyone in heaven and on earth and under the earth will bow and every tongue will confess that Jesus Christ is Lord (Phil. 2:9-11).

Jesus now rules in the hearts of believers. At His second coming, Jesus will return with His own to rule over the entire world for a thousand years. Ultimately He will reign with God the Father in the new heaven and earth for all eternity.

This week we have seen Christ presented as the *Lion of the tribe of Judah* and as the *Root of David*. In Revelation 5, He is seen as the One who is worthy to take the scroll and open its seals. Christ alone is worthy to receive all power, wealth, wisdom, and strength. All honor, glory, and praise are His. He is being worshiped in Heaven by everything and in every way. May we join them in worshipping Jesus Christ as King of kings and Lord of lords!

"Back to the Future"
End Times Prophecy, from Genesis to Revelation
Lesson 1 – Why Study Prophecy?

*** DAY 3: Prophecy Enables Us to *Recognize the Times*

1. What is the correlation between prophecy and Christ?
   Rev. 19:10

   John 1:45

   Luke 24:27

2. Looking at Acts 3:17-18 and 13:27-29, answer the following:
   a. Why did the people of Jesus' time not recognize Him?

   b. How were their actions a fulfillment of prophecy?

3. What were the consequences of their ignorance?
   Luke 19:44

   Mt. 21:42-44

   Acts 13:44-48

4. In Mt. 24:4-6, knowing the signs of the end times will prevent us from what? See also II Thessalonians 2:1-3.

5. In Mt. 24:30-33, what does the lesson of the fig tree teach us?

6. What two things does Jesus urge us to do in Mt. 24:42-44?

ON A PERSONAL NOTE . . .
- Can you think of a time when knowing what God says about the future kept you from being deceived or fearful?

- What are some of the deceptions Satan is using today to mislead people about the end times?

- From what you know of prophecy, what are some of the signs you see today that indicate Jesus' return is near?

- Doctors often will tell a dying patient to "get their affairs in order." What does God want you to do to "be ready" for Jesus' return?

"Back to the Future"
End Times Prophecy, from Genesis to Revelation
Lesson 1 – Why Study Prophecy?

REVIEW:

Jesus came to earth the first time presenting Himself as the Messiah and offering the Jews the Kingdom of God. If the people of Jesus' day had been attentive to the Scriptures, they could have recognized who Jesus was, since He fulfilled the many OT prophecies concerning the Messiah. John the Baptist heralded Jesus as the Messiah. Jesus claimed to be King, His miracles proved His authority to be King, and His teaching presented the Kingdom of heaven to the nation of Israel. Had they responded in faith, Jesus could have set up His kingdom on earth at that time.

The nation's rejection of Jesus as their King resulted in postponement, from the human standpoint, of Christ's physical rule over Israel and all the earth. The offer of the Kingdom was withdrawn until the time of a future "generation," who will turn in saving faith to their Messiah. Furthermore, the Jews' rejection of Christ resulted in the presentation of the Gospel to the gentiles. While the "rejected king" is back in heaven, a different form of the kingdom is in effect. Jesus our King is spiritually reigning in the hearts of believers during the Church Age. The Church is now God's instrument in holding out the offer of salvation.

How sad it would be to live at a time when God is doing a special work and miss it because of ignorance of His Word. God's Word gives us many signs of Jesus' Second Coming, when He will overcome His enemies and set up His Kingdom on earth for 1000 years. In particular, Matthew 24:4-14 gives general signs, events, and situations which will occur with growing intensity as the end of the age approaches.

While the parable of the fig tree in Matthew 24:32-33 specifically relates to those at the end of the age looking for the Second Coming of Christ, this passage has a general application for those of us in the Church who are awaiting the Rapture. As the birth pains of God's fearful judgment intensify, many will become frightened, discouraged, and hopeless. But knowing that these signs mean Jesus' return is "near, right at the door," we can be encouraged, confident, and hopeful as we joyfully ready ourselves and watch for His return.

"Back to the Future"
End Times Prophecy, from Genesis to Revelation
Lesson 1 – Why Study Prophecy?

*** DAY 4: Prophecy Gives Us an *Eternal Perspective*

Let's take a look at WHY we should have an eternal perspective by reading the following verses and filling in the blanks.

1. God is _____. (Deut. 32:40; Isa. 26:4; Rev. 1:8, 4:9-10, 10:6, 15:7)

    His _____ is eternal. (Ps. 119:89, 144, 52)

    His _____ is eternal. (Rom. 1:20)

    His _____ is eternal. (Jer. 31:3, Ps. 118:1-4)

    His _____ are eternal. (Ps. 16:11, 21:6)

    To Him belongs eternal _____. (Ps. 41:13, 111:10; I Tim. 1:17)

2. God has put eternity in our _____. (Eccl. 3:11)

3. We will one day be given an imperishable _____. (I Cor. 15:42-44; II Cor. 5:1-5)

4. Christ died to settle *where*, and not *if*, we will live for _____.
   (John 3:16, 36; Dan. 12:2; Mt. 25:46; Gal. 6:8; Rev. 1:18; II Thess. 1:8-9)

5. Our _____ _____ is short, (Ps. 90:10-12; Ps. 39:5-7;

    but eternity is _____!   Ps. 23:6)

6. God commands us to set our _____ and _____ on eternity. (Col. 3:1-2; Mt. 6:19-21; Phil. 3:19-20)

ON A PERSONAL NOTE . . .
- Read II Cor. 4:13-18 and I Pet. 1:3-9.
  How does having an eternal perspective help you in your day-to-day life?

- Read Rom. 8:28 and Phil. 2:13.
  Has there been a time when circumstances didn't make sense to you or seemed to be bad, but looking back you can see God's perfect plan for good?

  What current situation in your life do you need to trust makes sense from the perspective of God's eternal plan/purpose?

- What temporal things in your life are taking your focus off eternal things?

- Spend time in prayer asking God to change your *daily* perspective to an *eternal* one.

"Back to the Future"
End Times Prophecy, from Genesis to Revelation
Lesson 1 – Why Study Prophecy?

REVIEW:
We serve a God who is eternal – Who *Was* and *Is* and *Is to Come*. His presence, His love, His faithfulness, His word, His rewards, His power–everything about Him is certain forever. He alone is our eternal Rock.

Dear sisters, we must never forget that the eternal Creator created each of us for eternity. He set eternity in our hearts and minds. And when Jesus comes again, we will receive resurrected bodies that are imperishable (at the rapture of the Church Age saints).

God desires to live with us for eternity. Revelation 21 promises that those who come to Him through Jesus will live forever with God in the Holy City of the new heaven and earth. But He never forces His presence on anyone. In Revelation 20:11-15, we see that those who reject God (and His Son) will suffer eternity apart from Him in the Lake of Fire. We will spend eternity somewhere. If you are not sure of your eternal destination, please go no further in this study until you have read Appendix One: *The Best Decision of Your Life*.

Knowing what God's Word says about our future causes us to see our life here on earth differently. When we live our life with an eternal perspective, everything changes. We become more and more focused on the things of God, not on the things of earth. We live our lives for eternal blessings and not for the temporal things of this earth. We realize that the eternal glory we will share with Christ is worth far more than any reward this earth can give. While there is nothing wrong with making money, getting married, or having children, we realize that God has far more in store for us. Those things may be important now, but our lives mean far more than temporary, earthly pleasures. We were created for much, much more. Our true home and inheritance awaits us in heaven.

It was once explained to me this way. Excuse the geometry terms, but our life is like a line:
    Birth --→ eternity

Any given moment or situation is like a point on that line:
    Birth -----------------------•---------------------→ eternity

The question to constantly ask yourself is: In your attitudes and actions, are you living for the "point" or for the "line"?

Are you focused on the here and now or on eternity? Is your citizenship here on earth or is it in heaven? When we live "for the line," our priorities change, our values change, and we live our lives for God instead of for self. Our momentary troubles seem lighter, and our spirits are lifted.

As we study prophecy and learn more about God's plans for our future, our perspective cannot help but change to an eternal, heavenly one. As the song says, "Turn your eyes upon Jesus. Look full in His wonderful face. And the things of earth will grow strangely dim in the light of His glorious grace."

"Back to the Future"
End Times Prophecy, from Genesis to Revelation
Lesson 1 – Why Study Prophecy?

*** DAY 5: Prophecy Gives Hope, *Purifies the Believer*

1. How does Hebrews 11:1 define faith?

2. Looking at Titus 1:2,

    a. What is the hope of those chosen of God?

    b. When did God promise us this?

    c. Where will we spend eternity? (II Peter 3:13; Rev. 21:1-4)

3. According to Titus 2:11-15,

    a. What is called "the blessed hope"?

    b. When will Christ appear to claim His Church? (I Thess. 4:14-18)

4. From Romans 8:23,

    a. What promise are we given?

    b. How is our resurrection body described in I Corinthians 15:53?

    c. Not only will our bodies be like His physically, but intellectually and morally as well. What is our hope in I John 3:2-3? (see also Romans 8:29)

5. What do I Peter 1:3-5 and Eph. 1:18 say is waiting for us in heaven?

    a. What is waiting for us in heaven?

    b. What is the guarantee of our inheritance? (Eph. 1:13-14)

    c. When will we receive this inheritance? (Eph 1:14; I Peter 1:5)

    d. What does Romans 8:17 call us?

"Back to the Future"
End Times Prophecy, from Genesis to Revelation
Lesson 1 – Why Study Prophecy?

6. Because of our hope, how should we live our lives?

    a. II Cor. 7:1

    b. Titus 2:12, 15

    c. II Peter 3:11, 14, 17-18

    d. I Peter 1:13-16

7. Who is the agent of our purification? (I Thess. 5:23; Gal. 5:16, 25)

8. When will our purification process be complete? (Phil.1:6; Col. 3:4)

ON A PERSONAL NOTE . . .
- How does knowing prophecy give us a better understanding of other related Bible truths (salvation, work of Christ, heaven and hell, nature of the Church, etc.)?

- How does "becoming more like Him" make you more effective for the cause of Christ?

- II Peter 3:9 says the Lord is patient, "not wanting anyone to perish, but everyone to come to repentance." How does knowing prophecy promote evangelism?

- How does *your hope* affect the way you live your life?

"Back to the Future"
End Times Prophecy, from Genesis to Revelation
Lesson 1 – Why Study Prophecy?

REVIEW:
*"Blessed be the God and Father of our Lord Jesus Christ, who according to His great mercy has caused us to be born again to a **living hope** through the resurrection of Jesus Christ from the dead . . ."* (I Peter 1:3).

Through prophecy, God gives us hope in a hopeless age and confidence in our future with Christ forever. It has been said that "Life without Christ is a hopeless end, but life with Christ is an endless hope."

God has promised us eternal life before the beginning of time (Titus 1:2). Because of Christ's death and resurrection, His followers look forward to an eternal glorious life beyond the grave. If we only have hope in this life, we are to be pitied more than all men (I Cor. 15:19). But Christ's resurrection and victory over death assures us of much, much more than this world has to offer. We have a far better life awaiting us.

After our salvation, we as Christians live the rest of our lives looking for what Titus 2:11 calls "the blessed hope" – the glorious appearing of our Lord Jesus Christ. For Christians, this will be at the Rapture when, according to I Thess. 4:13-18, Christ will appear in the clouds for His own. Christ will bring with Him from heaven the spirits of all New Testament believers who have died. At the Lord's command, their bodies will be resurrected (glorified). Then, in the twinkling of an eye, all living believers will be "caught up" in the air with Christ, their bodies instantly changed into glorified bodies (I Cor. 15:51-53).

From that moment on, the Church will live eternally in Christ's presence, receiving the eternal rewards and pleasures of our promised inheritance (I Peter 1:3-5). We will return to earth with Christ at His Second Coming and will rule with Him during His Millennial Kingdom (Rev. 20:6). We will also reign with Him eternally from the New Jerusalem in the New Heaven and Earth (II Tim. 2:12; Rev. 2:26; Rev. 22:5).

In II Cor. 7:1, Paul exhorts believers, *"Since we have these promises, dear friends, let us purify ourselves from everything that contaminates body and spirit, perfecting holiness out of reverence for God."* And John writes in I John 3:2, *". . . when He appears, we shall be like Him for we shall see Him as He is. Everyone who has this hope in Him purifies himself, just as He is pure."* Purity of life on the outside is the result of hope on the inside. Our becoming like Him includes the three stages of our salvation.

At the point of accepting Christ as our Lord and Savior, we are (1) **justified**—redeemed from the *penalty of sin*. Justification is the legal act of God in which He forgives our sins, gives us the righteousness of Christ, and declares us righteous in His sight. We are seen as "pure" in God's eyes.

Although we are declared righteous, we have not been made righteous. Our (2) **sanctification** progresses daily from that moment, as we live our lives dependent on the power of the Holy Spirit to overcome the *power of sin*. At our death, sin is removed from our hearts and we are made perfectly holy.

Finally, at the resurrection of our bodies, we will be (3) **glorified**. All believers will be given perfect, immortal, imperishable bodies. From that moment, we will live with God apart from the *presence of sin,* enjoying all that Christ secured for us at the cross.

Our hope is the anchor of our soul (Heb. 6:19), and our hope of these good things to come is Christ-centered (Col.1:27). We rejoice in our hope (Rom. 12:12). We not only know about the good things in store for us but look forward to them with great joy. This joy is a very powerful force that drives us to be zealous for God and things of God. It gives us strength and determination to overcome sin and live righteously. Knowing what the future holds for us compels us to holiness. As we grow in the grace and knowledge of Jesus Christ, we become more effective for the cause of Christ, resulting in God being glorified both now and forever (II Peter 3:18).

Our God is a God of *Hope*. We rejoice in Him. Let us be filled with increasing joy and peace as we learn what His word says about our future. All praise and glory and honor are His forever and ever!

"May the God of hope fill you with all joy and peace as you trust in him, so that you may overflow with hope by the power of the Holy Spirit" (Rom. 15:13).

"Back to the Future"
End Times Prophecy, from Genesis to Revelation
Lesson 2 – Jesus, The Promised Messiah

*** DAY 1: The Messiah Promised

Man's Creation and Fall

1. How was "man" originally created? Gen 1:26, 31

2. In Gen. 1:28, what commands did God give Adam and Eve?

3. Gen. 2:16-17 issues the first prophecy of judgment. What is the prophecy?

4. In addition to the curses God pronounced in Gen. 3:14-19, what else happened?

    a. Genesis 3:8

    b. Genesis 5:5

God's Provision

5. Gen. 3:15 issues the first prophecy of salvation through Christ.

    a. How is the virgin birth prophesied?

    b. When did the serpent bruise Christ's heel?

    c. When did Christ crush the serpent's head?

6. What principle does Genesis 3:21 introduce?

ON A PERSONAL NOTE . . .
- Is there a Biblical command or a conviction from God that you are choosing to disobey? What are the results of your disobedience? How would following God's will for you result in your good and His glory?

"Back to the Future"
End Times Prophecy, from Genesis to Revelation
Lesson 2 – Jesus, The Promised Messiah

REVIEW:

Genesis 1 - 2 reveals God as the Sovereign Creator of all mankind. We know that in the beginning God created the heavens and the earth and everything in them. On the sixth day of creation, He created Adam and Eve in His own image and likeness and put them in the Garden of Eden. They were commanded to be fruitful and multiply, to fill the earth and subdue it, and to rule over the fish, the birds, and all creatures that move on the ground (Gen.1:27-28).

Adam and Eve, having no sin nature, were placed in the Garden of Eden where God provided for their every need. He gave them only one prohibition - not to eat from the tree of the knowledge of good and evil. In the first recorded prophecy of the Bible, God told Adam,"...for when you eat of it you will surely die" (Gen 2:17). As long as they obeyed God's command, they would be able to eat of the Tree of Life and live forever in their Garden of Paradise.

Then entered Satan - a created holy angel who had fallen into sin long before the world's creation (Isaiah 14:12-13; Eze. 28:12-19). We are told in Genesis 3 that Satan appeared to Eve as a serpent in the Garden of Eden. By misquoting, questioning, and denying God's word, Satan led Eve to doubt God's character and provision. Eve not only ate the forbidden fruit, but gave it to Adam who ate as well.

Because of their disobedience, sin entered the world; and judgment was immediate. John Walvoord writes, "The result of their sin was to bring upon them immediate spiritual death and ultimately physical death (Gen.5:5). Because of their sinful state and disobedience they were alienated from God and afraid of His holy presence (3:8), as is humankind today apart from the grace of God" (Major Bible Prophecies, p. 18). God immediately pronounced curses upon the serpent, upon Eve, upon Adam, and upon creation itself. Mankind and even the earth itself have since existed in a fallen state and will continue to do so until the Millennial Kingdom of Christ.

In the midst of these dark judgments, however, shines the light of Genesis 3:15. God first curses the serpent, saying that he would crawl on his belly and eat dust all the days of his life. He next turns to Satan, the "power" behind the snake. In Gen. 3:15a, God reveals that the woman and *her* offspring will enter into spiritual warfare against Satan and his offspring, both demonic forces and those on earth who serve him. Then in Gen. 3:15b the first prophecy concerning Jesus, our Victorious Redeemer, is recorded as God promises mankind victory over sin and death. Though the first part of the verse deals with *offspring* in plural, the second part says "*he* will crush *your* head and *you* will strike *his* heel." *He*, the seed of the woman, ultimately refers to Christ, who was physically descended from Eve through Mary, not through Joseph. Satan bruising the heel of Christ points to the sufferings of the cross (in fact Christ's feet were pierced and nailed to the cross). But the words "crush your head" indicate that Christ will inflict a mortal wound upon Satan. At Christ's resurrection, He triumphed over Satan, gaining victory over sin and death. Christ struck a fatal blow to the devil that can never be healed. In the end He shall totally destroy Satan and his kingdom. Satan and all who follow him will be thrown into the Lake of Fire forever (Rev. 20:10-15).

After promising salvation to Adam and Eve, God replaces their inadequate handmade garments of leaves with garments of skin. This is the first record of physical death on earth. By the slaying of an animal and the shedding of blood, God was introducing the principle of a blood sacrifice for the redemption of sin. He was also demonstrating that our acts of righteousness are but filthy rags and that only when we are clothed with the righteousness of Christ are we truly saved.

Adam and Eve were banished from the garden, prohibiting them from having access to the Tree of Life and physical immortality. Though this was an act of judgment on God's part, it was also an act of mercy and grace. How horrible it would be to live forever in a fallen state. How much better it is for us that our bodies die and return to earth. It will be with resurrected glorified bodies that we will live with Christ in God's presence forever.

"Back to the Future"
End Times Prophecy, from Genesis to Revelation
Lesson 2 – Jesus, The Promised Messiah

*** DAY 2: The "Godly Seed" from Adam to Abraham: Genesis 4 - 11

1. Which of Adam and Eve's sons was favored by God? Gen. 4:4-5

2. What does the Bible say in Gen. 4:25-26 about Seth; about his son Enosh?

3. Who descended from Seth? Gen. 5:32

4. Who were the three sons of Noah? Gen. 9:18

5. What does the Bible say about their descendants? Gen. 9:19; 11:1-9

6. Review a map of the Table of Nations (taken from Genesis 10) in either your Bible or a Bible Atlas. See if you can determine which of Noah's sons is your ancestor.

7. In Gen. 9:20-27, to which son does Noah extend God's blessing?

8. And who ultimately descended from Shem? Gen. 11:26

ON A PERSONAL NOTE . . .
- Who in your family has either directly or indirectly influenced your walk with the Lord? How?

- While only God can draw one to Himself, what are you doing/can you do to encourage a Godly lineage in your family?

- We all are descendants of Adam through Noah. How does this change your attitude towards other people or groups? What prejudices do you need to confess before God?

"Back to the Future"
End Times Prophecy, from Genesis to Revelation
Lesson 2 – Jesus, The Promised Messiah

REVIEW:
Beginning in Genesis 4, we see God pass the promise of a Redeemer and Savior down through His selected godly line, beginning with Adam and ending in Christ. The rest of today's lesson traces this line from Adam to Abraham, as recorded in Gen. 4-11.

We find in Gen. 4:4 that Abel, not Cain, was looked on by God with favor. After Abel's murder, the Bible records that God "replaced" Abel with Seth. In Gen. 5 God's righteous line is recorded through Seth down to Noah. In Genesis 6 we are told that Noah was a righteous man and that he and his family alone found favor in the eyes of the Lord.

God instructed Noah to build an ark for him and his family and for representatives of all the land animals and the birds. After they were safely inside, God closed the door and sent a universal flood. All the wickedness on earth was destroyed, and God repopulated the earth with those that were on the ark. He also promised never to destroy the earth by a flood and set his rainbow in the clouds as a sign of His covenant with Noah.

Noah's three sons who came off the ark were Shem, Ham, and Japheth. Genesis 9 records Noah's drunkenness and his sons' responses. As a result, Noah issues a curse on Ham's line through Canaan and specifies that the righteous line will continue through the descendants of Shem. Noah also blesses Japheth, the father of the Gentile nations. Noah's words, "may Japheth live in the tents of Shem," not only indicate that the Japhethites would live with the Shemites on friendly terms, but also point to the time of the conversion of Gentiles to the faith of Christ (See also Isaiah 42:4).

We are told in Gen 9:19 that from Noah's three sons came all the people scattered over the earth. It is, in fact, after man's rebellion at the tower of Babel that we see God confuse the languages of the people and scatter them over the face of the earth (Genesis 11:9). The Bible next traces the righteous line from Shem down to Abraham. And, as we shall study tomorrow, it is through Abraham that the promise of a Savior continues and that the nation of Israel is formed.

By looking at the fulfillment of the prophecies concerning God's judgment upon sin and concerning the flood, we see the importance of interpreting prophecy literally. Death entered the world as a result of Adam and Eve's disobedience, and there was a literal flood which destroyed life on earth. This leads us to the conclusion that God says what He means and means what He says. We can expect both literal and detailed fulfillment of all Bible prophecy.

"Back to the Future"
End Times Prophecy, from Genesis to Revelation
Lesson 2 – Jesus, The Promised Messiah

*** DAY 3: The "Godly Seed" from Abraham to the King David

1. What were the specifics of God's call to Abraham in Gen. 12:1?

2. Promises of the Abrahamic Covenant: Gen. 12:1-3

    a. "Go ... to the _____ I will show you; (see also v.7)

    b. I will make you into a _____

    c. and I will _____; I will make _____, and you will be a _____.

    d. I will bless those who _____, and whoever _____ I will curse;

    e. and _____."

3. The promises of the covenant pass from Abraham to the tribes of Israel, according to God's will, not man's.

    a. In Gen. 17:19; 21:12; and Gen 26:3-5
       the promises of the covenant continued through _____, not Ishmael.

    b. Reading Gen 25:23 and 28:3-4, 13-15
       God's promises are to continue through the line of _____, not Esau.

    c. In Gen. 35:9-13,
       God again reviews the covenant and changes Jacob's name to _____.

    d. From Genesis 35:23-26, list the 12 sons of Israel.

4. From which tribe does Jacob prophesy the Messiah will come? Gen. 49:9-12

5. And looking at the genealogies of Christ which are given in Matthew 1:2-6 Luke 3:31-34, from which tribe was David descended?

ON A PERSONAL NOTE . . .
- Read Rom. 4:16. Think of promises you have as a *spiritual descendant* of Abraham. Go to God in prayer, thanking Him for these promises.

"Back to the Future"
End Times Prophecy, from Genesis to Revelation
Lesson 2 – Jesus, The Promised Messiah

REVIEW:

In Genesis 12 Scripture takes a new turn. Up until Genesis 12, we have seen God dealing directly with all mankind as the righteous line of mankind descended from Adam to Abraham. With the call of Abraham, we see God begin to set aside a "people" for His very own. John Walvoord writes, "The importance of God's choosing a people becomes obvious as His plan for redemption unfolds. From Genesis 12 through Revelation, Israel is shown to be one of the major purposes of God."[1]

To Abraham was made known the special purpose of God in calling out a people to be His express channel of revelation. God revealed Himself through the prophets of Israel, the judges and kings of Israel, the twelve apostles, the writers of the New Testament, and through Jesus Christ, our Lord and Savior.

In Genesis 12:1-3, we see God's initial call to Abraham, with God's promises to Abraham stipulated. God promises Abraham that he will be the father of a great nation who will dwell in the land God is going to show him. God pledges to bless both Abraham and the nation we now know as Israel. Furthermore, in Gen. 12:3 God says that "all peoples on earth will be blessed through you." We will study the Abrahamic Covenant in much more detail next week.

In Genesis 21, Isaac, the long awaited heir of the promises (Gen. 17:19), is born to Abraham and Sarah. In the remaining chapters of Genesis, we see the promises given to the nation Israel pass from *Abraham* to *Isaac*, not Ishmael; to *Jacob*, not Esau; and to *the twelve sons of Jacob*. We see Jacob (whose name God changed to Israel in Gen. 35:10) and his family migrate to Egypt as had been prophesied in Gen. 15:13-16. There under God's protection, Jacob's descendants increased from a small group of 70 to a large nation of over 2 million.

Before Jacob's death we see him issue prophetic blessings on his 12 sons. In his blessing of Judah, he issues the prophecy that "the scepter will not depart from Judah, nor the ruler's staff from between his feet" (Gen. 49:10), indicating that the long-awaited Messiah/King of the Israelites will come from the tribe of Judah. The Bible specifically traces the line from Judah to Jesus through King David.

---

1. John Walvood, <u>Major Bible Prophecies</u>, p. 39.

"Back to the Future"
End Times Prophecy, from Genesis to Revelation
Lesson 2 – Jesus, The Promised Messiah

*** DAY 4: Jesus – Heir to the Throne of David

1. Read II Samuel 7:8-17. (See also Ps. 89:36)
   a. In v16 what does God promise King David?
      Your _____ and your _____ will last forever.

   b. In v13 what is God's promise concerning King Solomon, David's son?
      His _____ will be established forever.

   c. What does this difference in the two promises mean?

2. In Jer. 22:30 the Lord issued a curse against King Jeconiah, a descendant of Solomon. Although the legal right to the throne passed through Jeconiah, what does the Lord say about Jeconiah's offspring?

3. In Christ's genealogy in Matthew 1:6 (through Joseph), from which son of David is Jesus descended?

4. And in Christ's genealogy in Luke 3:31 (through Mary), from which son of David is Jesus descended?

5. How do the curse and the genealogies of Mary and Joseph combine to support the virgin birth of Jesus, THE Promised Messiah?

ON A PERSONAL NOTE . . .
- Spend time in prayer thanking God for His perfect plans, promises, and provisions. As a result of today's study, what qualities or characteristics can you attribute to God in praise?

"Back to the Future"
End Times Prophecy, from Genesis to Revelation
Lesson 2 – Jesus, The Promised Messiah

REVIEW:

We saw yesterday that in his blessing of Judah, Jacob prophesied that "the scepter will not depart from Judah, nor the ruler's staff from between his feet" (Gen. 49:10).

Fast-forward to the time of King David when he desires to build a temple for the Lord. God tells David through the prophet Nathan that David's son, yet to be born, will be the one to build the temple and that God has even greater plans for David. God then makes unconditional promises to David, expanding upon the kingdom or seed aspect of the Abrahamic Covenant. In the Davidic Covenant, God promises to make David's name great, plant Israel in her land, and give her rest from her enemies.

In II Samuel 7:12, God tells David that a son coming from his own body will succeed him. It will be this son Solomon who will be the one to build the temple, and God will establish the *__throne__* (legal right to rule over Israel) of Solomon *forever* (II Sam. 7:13). God goes on to say in II Sam. 7:14-15 that this is an unconditional promise. As for David, God promises in II Sam. 7:16 that both his *__throne__* (the right to the throne of Israel) and his *__house__* (lineage of kings) will last *forever*. This prophecy, as we are about to see, proved to be amazingly accurate in all details.

We know that in the later history and apostasy of the Israelites, prior to the Babylonian captivity, a curse was put upon Solomon's descendant King Jeconiah (a.k.a. Jehoiachin). Jeremiah 22:24-30 says, "None of his offspring will prosper, none will sit on the throne of David or rule anymore in Judah." This meant that no descendant of Jeconiah would be able to fulfill the messianic promise of ruling on the throne of David. Although Jeconiah did have offspring (I Chronicles 3:17-18) and the legal right to the throne continued to pass through Solomon's descendants down to Joseph, no one descended from Jeconiah ever occupied the throne of David.

Solomon's *house* (physical line to the throne) ended with Joseph. Christ, as Joseph's adopted son, was the legal heir to the *throne* of David. But if Jesus had been the physical offspring of Joseph, he could have never claimed to be the Messiah because of the curse. Therefore, Christ's physical claim to being *"of the house of David"* had to come from a different line.

In Mary's genealogy (Luke 3:23-38), we find that Mary also was a physical descendant of King David through David's son Nathan. Jesus' physical claim of being King David's descendant came through Mary and through Mary alone. Therefore the doctrine of the virgin birth is validated, and Christ fulfills the prophecies of the Davidic Covenant in every detail. Furthermore, since both the legal right to the throne and the physical right to the throne stopped with Christ, He is the only one who could ever fulfill these Messianic prophecies.

"Back to the Future"
End Times Prophecy, from Genesis to Revelation
Lesson 2 – Jesus, The Promised Messiah

*** DAY 5: Jesus' Family Tree

- Today we will review the lineage from Adam to Jesus, the Promised Messiah. See if you can draw Jesus' family tree based on the names we have looked at in this week's study (both Joseph and Mary's line will merge at King David).

"Back to the Future"
End Times Prophecy, from Genesis to Revelation
Lesson 3 – Israel and Her Promises

*** DAY 1: The Abrahamic Covenant – Part I

1. Review the promises of the Abrahamic Covenant: Gen. 12:1-3
   a. "Go ... to the _____ I will show you; (see also v.7)
   b. I will make you into a _____
   c. and I will_____; I will make _____, and you will be a _____.
   d. I will bless those who _____, and whoever _____ I will curse;
   e. and _____."

2. The first aspect of the covenant we will look at is the promise of the *land*.
   What further revelation is given concerning this promise in the following verses?
   a. Gen 12:1,5,7

   b. Gen. 13:14-15, 17

   c. Gen. 15:7, 18-21

   d. Gen. 17:7-8

3. The second aspect of the covenant is the promise of the *seed* (offspring). Let's follow the development of this promise through Genesis.
   a. Gen. 12:2

   b. Gen. 13:16; 15:5

   c. Gen. 15:4

   d. Gen. 17:2-6

   e. Gen. 17:15-16,19-22

4. The third aspect of the covenant is the promise of the *blessing*. We see God promise to bless Abraham, His promised seed (Israel), and even the entire world.
   a. Gen. 12:2-3

   b. Gen. 17:7

   c. Gen. 22:17

"Back to the Future"
End Times Prophecy, from Genesis to Revelation
Lesson 3 – Israel and Her Promises

ON A PERSONAL NOTE . . .

- God offers salvation to those who repent of their sin and turn to Christ as their Lord and Savior. Again, if you have not taken this important step please read Appendix One: *The Best Decision of Your Life*.

- What blessings are promised to those who enter into a saving relationship with Christ? Spend time in prayer thanking God for these blessings.

"Back to the Future"
End Times Prophecy, from Genesis to Revelation
Lesson 3 – Israel and Her Promises

REVIEW:
In Genesis 12:1-3 we see God's initial call to Abraham and God's promises of the covenant stipulated. The covenant is confirmed and enlarged in Genesis 12:6-7; 13:14-17; 15:1-21; 17:1-14, 19-22; and 22:15-18.

By comparing all the passages concerning the Abrahamic Covenant, we see that some of the promises were individual promises given to Abraham, some were promises concerning the nation Israel, and some were universal promises made to all the nations of the earth.

Promises to Abraham
In Genesis 12:2, Abraham was promised that he would be the *father of a great nation*, and in Gen. 17:5-6, we see that he would in fact be the *father* of *many nations* and that *kings would come from him*. It is to the nation of Israel that the covenant promises passed, and it is through David and his descendants that the promise of kings was primarily fulfilled. However Abraham is also the founding patriarch of the:

Ishmaelites	through Ishmael	Gen. 25:12-18
Edomites	through Esau	Gen. 36
Midianites and kindred peoples	through Keturah	Gen. 25:1-4

Abraham is also told in Gen. 12:2 that God would *bless him*, that his *name will be great,* and that *he will be a blessing*. We know from the Bible that God made him a very rich and powerful man. He also was blessed spiritually as he lived a life in close communion with God. Abraham is one of the most important characters of the Old Testament. His name is mentioned over 300 times in Scripture. Abraham was a blessing to his family and to those around him. His faith and obedience to God has been an example to believers since his time. Furthermore, it was through his seed that both the Bible and Jesus, the Savior of the World, came.

Promises to Israel
Israel, Abraham's **seed** is promised in Gen. 12:2 that it will be a great nation. In Gen. 13:16 and Gen. 15:5, God promises that the number of Israelites will be as numerable as the dust and as the stars in the sky. Gen. 5:4 specifies that the seed will come from Abraham's body, and Gen. 17:19 promises that the seed will be from Sarah's body as well. Genesis 17 also adds that this seed will produce many kings.

In Gen. 12:1, 7; 13:14-17; 15:18-21; and 17:8, Israel is promised *everlasting* possession of a literal *land* with *literal* boundaries.

In Gen. 17:7, God promises He will be their God - they will experience His **blessings**, provisions, and protection. And in Gen. 22:17, God pledges that Israel will be victorious over the cities of her Canaanite enemies. As with Abraham, we have seen throughout history that God has blessed nations that have been kind to Israel, while nations that have come against Israel have come under God's judgment.

Universal Promises
The greatest and most exciting promise given to Abraham was that "*all peoples on earth will be blessed through you*" (Gen. 12:3). We saw last week that blessing has come to the whole world through the revelation that God has given of Himself through the nation of Israel. However, this promise finds ultimate fulfillment in Jesus Christ, through whom salvation is available to all. Galatians 3:8 says, "The Scripture foresaw that God would justify the Gentiles by faith, and announced the gospel in advance to Abraham: 'all nations will be blessed through you.'"

"Back to the Future"
End Times Prophecy, from Genesis to Revelation
Lesson 3 – Israel and Her Promises

*** DAY 2: The Abrahamic Covenant – Part II

1. What initial act of faith and obedience did Abraham have to make before God would enter into a covenant with him? Gen. 12:1; Hebrews 11:8

2. In Gen. 15:8-21, God appears to Abraham in a vision.
   a. In v.8 what does Abraham ask God?

   b. At God's request, what does Abraham do? vv. 9-10

   c. What happened to Abraham after that? v. 12

   d. After sunset, what happened? v. 17

3. God again appears to Abraham in Gen. 17, enlarging the covenant and instituting the sign of the covenant.
   a. What instructions did God give Abraham? vv. 10-14

   b. How does God himself describe the covenant in vv. 7, 13, 19?

4. After Abraham was tested in Gen. 22, God again confirmed His covenant to him.
   a. By whose name did He swear? v. 15

   b. Why did God confirm the covenant with an oath? Hebrews. 6:13-17

5. God personally passes the covenant promises to Isaac in Gen. 26:3-5 and then to Jacob in Gen. 28:13-15; 35:9-13. Look up these passages and underline the different aspects of the covenant mentioned in each.

6. How long do both I Chron. 16:15-17 and Ps. 105:6-10 say God will remember his covenant to Abraham, Isaac, and Jacob?

7. In Jer. 31:35-36, how long does Jeremiah say that the nation of Israel will remain in a covenant relationship with God?

ON A PERSONAL NOTE . . .
- Abraham had to leave his county, his people, and his father's household before entering into the covenant with God and receiving His blessings. What in your life do you need to "leave behind" in faith and obedience before God can further bless you?

"Back to the Future"
End Times Prophecy, from Genesis to Revelation
Lesson 3 – Israel and Her Promises

REVIEW:
In Old Testament times, covenants were very common. A covenant was an agreement between two parties, binding them together with common interests and responsibilities. They were often made between individuals and often made between nations as well. Covenants were very serious and sacred, with the reputation of the covenant maker at stake.[1] Before moving on, it is important that we look at the nature of the Abrahamic Covenant. It is an unconditional, everlasting, and literal covenant.

1. <u>Unconditional covenant</u>
    In Genesis 12, God instructs Abraham to go to the land He will show him. While it is true that obedience was required on Abraham's part in order to enter into the covenant, there are no conditions given to Abraham concerning the covenant itself.

    God makes it very clear in Genesis 15 that this is an *unconditional covenant*, not dependent on Abraham or his descendants in any way. In that time, people would confirm a covenant by killing animals, dividing them into two pieces, and laying them opposite one another. The two parties involved would then walk between the pieces to ratify the covenant. In this case however, Abraham is put into a "deep sleep" and *God alone confirms the covenant.*

    In Genesis 17, the rite of circumcision is given to Abraham, not as a condition but as a sign of the covenant. All the males of Abraham's household for generations to come must be circumcised. While it is true that an *individual* who was not circumcised would forfeit the blessings of the covenant, the *nation's* covenant relationship with God was still intact.

    This principle has held true down through history. Sin and disobedience on the part of an *individual* or even on a *generation of people* have resulted in their loss of covenant blessings, but that does not mean the covenant has been cancelled. The complete and final fulfillment of the Abrahamic Covenant depends on *God alone*.

2. <u>Everlasting covenant</u>
    Several times in Genesis God declares that His covenant with Abraham and his descendants is an *everlasting covenant*. In his book Israel in Prophecy, John Walvoord writes, "The Hebrew expression for 'everlasting' is *olam,* meaning 'in perpetuity.' . . . It is the strongest expression for eternity of which the Hebrew language is capable." (p.37)

    Other scriptures as well clearly indicate that the covenant between God and Israel is an everlasting one. I Chronicles 16:15-17 and Ps. 105:6-10 say God will remember his covenant to Abraham, Isaac, and Jacob *forever.* And in Jer. 31:35-36 God declares that the nation of Israel will remain in a covenant relationship with Him *as long as the sun, the moon, and the stars continue to shine*.

3. <u>Literal covenant</u>
    The Abrahamic Covenant is a *literal covenant* - the promises should be understood literally. It was made with a *literal people* - Abraham, Isaac, Jacob, and the nation of Israel. The land that was promised was a *literal land* (specific boundaries). And the promises fulfilled so far have been *fulfilled literally.* Since the promises of the covenant that have been fulfilled have been fulfilled literally, we can conclude that the *unfulfilled promises will also be fulfilled literally*.

As ordained by God, the promises of the Abrahamic Covenant passed through Isaac (Gen. 26:2-6) and then through Jacob (Gen. 28:13-15) to his twelve sons (Gen.35:11-13). The house of Jacob refers to Israel, the literal and physical descendants of Jacob. To them belong the promises of the Abrahamic Covenant forever.

During the next three days, we will look at three additional covenants that God made concerning the House of Jacob (Israel) which amplify or enlarge the Abrahamic covenant. Being sub-covenants of the Abrahamic Covenant, they too are literal, unconditional, and eternal.

---

1. Paul N. Benware, Understanding End Times Prophecy, p. 36.

"Back to the Future"
End Times Prophecy, from Genesis to Revelation
Lesson 3 – Israel and Her Promises

*** DAY 3: The Land Covenant – *amplifies the "land" promises*

1. The Land Covenant: Deuteronomy 30:1-10
   7 main features:

   v. 1   The nation will be _____ for its unfaithfulness.

   v. 2   There will be a future repentance: you will _____ to the Lord and _____ Him.

   vv. 3-4   God will _____ Israel from _____, have compassion on them, and _____ them from all the nations.

   v. 5   Israel will be brought back to the _____ and _____ it.

             He will _____ Israel and _____ them more than their fathers.

   v. 6   God will _____ their hearts (and those of their descendants), giving them a new will to love Him.

   v. 7   Israel's _____ will be judged.

   v. 9   God will make them _____ in every way.

2. What boundaries of the Promised Land did God specify to Abraham? Gen 15:18

3. What were the boundaries of the territory the Lord told Joshua he would give Israel? Joshua 1:4-5

4. What were the boundaries of Israel over which King Solomon ruled? I Kings 4:20-21

5. How do the following verses support that the Land Covenant is *eternal*?
   a. Jer. 31:38-40
   b. Joel 3:17-21
   c. Amos 9:14-15
   d. Micah 4:6-7

ON A PERSONAL NOTE . . .
We see that although the land was given to the nation of Israel unconditionally and eternally, a particular generation could be banished from the land due to their disobedience and unfaithfulness. After accepting Christ as Lord and Savior, our salvation is also unconditional and eternal. However our disobedience and unfaithfulness can cause us to forfeit God's blessings in our own life.
- What sin in your life is currently causing you to miss out on God's blessing? Go to God in repentance and turn that area over to God, knowing that our omniscient, omnipotent and omnipresent God will provide for your needs in a higher and better way.

"Back to the Future"
End Times Prophecy, from Genesis to Revelation
Lesson 3 – Israel and Her Promises

REVIEW:
Before we review today's questions, a word of explanation is needed. For years, the promises made to the Jewish people in Dt. 30:1-10 have been referred to as the *Palestinian Covenant*, although the name *Palestine* was given to the land years after the covenant was made. Today, however, the name *Palestine* is more associated with Arabs than with the Jews, and using the term *Palestinian Covenant* opens the door for much confusion. Therefore, like many Bible students of today do, we will refer to this covenant as the *Land Covenant*.

When Joshua and the Israelites returned from Egypt and were set to enter the Promised Land, it seemed a daunting task. The land was filled with Israel's enemies – who were not just going to invite them in to settle. Moses had just reminded them of the Mosaic Covenant that they were under, with its curses and blessings based on obedience. In view of these things, they wondered if they could ever hope to permanently possess their land. The Land Covenant was confirmation of God's original covenant with Abraham, enlarging upon its *land* aspect.

In Deuteronomy 29:12-13, God had told the people that Israel's inheritance to the land was not based on anything they had done, but on the promises He had made with Abraham. **However, God had made it clear that the condition of a particular generation's enjoyment of the land was its continual obedience to Him** (Dt. 29:16-29).

In the Land Covenant of Dt. 30:1-10, God reveals that, in fact, the nation will rebel in the future, resulting in their dispersion from the land (v. 1). But their disobedience would not invalidate the covenant. Its blessings would be reserved for a generation that will call upon Him (v. 2). At that time, the Lord himself will gather them from all the nations and return them to the land (vv. 3-5). They will prosper as a nation (vv. 5, 9), God will grant the nation of Israel a new will to love and obey Him (vv. 6, 8), and Israel's enemies will be punished (v.7). The Land Covenant is, as the Abrahamic Covenant, a *literal*, *eternal* and *unconditional* covenant. Although there *seems* to be a "condition" given in v. 10, "turn to the Lord with all your heart," we will see in the new covenant that one day it is *God* who will enable the nation to obey him wholeheartedly.

In Gen 15:18, God told Abraham his descendants would be given the land from the river of Egypt to the great river, the Euphrates. The specific boundaries of the Promised Land can be established by combining the scriptures of Numbers 34:1-12, Joshua 15:1-12, and Ezekiel 47:15-20. Note that there is a difference between *owning* the land and *living* in the land.

There are some who think that the Land Covenant was fulfilled when Joshua conquered the land. However large areas of the Promised Land were never taken in Joshua's time (Joshua 23:1-7). In Judges 1:21-36 we see that there were many people groups living in the land that the Israelites were not able to dislodge.[2]

There are others who say the Land Covenant was fulfilled during the reign of King Solomon. While the Kingdom of Solomon stretched over more of the Promised Land than at any other time, Israel did not actually possess and occupy the entire land area. Other kings still ruled, but "brought tribute and were Solomon's subjects all his life" (I Kings 4:21).[3]

Even if the scope of the land in either case had matched the boundaries of the Promised Land, neither instance resulted in a permanent possession of the land for the Israelites. It is evident from the scriptures that the OT prophets expected a future fulfillment of the Land Covenant when the Israelites will be gathered from the four corners of the world to possess their land *forever*. God will then turn the Israelites' hearts to him, fulfilling completely and literally His covenant promises.

---

2. Ibid., pp. 57-58.
3. Ibid., p. 58.

"Back to the Future"
End Times Prophecy, from Genesis to Revelation
Lesson 3 – Israel and Her Promises

*** DAY 4: The Davidic Covenant – *amplifies "seed" promises*

1. In II Sam. 7:12-16 God appears to David and establishes the Davidic Covenant, enlarging and confirming the seed promises of the Abrahamic Covenant. From these verses, answer the following questions:
   a. God will raise up David's _____ (Solomon) to succeed him. God will establish Solomon's _____. (v.12)

   b. Solomon is the one who will build a _____. (v.13) God will establish the _____ of Solomon's kingdom ___, even though his sins will justify God's punishment. (vv. 14-15)

   c. David's _____ and _____ will endure forever; David's _____ will be established forever. (v.16)

   d. As we saw last week, what is the difference between the promises to David and the promises to Solomon?

2. Read Psalm 89:3-4, 34-37. Circle every occurrence of the words "line" and "throne." Underline words and phrases that indicate how long God's covenant with David and God's love for David will last.

3. Read Jeremiah 33:25-26. In v. 26 who does God say will rule over the Israelites when He restores their fortunes?

4. In Isaiah 9:6-7 the prophet writes about the future and final King who will reign over the descendants of Jacob from David's throne. List titles for this great king. How long will His reign last?

5. What was the angelic message given to Mary concerning Jesus? Luke 1:30-33

ON A PERSONAL NOTE . . .
- Take today to lift up your offspring in prayer. Pray that they will continue the godly line in your family. If you do not have children, pray for someone else in your extended family.

"Back to the Future"
End Times Prophecy, from Genesis to Revelation
Lesson 3 – Israel and Her Promises

REVIEW:
We have seen that the promises of the Abrahamic Covenant passed through Isaac and then through Jacob to the twelve tribes of Israel. Later the promise of a kingdom and throne was given to the tribe of Judah (Gen. 49:10). The Davidic Covenant expands upon the *seed (kingdom)* aspect of the Abrahamic Covenant and narrows the focus to one family within the tribe of Judah - that of David's. This covenant, being a sub-covenant of the Abrahamic Covenant, is also a literal, unconditional, and everlasting covenant.

In II Samuel 7:9-11 God promises David that He will make David's name great and that David will have rest from all his enemies. Both promises came to fruition. However the most important promise of the Davidic Covenant is found in II Samuel 7:11, 16. God promises David that his *house* and his *kingdom* and his *throne* would last *forever*.

The term "*house*" refers to the physical line of David, his physical descendants. This royal line of David will endure forever and never be cut off. The term *"kingdom"* refers to David's political kingdom. A kingdom involves a literal king, literal subjects, and literal sphere of rule. And the term *"throne"* refers to the place of ruling authority. The legal right to rule would always belong to the Davidic dynasty and would never pass away permanently. The covenant did not require an unbroken succession of kings. In fact, Hosea 3:4-5 indicates that the Israelites will live "many days without a king." Even during time when the kingdom has been temporarily interrupted or taken away due to disobedience, there has always been a legitimate heir to the throne.

God also tells David that it will be his son, not David, who will build a house for the Lord. We know it was David's son Solomon who did, in fact, build the temple. God goes on to say in verses 12-15 that although Solomon will be disobedient and experience God's punishment, Solomon's *kingdom* and *throne* will continue forever. Solomon's royal line ended physically in Joseph who passed the *legal* right to the throne to his *legal* son, Jesus. As stated earlier, the physical line from David passed to Jesus through Mary.

It is Jesus whom the prophet Isaiah referred to as *Wonderful Counselor, Mighty God, Everlasting Father,* and *Prince of Peace.* And it is Jesus of whom the angel who appeared to Mary said,
> "He will be great and will be called the Son of the Most High. The Lord God will give him the throne of his father David, and he will reign over the house of Jacob forever; his kingdom will never end."

This Davidic King, who will rule over the nation of Israel forever, is the Messiah that the Jewish people were looking for at Christ's first coming to earth. However, the promises of the Davidic Covenant will not be fulfilled until His Second Coming when Christ will reign not only as King of Israel but also as King of the entire world.

"Back to the Future"
End Times Prophecy, from Genesis to Revelation
Lesson 3 – Israel and Her Promises

*** DAY 5: The New Covenant – *amplifies "blessing" promises*

1. **The New Covenant announced: Jeremiah 31:31-33**
   a. With whom will God make His new covenant?

   b. It will not be like what prior covenant? (v. 32)

   c. When will the covenant be established? (compare v. 33 with Jer. 30:7; 31:23, 27-28)

   d. Circle each time God says, "I will." List five things God declares He will do.

   e. Underline each time God says "*they will*" or "*they shall.*" What three things will be true about God's people at this time?

2. The following scriptures describe the time when Israel will be living under the New Covenant. What information do we learn from each passage?
   a. Is. 61:8-9

   b. Jer. 32:37-41

   c. Eze. 37:21-28

   d. Romans 11:25-27

   e. Is. 45:17

   f. Is. 59:20-21

ON A PERSONAL NOTE . . .
- Isaiah 61:6-9 says that all who see Israel during this time will acknowledge that Israel is a people whom the Lord has blessed. What do you think people see in your life? In what ways are others attracted to Christ through your life? In what ways might your life "turn off" others to the Christian life?

"Back to the Future"
End Times Prophecy, from Genesis to Revelation
Lesson 3 – Israel and Her Promises

REVIEW:
So far we have seen that the Land Covenant enlarged the *land* aspect of the Abrahamic Covenant, confirming that the title to the Promised Land did indeed belong to Israel and that they would one day live in the land as a redeemed and prosperous people, never to be uprooted again. We have also seen that the Davidic Covenant expanded upon the *seed* or kingdom aspect of the Abrahamic Covenant, saying that the right to the throne of Israel would remain with David's line forever. Now in Jeremiah 31:31-34, we see God speak of entering into a new and future covenant with Israel, expanding upon the *blessing* feature of the Abrahamic Covenant.

We see from the prophecy of the New Covenant that this too is a literal, everlasting, and unconditional covenant resting on the grace ("I will") of God. In Jer. 31:33 God promises that the house of Israel will receive a renewed mind and heart and will be restored to God's favor. This refers to the indwelling of the Holy Spirit, necessary for regeneration (see Eze. 36:26-27). Indication of the Holy Spirit's teaching ministry is given in Jer. 31:34 when God says, "no longer will a man teach his neighbor . . . because they will all know me." Also in v. 34, God promises to forgive their sin and remember it no more.

Many additional passages in the Old Testament refer to this future time of the covenant. Adding these verses to Jer. 31:31-37, the following observations can be made:

1. This covenant relates to a restored Israel, descendants of Jacob.
2. This covenant is in contrast to the Mosaic Covenant and will extend into eternity. The Mosaic Covenant was dependent on obedience; this one is dependent upon God's grace. The old one was written on tablets of stone; the new one will be written "on their hearts".
3. The major provision of this New Covenant will be fulfilled after Israel's time of trouble (Great Tribulation).
4. The New Covenant will feature great spiritual blessing for the people of Israel, and the nation, identified with God, will be exalted above all the nations.
5. All will know that Jesus is King of Kings and Lord of Lords.
6. This covenant features forgiveness, grace, and blessing for Israel.
7. God will gather the people of Israel from all over the world and plant them in their land to live in safety.
8. Israel and Judah will be reunited with one king reigning over them.
9. The nation will be cleansed from sin.
10. David will be resurrected and will reign with Christ as Israel's prince.
11. God will dwell with his people and they will be set apart for his holy use.[4]

Neither the physical or spiritual restoration of Israel could occur until the saving work of Christ occurred. While the New Covenant depended upon the shedding of Christ's blood upon the cross, the new covenant was not fulfilled at Christ's first coming. The promise of salvation for Israel as a nation has yet to be fulfilled. In Romans 11:25-27, the apostle Paul was still looking forward to this time when Israel as a nation (the leaders and a great mass of people, but not necessarily every Israelite) will be saved. From the prophets we know that the fulfillment of the New Covenant is connected with the second coming of Jesus, Israel's Messiah. It is then that, by God's grace alone, the nation will be cleansed and forgiven by God, be indwelt by the Holy Spirit, and have a full knowledge of the Lord. They will be planted in their land to enjoy both the spiritual and material blessings of the Millennial Kingdom.[5]

God has promised the Israelites that they will be a great PEOPLE living under God's BLESSING in their own literal, earthly LAND, and that there will be a ruler on the throne of David forever. We know that to this point the land has never been possessed in full by the Israelites. While the throne of David is a literal, political throne on earth, there is no current King of Israel. And although there have been some Jews who have come to Christ as their Lord and Savior, the nation as a whole still rejects Christ as its Messiah.

The ultimate fulfillment of the Abrahamic, Land, Davidic, and New Covenants will begin at the Second Coming of Christ. God will regather the Jewish people from the four corners of the earth, plant them safely in their land, and bring about their spiritual renewal. Jesus will rule over them from the throne of David, first during the Millennial Kingdom and then in the New Heavens and Earth *forever*.

"Back to the Future"
End Times Prophecy, from Genesis to Revelation
Lesson 3 – Israel and Her Promises

We will learn more about the Millennial Kingdom later, but for those interested in more reading now, Eze. 34:11-31; 36:24-48,37; and 39:25-29 offer amazing insights into this period, as does Isaiah 11:1-9.

4. Walvoord, <u>Major Bible Prophecies</u>, pp. 181-182.
5. Benware, op. cit., pp. 73-75.

"Back to the Future"
End Times Prophecy, from Genesis to Revelation
Lesson 4 – Israel: Her Fate and Her Future

*** DAY 1: The Kingdom Divided and Exiled
Hold onto your hats, we're flying through history today!

1. Read I Kings 11:9-13.
   a. Why did the Lord become angry with Solomon?

   b. What did God tell Solomon concerning the Kingdom?

   c. In I Kings 11:43, which son succeeded Solomon as king?

2. Read I Kings 11:26-36.
   a. What do we know about Jeroboam from vv. 26-28?

   b. What did the prophet Ahijah do upon meeting up with Jeroboam and what did this action signify?

   c. When would this happen?

   d. Why would one tribe be left with Solomon's son?

3. Read I Kings 12:12-24 (Kingdom Divided).
   a. In the rebellion against Rehoboam, which tribe remained loyal to the house of David? v. 20

   b. Which tribe joined the forces of Rehoboam? v. 21

   c. What prevented the fighting? vv. 22-24

4. Skim II Kings 17 (Northern Kingdom Exiled).
   a. Who was king over Israel when the Assyrians invaded Samaria? v. 6

   b. Where were the Israelites deported? v.6

   c. Were they ever returned to the land? v. 23

   d. Who did the king of Assyria bring in to live in the land of Samaria? v. 24

5. Read II Chronicles 36:11-23 (Southern Kingdom Exiled)
   a. Who was the last king to reign over the House of Judah? v.11

   b. What nation and king conquered the land of Judah? v.17

   c. What happened to those who escaped the sword? v. 20

   d. According to v. 21 and Jer. 29:10, how long did this exile last?

"Back to the Future"
End Times Prophecy, from Genesis to Revelation
Lesson 4 – Israel: Her Fate and Her Future

REVIEW:
You were not given a personal application today, but we should all heed the warning given by God through Samuel as Israel's Kingdom Era began:

> *"If you fear the LORD and serve and obey him and do not rebel against his commands, and if both you and the king who reigns over you follow the Lord your God - good! But if you do not obey the Lord, and if you rebel against his command, his hand will be against you as it was against your fathers."* I Samuel 12:8

While you may feel like you didn't sign up for a class on the history of Israel, it is important to know what happened to the descendants of Jacob, as they are the people to whom the promises of the Abrahamic Covenant belong. It is also important to see that, although the line to the Messiah was preserved, at no time during the Kingdom Era were the promises of the covenant ever fulfilled.

When King David died, he left a powerful, wealthy, and united Hebrew nation - eager to honor and celebrate God (I Chron. 29:26-28). David's son Solomon then reigned over Israel for 40 years. The 80 years that David and Solomon ruled were known as *Israel's Golden Age*. During this time, the nation was powerful and prosperous. The kingdom dominated the Middle East during this time.

Despite his youthful dedication to God, King Solomon turned away from the Lord in his later years (I Kings 11). In disobedience to God's law, he cemented treaties with many nations by marrying women of foreign royal families. Solomon had 700 wives of royal birth and 300 concubines. He also allowed pagan worship in Jerusalem. These choices led directly to tragedy. Solomon, who had every advantage, turned away from God, as did the people of his kingdom.

As a result of Solomon's spiritual backsliding, the Lord appeared to him and revealed that after Solomon's death, God would tear the kingdom from his son Rehoboam's hands. However for David's sake (and the sake of the Covenant) one tribe would remain with Rehoboam.

After Solomon, the Kingdom became a divided kingdom. The 10 tribes following Jeroboam became the *Northern Kingdom* and retained the name *Israel*. The tribes composing the Northern Kingdom included

| Reuben | Simeon | Issachar | Zebulun |
| Dan | Naphtali | Gad | Asher |

Ephraim and Manasseh (Joseph's sons)

* Note: the tribe of Levi was set apart by God as priests and was not allotted its own portion of the land (Numbers 18:20-24). Instead they were given towns in each of the territories (Numbers 35:1-5; Joshua 21).

King Jeroboam was given the same promise from God that David and Solomon had been given, "If you do whatever I command and walk in my ways and do what is right . . . I will be with you. I will build you a dynasty as enduring as the one I built for David . . ." (I Kings 11:38). However, Jeroboam rebelled against the Lord and proved to be evil and unrighteous, as were the other 18 kings who succeeded him during the 250-year life of the Northern Kingdom. Even though God sent prophets to warn Israel and turn the nation back to him, the people did not listen. Finally, God raised up Assyria who conquered the Northern Kingdom and scattered his people "to the four winds." Israel fell to the Assyrians in 722 B.C., and the kingdom was never restored.

Under Rehoboam's reign, Benjamin and Judah made up the *Southern Kingdom*. Because the tribe of Benjamin was so small, they adopted the name *Judah*. Ruling from Jerusalem, Rehoboam did evil in the Lord's eyes, stirring up God's jealous anger. David's descendants continued to rule Judah until the nation fell to Babylon in 586 BC. Seven of these kings were righteous, prolonging the life of the Southern Kingdom. But the sins that led to Israel's defeat became deeply entrenched in Judah as well. Despite revivals under King Hezekiah and later under King Josiah, Judah experienced a spiritual and moral decline.

"Back to the Future"
End Times Prophecy, from Genesis to Revelation
Lesson 4 – Israel: Her Fate and Her Future

The Southern Kingdom survived the Assyrian invasion that destroyed Israel. God answered the prayers of godly King Hezekiah and delivered them from the Assyrians. Seven kings later God finally brought judgment on the Southern Kingdom by raising up Babylon (which had conquered Assyria) to conquer Judah in 586 B.C. All the leaders, artisans, musicians, and healthy children were taken away to captivity in Babylon.

The captives were exiled in Babylon for 70 years. It was during this time (Daniel 9:1-3) that God revealed to Daniel the outline of the history of the world from Daniel's day until Christ's Second Coming, both from the Gentile perspective and from Israel's perspective. These outlines will be the topic of our study over the next few days.

"Back to the Future"
End Times Prophecy, from Genesis to Revelation
Lesson 4 – Israel: Her Fate and Her Future

*** DAY 2: God's Revelation of the Future – The Gentile Program

1. Daniel 2:31-35   Daniel Relates / Interprets Nebuchadnezzar's Dream
    <u>Statue</u>
    v. 32   head of _____

    chest and arms of _____

    belly and thighs of _____

    v. 33   legs of iron, feet partly of _____ and _____

    <u>Rock</u>
    v. 34   not cut by _____ _____

    strikes statue on its _____ and _____ them

    v. 35   statue _____; swept away by wind without leaving a

    _____

    rock becomes a _____ _____ filling the whole _____.

2. Daniel 2:36-45   Daniel Interprets Nebuchadnezzar's Dream
    <u>Statue</u>
    vv. 36-38   head of gold: _____ kingdom (Babylonian)

    v. 39   chest and arms of silver: _____

    v. 39   belly and thighs of bronze: _____

    v. 40   legs of iron: _____

    v. 41   _____ kingdom,

    v. 42   partly _____ and partly _____,

    v. 43   people will be a _____.

    <u>Rock</u>
    v. 44   the rock: God's kingdom

    will never be _____,

    will never be left to _____,

    will ____ prior kingdoms, bring them to _____,

    will endure _____.

3. In Daniel 2:45, whom does Daniel credit for interpreting the dream?

ON A PERSONAL NOTE . . .
- Read Romans 13:1-5. What does God say about the governing authorities over us and how we should respond to them?

- In Daniel 4:17, Daniel proclaims that "the Most High is ruler over the realm of mankind, and bestows it on whom He wishes and sets over it the lowliest of men." How can relying on God's sovereignty calm you in today's world?

"Back to the Future"
End Times Prophecy, from Genesis to Revelation
Lesson 4 – Israel: Her Fate and Her Future

REVIEW:
In the prophecies of Daniel, we see the revelation of world history in outline. Walvoord writes, "To Daniel the prophet was given the rare privilege of outlining not only Gentile history from his day until the second coming of Christ, but also the parallel pathway of Israel, beginning with the rebuilding of Jerusalem in the time of Nehemiah and culminating in the second coming of Christ."[2]

Our study today deals with Daniel 2, but additional facts concerning the Four Final Gentile Kingdoms can be gained by also looking at Daniel's visions in Daniel 7-8 and 10-12 (optional studies).

In Daniel 2:37-38, Daniel begins his interpretation of the King's dream by pointing out that the head of gold represents Nebuchadnezzar and the Babylonian empire. This kingdom had been God's instrument in the destruction of Jerusalem and the captivity of the kingdom of Judah. Under Nebuchadnezzar, Babylon had become one of the wonders of the world, with great palaces, temples, and other buildings. Nebuchadnezzar did not actually reign over the entire world; but in Daniel's time, it seemed as if the entire earth was under his dominion.

In Daniel 2:39, Daniel says that a second kingdom, indicated by the chest and arms of silver, will arise. Prophecies in Daniel 7 and 8 clearly specify that this kingdom is that of Medo-Persia. Just as the statue had two arms, this kingdom was made up of the Medes and the Persians. Just as silver is less valuable than gold, this kingdom was inferior to the Babylonian kingdom. The fall of the Babylonians to the Medes and the Persians was actually recorded in Daniel 5; though chronologically, it happened between Daniel 8 and 9. It was during the rule of the Medo-Persian empire that God allowed the Israelites to return from captivity to rebuild Jerusalem. It was also during this time that the last six books of the OT were written.

The next kingdom to come is represented by the statue's belly and thighs of bronze. Daniel 2:39 just refers to it as a "third kingdom," but Daniel 8:5-8, 20-21 identifies it as the Grecian Empire. History records the fall of the Medo-Persian empire to Alexander the Great from 334-330 B.C. Little is found in scripture concerning the Grecian Empire because it existed in the period between Malachi and Matthew.

In Daniel 11:1-35, there are approximately 135 prophecies concerning the course of the Medo-Persian and the Grecian empires that have been so accurately fulfilled that liberal scholars rejected the idea that the book of Daniel could have been written beforehand. The discovery of a copy of Daniel in the Dead Sea Scrolls proves that it was so written.

Finally, in Daniel 2:40-43, Daniel describes a fourth kingdom which will emerge. This kingdom was represented by the statue's "legs of iron and feet partly of iron and baked clay" (Daniel 2:33). Daniel 7 also describes this fourth kingdom. Though not specifically named in Daniel, this empire is clearly the Roman Empire, which conquered the Grecian Empire in 63 B.C. The Roman Empire was the most powerful, most extensive, and longest in duration of all the empires. It devoured the lands and the peoples of the previous three empires. Other details of this empire are given in Daniel 7. It was the Roman Empire which dominated the world during the lifetime of Jesus and his apostles.

Daniel continues in 2:44-45 by explaining the meaning of the rock that strikes the statue at its feet of iron and clay, causing the whole statue to break and disintegrate (Dan. 2:24-25). Once the statue disappears, the rock becomes a mountain and fills the earth. The rock is Jesus, and the blow struck to the statue represents the second coming Christ, when He will return to rule over all the earth. Daniel reveals that this fifth kingdom, Christ's kingdom, will never be destroyed, but will endure forever. Christ will reign on earth during the Millennium and then in the New Heavens and Earth for eternity.

The Roman Empire was never destroyed, but gradually disintegrated over time. The final destruction of the Roman Empire described in Daniel 2 and 7 has never been fulfilled. Like many other prophecies in the Old Testament, this vision seems to skip from the time of Christ's first coming to that of His second. While the two legs of iron represented the eastern and the western part the empire, nothing so far has corresponded to the feet of clay and iron with ten toes (the ten kings that will come from this kingdom - 7:24). Therefore, total fulfillment of Daniel 2 and 7 requires that there be a revival of the Roman Empire before Christ's return.

"Back to the Future"
End Times Prophecy, from Genesis to Revelation
Lesson 4 – Israel: Her Fate and Her Future

*** DAY 3: God's Revelation of the Future – Program for Israel

The Jews had a "seven" of years as well as a "seven" of days. To a Jew, a "week" could refer to either seven days or seven years. Interpreters are in agreement that Daniel was thinking in terms of years. In the prophecy given in Daniel 9:24-27, the term "seven" or "week" refers to a seven year period.

1. **Reading Daniel 9:24,**
    a. How many years does this prophecy span?

    b. Who is meant by the term "your people"?

    c. To what does the "holy city" refer?

    d. What six things does God purpose to do for Israel?
        1) _____ 4) _____
        2) _____ 5) _____
        3) _____ 6) _____

2. **In Daniel 9:25,**
    a. How many years are spanned?
        ____ "sevens" (49 years)   +   ____ "sevens" (434 years)

    b. What will be the start of this timetable?

    c. What ends the 62 sevens?

3. **Looking at Daniel 9:26,**
    What two things will happen after the 62 sevens?
        1)

        2)

4. **And in Daniel 9:27,**
    a. To whom does "he" refer?

    b. What event will signal the start of the last "seven"?

    c. What will happen in the middle of this "seven"?

ON A PERSONAL NOTE . . .
- In Daniel 9:1-4 what godly disciplines do we see Daniel doing?

- What components of prayer do you see in Daniel 9:4-19?

- What reason does Daniel give God for answering his prayers?

- How does Daniel's example motivate you to change your time with God?

"Back to the Future"
End Times Prophecy, from Genesis to Revelation
Lesson 4 – Israel: Her Fate and Her Future

REVIEW:
Daniel was still in captivity in Babylon when the Medes and Persians conquered Babylon, fulfilling the earlier prophecy that had been given him. While reading, Daniel came upon prophecies in Jer. 25:1 and Jer. 29:10 that Israel would return to her homeland after 70 years of captivity. Realizing that the time was near, Daniel began praying for fulfillment of the return of his people and the restoration of Israel. While he was still praying, God sent Gabriel with a new vision. Because the prophecy in Jeremiah only revealed God's plan for Israel up to end of the Babylonian captivity, this new vision revealed God's program for Israel from the end of the Babylon captivity until the time when the Messiah would come to set up His Kingdom on earth.

The prophecy opens by stating that the period of time that the prophecy spans is 70 times 7 (years), or 490 years. In v. 24, the angel specifies that the prophecy concerns Daniel's people (Israel) and his holy city (Jerusalem). Next the angel announces six things that God will have completed by the end of the 490 years. The following explanation of these six elements by J. Dwight Pentecost is found in The Bible Knowledge Commentary, by Walvoord and Zuck, pp. 1361-1362.

> "1. 'Finish transgression' - Israel's disobedience will be brought to an end when she repents and turns to Him as her Messiah and His 2nd coming. She will then be restored to the land and blessed.
>
> 2. 'Put an end to sin' - Israel's sin which had gone unpunished would be punished through Jesus who would bear her sins (and the world's) on the cross. At His return, He will remove Israel's sin.
>
> 3. 'Atone for wickedness' - The provision for Israel's atonement was made at the Cross. God's final atonement of Israel will be when she repents at Christ's 2nd coming.
>
> 4. 'Bring in everlasting righteousness' - The millennial kingdom will be characterized by righteousness.
>
> 5. 'Seal up vision and prophecy' - All of God's promises to Israel in His covenants will be fulfilled in the millennial kingdom.
>
> 6. 'Anoint the most holy' - This could either refer to the dedication of the most holy place in the millennial temple (Eze. 41-46). Or it could speak of the enthronement of Christ as King of kings and Lord of lords in the Millennium."

Pentecost also writes that, "The first three have to do with sin and the second three with the kingdom. The basis for the first three was provided in the work of Christ on the cross, but all six will be realized by Israel at the Second Advent of Christ." He later points out that, "The six summarize God's whole program to bring the nation Israel the blessings promised through His covenants . . ."

In Daniel 9:25, Gabriel reveals to Daniel three major divisions in God's program for Israel. The entire period will begin when the decree to restore and rebuild Jerusalem is issued. There are several decrees recorded in the scriptures that deal with the Jews' restoration from their captivity (Ezra 1:1-3; Ezra 6:3-8; Ezra 7:7; and Nehemiah 2:1-8). The first three decrees, however, deal only with rebuilding the temple. Only in the final decree given by Artaxerxes in 445 B.C. to Nehemiah do we see permission granted to rebuild the *city* of Jerusalem.

After the decree to rebuild Jerusalem there will be 7 "sevens" and 62 "sevens" until the "Anointed One" comes. The first 49 years, then, refer to the rebuilding of the city of Jerusalem "with streets and a trench" (Daniel 9:25). The second part, the 434 years, follows immediately. We are not told about anything specific happening during this time, but we can assume that the restoration of Jerusalem continues. This period is to end when the "Anointed One" comes. This refers to the Triumphal Entry of Christ on the Sunday of the week of His death.

Two signs are given that will happen after the end of the first 434 years. First the Anointed One will be cut off, referring to Christ's crucifixion. Second, "The people of the ruler who will come will destroy the city

"Back to the Future"
End Times Prophecy, from Genesis to Revelation
Lesson 4 – Israel: Her Fate and Her Future

and the sanctuary." This describes the destruction of Jerusalem and the Temple in 70 A.D. by the Roman Empire. The "ruler to come" is the final head of the revived Roman Empire or the antichrist. Note though that it is his people, not him, that will destroy Jerusalem and its Temple. These two signs are said to be after the 62 sevens but not in the final 7 years. This implies that there is a gap between the end of the 483 years and the beginning of the last 7 years. The Church Age, which began at Pentecost, is included in this gap, and both will continue until the time of the Rapture.

The last "seven" (7 years) refers to the Tribulation. It will begin when the "ruler to come" confirms a peace covenant with Israel. We know from other scriptures that he will become the final world ruler. But after 3½ years, he will break his covenant with Israel. Great tribulation will come upon the people of Israel, as well as the entire world. The antichrist will also abolish the Jewish system of religion. He will set up an image in the temple and cause the world to worship him. This unfulfilled "week" is also known as: the "time of Jacob's distress" (Jer. 30:3-11); the "Day of Vengeance" (Is. 61:2); and a "time of great distress, unequaled from beginning of world until now" (Mt. 24:21). While this time seems cruel, it is actually an act of God's mercy, since millions will turn to Him in faith (Rev. 7:9-17). This brings us to the end of the 490 years when Christ will come and destroy the antichrist and all of his armies. We are told in Rev. 19:20 that the antichrist and his false prophet will be cast in to the lake of fire for eternity. A purified Israel will then enter the Millennial Kingdom with their Messiah.

To Summarize, God's program for the nation of Israel is divided as follows:
        7 "sevens" + 62 "sevens" + 1 "seven" = 70 "sevens"

- The first 69 "sevens" or 483 years have already occurred in history.

  <u>The Restoration Years</u>
  7 "sevens" (49 years)   from decree to rebuild Jerusalem until Jerusalem rebuilt; decree given to Nehemiah by Artaxerxes in 445 B.C. (Neh. 2:1-8)

  <u>The Silent Years</u>
  62 "sevens" (434 years)   up to Triumphal Entry in 33 A.D. (Zech 9:9; John 12:12-19)

- A gap in Israel's program began prior to the crucifixion of Christ and will continue up to the Tribulation. This period included the destruction of Jerusalem/the temple by Romans in 70 A.D. It also includes the Church Age and the Rapture.

- The final "seven" (7 years)
  <u>The Tribulation</u>
  1 "seven" (7 years)   begins when the antichrist signs covenant with Israel, ends with the 2nd Coming of Christ.

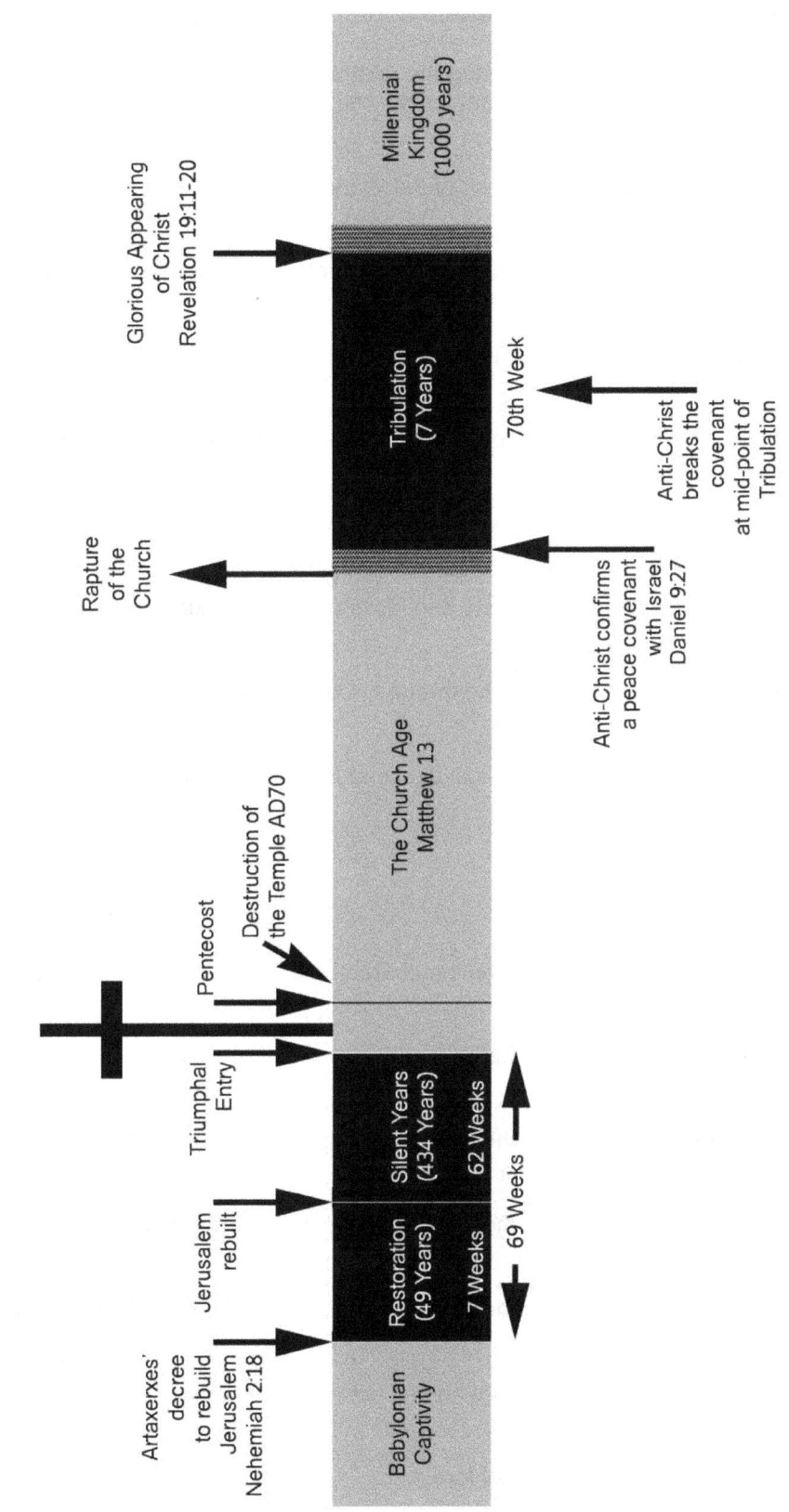

"Back to the Future"
A Biblical Study of End Time Prophecies
Lesson 4 - Israel: Her Fate and Her Future

*** DAYS 4 & 5: Review of Lessons 2 - 4

We have covered a lot of material during the past weeks. Before we move on, let's review what we have learned about Israel and God's program for His chosen people.

Week 2
1. The good news of Jesus, the Savior of the World, was first announced in what verse?

2. The godly line continued from Adam to Noah through which son of Adam?

3. Through which of Noah's sons did the godly line continue to Abraham?

4. Who fathered the twelve tribes making up the nation of Israel?

5. Through which tribe would the royal line of Israel come?

6. God promised whom that his throne and his house and his kingdom would last forever?

7. Jesus received the legal right to the throne through whom?

8. Through whom was Jesus a physical descendant of King David?

9. Why is this significant?

Week 3
1. What are three words that describe the character of the Abrahamic Covenant?

2. What are the three aspects of this covenant?

3. Which sub-covenant amplifies the land aspect of the Abrahamic Covenant?

4. Which sub-covenant amplifies the seed aspect of the Abrahamic Covenant?

5. Which sub-covenant amplifies the blessing aspect of the Abrahamic Covenant?

6. When will the Abrahamic Covenant and its sub-covenants find total fulfillment?

7. Who will ultimately rule over Israel forever?

"Back to the Future"
A Biblical Study of End Time Prophecies
Lesson 4 - Israel: Her Fate and Her Future

Week 4

1. Under which king was the Kingdom of Israel split?

2. Who became the first king over the Northern Kingdom (House of Israel)?

3. To what country were the people of the Northern Kingdom exiled and dispersed?

4. Which nation and king conquered the Southern Kingdom (House of Judah)?

5. How long were the survivors exiled in Babylon?

6. To which prophet did God appear to in Babylon and reveal the timelines of world history?

7. What three Gentile Kingdoms did God say would come after the Babylon Kingdom?

8. And whose kingdom would follow those three?

9. How many "sevens" did God decree for the nation of Israel?

10. With what event did this timeline for Israel start?

11. With what event will it end?

12. How many "sevens" are yet to be fulfilled?

13. What do call this last "seven"?

14. What is the time period that we are living in now called?

MOVING ON . . .
Because of her disobedience and unfaithfulness, God has temporarily set aside the program for Israel. We are now living in the time of the Gentiles. More specifically, since the death and resurrection of Christ and the advent of the Holy Spirit we are living in what is called The Church Age.

Because of God's literal, unconditional and everlasting promises to Israel have yet to be fulfilled completely, we know that one day Christ will return and establish His rule over a re-gathered, regenerated Israel. Christ will rule from Jerusalem – not only over Israel, but over the entire world. Once again, God's Presence will fill the temple, with Jerusalem and the House of Jacob the center of His program.

During the next few weeks, we will turn our attention to the Church and God's current program for her – mysteries not revealed in the Old Testament. Afterwards, we will return to our study of end times as we look at the Tribulation, Christ's Return, the Millennial Kingdom, and life in the eternal future.

"Back to the Future"
End Times Prophecy, from Genesis to Revelation
Lesson 5 – The Church

*** DAY 1: Anticipation of the Church

1. Shift in Jesus' Ministry:
   a. In Matthew 11:16-18, why does Jesus rebuke the Jews?

   b. What does Jesus say will happen to those who witnessed His miracles, yet still rejected Him? Matt. 11:20-24

   c. To whom does Jesus now extend His Kingdom invitation? Matt. 11:28-30

   d. What was the ultimate, unforgivable rejection of Jesus by the Pharisees? Matt. 12:22-32

   e. How do Jesus' words in Matt. 12:48-50 anticipate God's new program?

2. Jesus' Revelation of the Church to the Disciples:
   a. After washing the disciples' feet in the Upper Room and sending Judas away, what does Jesus reveal to His disciples? John 13:33

   b. What new command does Jesus give them? John 13:34-35

   c. What does Jesus exhort the disciples to do? John 14:1

   d. What does Jesus first promise the disciples? John 14:2-3 (also 13:36)

   e. What are the disciples assured of in John 14:6-7?

   f. What two privileges will those in Christ have? John 14:12-14

   g. At Jesus' request, whom will the Father send? John 14:15-17

   - How long will He be with us?

   - What does Jesus call Him?

   - Where will He live?

   h. What other promise does Jesus make in John 14:23?

"Back to the Future"
End Times Prophecy, from Genesis to Revelation
Lesson 5 – The Church

    i. What promises concerning the Holy Spirit does Jesus give in the following verses?
- John 14:26

- John 16:8-10

- John 16:12-13

    j. What promise is given in John 14:27? See also John 16:33.

ON A PERSONAL NOTE . . .
- What does having the indwelling Holy Spirit mean to you? (*If you have not made Christ your Lord and Savior, read Appendix One now.*) How has having the Holy Spirit changed your life? Praise God for His infinite wisdom and grace in giving us this gift.

- Jesus said to not let our hearts be troubled (John 14:1, 27). What do you need to entrust to the Father and to Jesus so that you can experience His peace (v. 27)? Why not do it now?

"Back to the Future"
End Times Prophecy, from Genesis to Revelation
Lesson 5 – The Church

REVIEW:
From Genesis to Revelation God's plan for the people of Israel and His plan for the Gentile world follow dual tracks. It is in the New Testament, however, that the special purpose of God in the present age is revealed - that of calling out His **church**, composed of both Jews and Gentiles. While every saved person in time fits somewhere in the plan of God, the Church is the subset of believers who are *baptized* by the Holy Spirit into the Body of Christ (I Cor. 12:13; Acts 1:5). The **Church Age,** spanning a yet undetermined number of years, started on the Day of Pentecost in A.D. 33 and will end with the Rapture. This Church Age is the parenthetical period between the 69th and 70th week of Daniel's Seventy Week prophecy.

The gospel of Matthew, written by a Jew for the Jews, clearly was written to prove that the Lord Jesus Christ was Israel's long-awaited Messiah who had come to offer them His Kingdom. In chapters 1-12, Matthew presents Jesus as the King. Jesus authenticates His claim by His ministry, His message, and His miracles. However in Chapter 11 we see opposition to Jesus begin to rise. Realizing that the Jewish nation, who had also rejected John the Baptist, was now rejecting Him, Jesus issues an open invitation to become His disciples to *all*, both Jews and Gentiles alike (Matthew 11:28-30).

As opposition to Christ increases in Chapter 12, it becomes evident that the Messianic Kingdom would not be set up until He returns to earth again, at the beginning of the Millennium. Although the final rejection of Christ and His Kingdom does not occur until later, Jesus indicates that He is setting aside all physical relationships (Israel and her promises) and establishing a new relationship based on faith (Matthew 12:48-50). Remember that although God's covenant program for Israel was *postponed (from a human standpoint)* for a time, it was *not abandoned* (Rom.11:25).

The focus of Jesus' ministry then shifts from the Israelites to His disciples. His message changes from one of offering the kingdom to one of what would result in view of Israel's rejection. The parables in Matthew 13 describe the conditions that will exist while the King is absent. The time between Christ's first and second coming is referred to as the Inter-advent Age. In these parables the *kingdom of heaven* refers to all who *profess* belief in Christ, whether they are truly saved or not. While the Kingdom of Heaven includes the church, it is not limited to the church. We will look at the Inter-advent Age in a later lesson.

As Jesus celebrates His last Passover with the disciples in the Upper Room (John 13-17), He reveals that a new program would be put into effect prior to the fulfillment of the millennial kingdom. By washing their feet, He shows them that in this new program, they will be *servants* of God rather than *rulers* of God. After sending away His betrayer Judas, Jesus announces His upcoming departure and glorification (John 13:31-33) and gives the disciples a new commandment: "As I have loved you, so you must love one another" (John 13:34). Jesus closes His Upper Room Discourse by revealing promises of this new program, which apply to all who are in the body of Christ.

To comfort the disciples, Jesus gives the first promise of the rapture (John 14:2-3). He assures them (and us) that after He goes and prepares a place for them in His Father's house, He will come back and take them there (John 14:1-3). The disciples do not understand at that time what Jesus is saying. It is not until Paul's later writing on the subject that the whole truth of the rapture is revealed.

Jesus also comforts them by telling the disciples that their salvation is certain. Jesus tells them that He alone is the only way to the Father and to heaven (John 14:6). He assures them that no matter what their earthly future may hold, they can be confident of their eternal future. In John 14:7-11, Jesus also says that to know Him is to know the Father. How calming it is to know that the sovereign, all-powerful God of the universe is also our loving Father Who constantly watches over us.

Because Jesus is going to the Father, where He will serve as our Mediator and High Priest, Jesus promises that 1) God will do even greater things through us and that 2) we have the assurance that our prayers will be heard and answered (John 14:12-14; also I John 5:14).

Not only does Jesus say that both He and the Father will live in us (John 14:23), but He also promises that in His physical absence the Holy Spirit will come to be with us and live in us *forever.* Although the Holy Spirit had been with the saints in the OT, now the Holy Spirit will indwell every believer. The Spirit will teach us all things and remind us of all truth (John 14:26) and will convict us of guilt concerning sin,

"Back to the Future"
End Times Prophecy, from Genesis to Revelation
Lesson 5 – The Church

righteousness, and judgment (John 16:8-11). Jesus promises the disciples that much more will be revealed to them when the Spirit of truth comes (John 16:12-15).

In John 14:27 Jesus promises to leave them His supernatural peace. His peace helps us to keep calm in times of trouble (John 14:1), dissolves fear (Phil. 4:7), and maintains harmony between believers (Col. 3:15).

Having told the disciples of new and wonderful things to happen and having comforted these confused and fearful men with His many promises, Jesus exhorts them to be courageous as they endure tribulation because He has overcome the world (John 16:33)! Likewise, we are promised in I John 5:4 that everyone born of God overcomes the world.

"Back to the Future"
End Times Prophecy, from Genesis to Revelation
Lesson 5 – The Church

*** DAY 2: Beginnings of the Church

1. **Coming of the Spirit:**
   a. After Jesus' resurrection, what did He instruct the disciples to do? Acts 1:4

   b. What did He say would happen? Acts 1:5

   c. What will the Holy Spirit bring? Acts 1:8

   d. Acts 2:1-13 records this event. Describe it.

2. **Peter preaches to the Jews:**
   a. After Peter confesses Jesus as the Christ (Messiah), what two things does Jesus tell Peter in Matthew 16:18?

   b. From Acts 2:5, 36, who is Peter's audience?

   c. How did Peter explain what had just happened? Acts 2:33

   d. What did Peter tell them they should do in Acts 2:38?

   e. What will happen?

   f. In Acts 2:39 Peter says this promise is for all whom the Lord will call.

      1) To whom does "you and your children" refer?

      2) To whom does "those who are far off" refer?

   g. How many Jews were added to the church on that day? Acts 2:41

3. **Peter preaches to the Gentiles:**
   In Acts 10:44-48, we see the first instance in Scripture of Gentiles being baptized by the Holy Spirit. Read also Acts 11:15-18. Describe this event.

4. **Paul chosen by God:**
   a. From Acts 9:15 and Col. 1:25-27, what was Paul chosen by God to do?

"Back to the Future"
End Times Prophecy, from Genesis to Revelation
Lesson 5 – The Church

    b. When had Jesus told His disciples that future revelation would be given? John 16:12-15

    c. How was Paul given wisdom concerning the Church? I Cor. 2:10; Eph. 3:2

    d. What was the mystery revealed to Paul by the Holy Spirit in Eph. 3:1-9?

    e. In Eph. 2:14-18 how are both Gentiles and Jews reconciled to God?

    f. In I Cor. 12:13 and Eph. 2:18, what distinguishes a believer as a member of the Body of Christ?

ON A PERSONAL NOTE . . .
- Peter and Paul had a specific role in God's plan to spread the gospel. Read Psalm 139:13-17 and Ephesians 2:10. Identify how God has used your gifts, your talents, and your past to uniquely mold you into His chosen instrument. Seek His wisdom and will for serving Him.

"Back to the Future"
End Times Prophecy, from Genesis to Revelation
Lesson 5 – The Church

REVIEW:

In Col. 1:24-27 Paul very clearly calls the divine program of the church a mystery. In Scripture the term "mystery" is used to refer to a purpose or program known to God from eternity but only now revealed. Although the Old Testament reveals that Gentiles would be saved, it was assumed that they would be Jewish converts. God's plan to reconcile both Jews and Gentiles in Christ into one body was not revealed in the Old Testament. Jesus announced the coming program to His disciples, but told them much more would be revealed after the Spirit of Truth had come (John 16:12-15).

Peter was chosen first by God to preach the gospel. In Matthew 16:18, Jesus calls Simon "Peter" (which means *rock)* and tells him, "upon this *rock* I will build My church; and the gates of Hades will not overpower it." The term "*rock*" refers to Peter's confession that Jesus is the Christ, the Son of the living God (v.16).

After the arrival of the Holy Spirit on the Day of Pentecost, Peter stood up and presented the gospel to God-fearing Jews from every nation. We are told that about 3000 accepted his message and were baptized. Later in Acts 10, God showed Peter in a vision that He does "not show favoritism, but accepts men from every nation who fear Him and do what is right (Acts 10:35). God confirms the vision in Acts 10:28-47 by sending Peter to preach to the Gentile house of Cornelius, where Peter and his companions were amazed to see the Holy Spirit fall upon those who believed.

In Acts 9:15 we see that Paul was God's chosen instrument to carry Christ's name to the Gentiles. Paul was also the one to whom God, through the Spirit of Truth, gave the full revelation of the church (Col. 1:25-29). Paul's writings make it clear that both Jews and Gentiles can be reconciled to God through the cross and that those who come to the Father through Christ are baptized by the Spirit into the one body, the Body of Christ. Paul's writings set forth the major doctrines of the church.

"Back to the Future"
End Times Prophecy, from Genesis to Revelation
Lesson 5 – The Church

*** DAY 3: Destiny of the Church

1. What does Phil. 3:20 say about a Christian's citizenship?

2. Therefore what are we to do? Col. 3:1-2

3. What are we eagerly awaiting? Phil. 3:20; Col.3:4

4. What two things are God's children called in Romans 8:17?

5. What is the guarantee of our inheritance? Eph. 1:13; II Cor. 1:22

6. What does I Peter 1:4-5 say about our inheritance?

7. In Romans 8:29 what is the hope of our salvation?

8. I Thess. 4:15-18 describes this time. Describe what will happen.

9. I Cor. 15:50-54 also describes this time. What information do you learn here?

10. What does Phil. 3:21 say about our resurrection body?

11. What will happen next? Romans 14:10-12

12. Where will Christ then take us? John 14:1-3

13. When we return with Christ to set up His kingdom on earth, what will Christ give us? Rev. 2:26, 3:21

14. After the Millennial Kingdom we will spend eternity with Christ in the New Jerusalem on the New Earth. From Rev. 22:3-6, what will be our role?

ON A PERSONAL NOTE . . .
- Compare and contrast what a *"citizen of heaven"* and a *"citizen of earth"* look like to us (externally) and to God (internally).

- Spend time in prayer praising and thanking God for our wonderful inheritance in Christ.

"Back to the Future"
End Times Prophecy, from Genesis to Revelation
Lesson 5 – The Church

REVIEW:

This week we have seen that although Jesus retuned to Heaven after the resurrection, He did not leave us alone and without hope. He sent the Holy Spirit to indwell those in Christ, baptizing them into the church, the Body of Christ. We have God as our Father, and Jesus is interceding for us at the Father's right hand. Through the Spirit, God's divine power "has given us everything we need for life and godliness" in this world (II Peter 1:4). However, it is not for this world that we live. Our citizenship is now in heaven (Phil. 3:20). We are to set our hearts and our minds on things above (Col. 3:1) as we eagerly await the Savior's return from there (Phil. 3:20). The destiny of the church is a heavenly destiny. All of our promises and expectations are heavenly in character.

Romans 8:17 tells us that when we became children of God, we also became co-heirs with Christ. In Ephesians 1:18, Paul prays that "the eyes of your heart may be enlightened in order that you may know the hope to which he has called you, the riches of his glorious inheritance in the saints, and his incomparably great power for us who believe." Many other passages speak of the Christian's glorious inheritance. We are told that the Holy Spirit in our hearts is God's seal of ownership on us, guaranteeing what is to come (Eph. 1:13; II Cor. 1:22). Our inheritance is one that can never perish, spoil or fade and is kept in heaven for us until the last time when Christ will return to take us to the Father's home (I Peter 1:4-5; John 14:3).

Although we received freedom from the penalty of sin at the moment of our salvation (justification) and we are currently being freed from the power of sin (progressive sanctification), we are not currently free from the presence of sin. Our bodies were born with a fallen nature into a fallen world. It will only be when our bodies are redeemed at Jesus' return that we will be free from the presence of sin. It is this bodily redemption (glorification) that is the hope of our salvation (Romans 8:22-25),

At what is referred to as the Rapture, the Lord will one day return, and the dead in Christ will receive their glorified bodies first. Next, the living in Christ will be *caught up in the air* and given glorified bodies. From that point on, the Body of Christ will be physically with the Lord forever. (I Thess. 4:15-18). This event will happen in the twinkling of an eye, and our bodies will be imperishable, immortal, and glorious like Christ's (I Cor. 15:50-54; Phil. 3:21).

Next we will each stand before the Judgment Seat of Christ (Romans 14:10-12). As all who appear at this seat are saved, this will not be a judgment of condemnation, but one of rewards for the deeds we have done while on earth which have eternal value (Eph. 6:7-9; II Cor. 5:10). As the purified Bride, we are united with Christ and taken to our new home in heaven, spared from the troubles of the Tribulation (Daniel's 70th week).

When Christ returns to earth to set up His promised kingdom on earth, we will return with Him (Rev. 19:14) and will rule with Him for 1000 years (II Cor. 6:1-3; Rev. 2:26, 3:21). Finally, we will live in the New Jerusalem on the New Earth. There we will be servants of God and of the Lamb and will reign forever and ever (Rev. 22:1-6).

As you can see, those in Christ have a glorious future, no matter what happens while here on earth. I am reminded of the passage in Isaiah 64:4 which is quoted in I Cor. 2:9 and says, "No eye has seen, no ear has heard, no mind has conceived what God has prepared for those who love him." It is because of these promises that Paul exhorts us to "purify ourselves from everything that contaminates body and spirit, perfecting holiness out of reverence for God (II Cor. 7:1).

"Back to the Future"
End Times Prophecy, from Genesis to Revelation
Lesson 5 – The Church

*** DAY 4: New Covenant of the Church

1. Read Gal. 3:6-14; 26-29.
   a. What did God promise Abraham concerning *all nations*? v. 8

   b. To what was God's promise to Abraham pointing? v. 8

   c. What made fulfillment of this promise possible? v. 13

   d. What do those in the faith receive? v. 14

   e. So who are considered to be the spiritual offspring of Abraham? v. 7

   f. What two terms describe those who belong to Christ? v. 29

2. Read Rom 4:9-17.
   a. What two specific groups make up Abraham's spiritual descendants? vv. 11-12
      (see also Romans 2:28-29)

   b. What is the promise that Abraham and those in the faith received? v.13

3. How do the following New Testament references relate the Church to the new covenant?
   a. Luke 22:20; Matt. 26:28; Mark 14:24; I Cor. 11:25

   b. II Cor. 3:6

ON A PERSONAL NOTE . . .
- Some people use *OT scriptures associated with the New Covenant* to support the "prosperity gospel" (Christians can expect worldly blessings). How would you correct their thinking?

"Back to the Future"
End Times Prophecy, from Genesis to Revelation
Lesson 5 – The Church

REVIEW:
The term "seed of Abraham" is used three different ways in Scripture. First the term is used to refer to the *physical* descendants of Abraham. As far as the Abrahamic covenant was concerned, God narrowed the *seed* to those who were descendants of Abraham through Jacob (see Romans 9:6-13).

Next, the term "seed of Abraham" can refer to the Israelites who were genuine believers (Romans 2:28-29). Scripture makes it clear that many of the promises of the covenant will be fulfilled only by the *believing natural seed*.

Finally the term "seed of Abraham" is seen to refer to Gentiles who have been saved through faith in Christ. (Gal. 3:6-9). They are heirs of the promise given to "all families of the earth" in Gen. 12:3. Nowhere, however, does Scripture say that the Church will inherit or fulfill the promises given to the physical descendants of the Abrahamic Covenant.

Romans 4:11-12 refers to both the second and third of these three groups. These verses tell us that the *spiritual seed* of Abraham encompasses true believers of all time, both the believing natural seed of Abraham and Gentles who have personally placed their faith in Christ.

Previously we studied the passages in the Old Testament regarding the New Covenant that God made with the Israelites. Its promises were to Israel as a nation, yet it also promised that those who knew Him would participate in the blessings of salvation. Since the Church was a mystery and not known, there was obviously no application of the New Covenant to the Church in the Old Testament. However the many New Testament references to the New Covenant make it evident that this is an important doctrine of the New Testament. Though most agree that the New Covenant has its ultimate fulfillment in Israel during the Millennial Kingdom, there are differing opinions as to how the New Covenant of the Old Testament relates to the New Covenant for the Church.

Some say the New Covenant is exclusively for Israel and deny that there is a New Covenant for the Church. They would say that at the Lord's Supper, Jesus was talking to the disciples, all Israelites, and that they clearly would have in mind the New Covenant pertaining to Israel. However, the Lord's Supper was clearly a time when the Lord was revealing the new program of the Church.

Another view is that the covenant was for Israel, but has applications for the Church - the Church inherited the promises of the New Covenant that were intended for Israel. This view confuses the promises to Israel, the physical offspring of Abraham, and the promises to the Church, the spiritual offspring of Abraham. Still others say that there are two new covenants in the Bible - one in the Old Testament for Israel and one in the New Testament for the Church.[1]

In my opinion, however, Walvoord offers the best explanation saying that "because the new covenant for Israel as well as the new covenant for the church both stem from the death of Christ... there is one new covenant, commonly recognized as the covenant of grace."[2] Romans 4:16 supports this thought: "*Therefore, the promise comes by faith, so that it may be by grace and may be guaranteed to all Abraham's offspring—not only to those who are of the law but also to those who are of the faith of Abraham. He is the father of us all.*"

Under the New Covenant, Christ's death is the grounds of salvation for everyone from Adam to the last person saved (Acts 4:12). It provides God's blessings for those people, whether Jew or Gentile, who do not deserve them. When Israel is restored in the millennial kingdom, it will be an act of grace, just as the Church receives its blessing as an act of grace. The New Covenant offers salvation to all in time through faith (not by works) by grace (dependent on the work of Christ). This covenant of grace is a gift from God and will be observed for eternity.[3]

The Church has been given the eternal role of demonstrating the grace of God and the power of His resurrection. Israel has a similar role of illustrating the how a gracious God fulfills his covenant promises in both the judgments and restorations of Israel. As Christians, some of the spiritual promises of the new covenant apply, but it will be during the Millennial Kingdom that both the physical and the spiritual promises of the New Covenant will be fully fulfilled. Walvoord sums it up by saying, "The doctrine of grace, as it relates to the Church, includes the provisions of the Church age, its completion, its rapture, and its eternal blessing. As far as Israel is concerned, the doctrine of grace especially relates to the millennial kingdom (Jer. 31:31-37)." [4]

> *But you have come to Mount Zion, to the heavenly Jerusalem, the city of the living God. You have come to thousands upon thousands of angels in joyful assembly, to the church of the firstborn, whose names are written in heaven. You have come to God, the judge of all men, to the spirits of righteous men made perfect, to Jesus the mediator of a new covenant, and to the sprinkled blood that speaks a better word than the blood of Abel.   Hebrews 12:24*

1. Walvoord, <u>Major Bible Prophecies</u>, p. 188.
2. Ibid., p. 189.
3. Ibid., pp. 189-191.
4. Ibid., pp. 187, 190.

"Back to the Future"
End Times Prophecy, from Genesis to Revelation
Lesson 5 – The Church

*** DAY 5: Distinctions of the Church

Hopefully you have seen that God has two entirely separate purposes and two entirely different programs for the nation of Israel and for the Church, a mystery not revealed in the Old Testament. The Church has not simply replaced Israel and inherited its promises, as some would say. In his book Systematic Theology IV, Lewis Sperry Chafer has compiled a list of distinctions between Israel and the Church. Study the chart on the following page, making sure you understand each distinction. List below any questions you wish to discuss in class.

This would also be a great time to review Appendix Two: Destination of the Dead, before we move on next week to our study of the Rapture.

"Back to the Future"
End Times Prophecy, from Genesis to Revelation
Lesson 5 – The Church

Distinctions Between Israel and the Church*

		Israel	The Church
1.	Extent of Biblical Revelation:	4/5th of Bible	1/5th of Bible
2.	Divine Purpose:	earthly promises in the covenant	heavenly promises in the gospel
3.	Seed of Abraham:	Physical seed	spiritual seed
4.	Birth:	physical birth that produces a relationship	spiritual birth that brings relationship
5.	Headship:	Abraham	Christ
6.	Covenants	Abrahamic and all the following covenants	Abrahamic and the new covenants
7.	Nationality:	one nation	from all nations
8.	Divine Dealing:	national and individual	individual only
9.	Dispensations:	seen in all ages from Abraham	seen only in the present age
10.	Ministry:	no missionary activity, no gospel to preach	a commission to fulfill
11.	Death of Christ:	guilty nationally, to be saved by it	perfectly saved by it now
12.	The Father:	by a peculiar relationship God was Father to the nation	we are related individually to God as Father
13.	Christ:	Messiah, Immanuel, King	Saviour, Lord, Bridegroom, Head
14.	The Holy Spirit:	came upon some temporarily	indwells all
15.	Governing Principle:	Mosaic law system	grace system
16.	Divine Enablement:	None	the Indwelling Holy Spirit
17.	Farewell Discourse:	Olivet Discourse	Upper Room discourse
18.	Promise of Christ's Return:	in power and glory for judgment	to receive us to himself
19.	Position:	a servant	members of the family
20.	Christ's earthly reign:	Subjects	co-reigners
21.	Priesthood:	*had* a priesthood	*is* a priesthood
22.	Marriage:	unfaithful wife	Bride
23.	Judgments:	must face judgment	delivered from all judgments
24.	Position in Eternity:	spirits of just men made perfect in the	church of the firstborn in the new heavens

*Lewis Sperry Chafer., Systematic Theology IV, pp.47-53.

"Back to the Future"
End Times Prophecy, from Genesis to Revelation
Lesson 6 – The Rapture

*** DAY 1: Christ's Second Coming

Christ's Second Coming Is Certain
- 318 references in NT to Lord's second coming
- mentioned or alluded to in 22 of 27 NT books
- Jesus promised he would return again
- angels, disciples, and Paul promised his return
- most important doctrine in the Bible, next to salvation
- next major event of prophecy

Christ's Second Coming Will Occur in Two Phases
The Rapture and His Glorious Appearing (return to earth) - different *places*, different *times*, for different *people*, for different *purposes*

Look up the scriptures relating to each phase. Using these scriptures and any prior knowledge of the two events, list as many differences between the Rapture and His Glorious Appearing you can find.

Rapture
I Thess. 4:13-18; I Cor. 15:51-53

Glorious Appearing of Christ
Joel 3:12-16; Zech. 14:1-5; Matt. 24:29-31; 25:31-46; Rev. 19:11-21

Rapture:	His Glorious Appearing:

ON A PERSONAL NOTE . . .
- Read II Peter 3:18. As there are many different interpretations of the scriptures we will look at this week, spend time in prayer asking God to direct you into all wisdom and knowledge through His Holy Spirit, living in you . . . to Him be the glory!

"Back to the Future"
End Times Prophecy, from Genesis to Revelation
Lesson 6 – The Rapture

REVIEW:
We have seen that there are two phases to the Lord's Coming to earth: the first time to provide salvation for all mankind and the second time to set up His Kingdom on Earth. Likewise, as we study the scriptures, we see there will be two phases of His Second Coming. The first phase, when Christ returns to take His church to His Father's house (John 14:1-3), is called the Rapture. The second phase begins with His Glorious Appearing (Rev.19), when Christ returns with the church to reign on earth.

As we study the Rapture this week, the differences between the two phases will become more apparent. Before beginning our study, familiarize yourself with the following table, drawn from the writing of J. Dwight Pentecost in <u>Things to Come,</u> pp. 206-207.

Rapture	Glorious Appearing
Removal of all believers	Appearing of the Son
Saints caught up in the air	Christ returns to earth
Christ comes to claim His bride	Christ returns with the bride
Removal of the church and start of tribulation	Establishment of Millennial Kingdom
Imminent	Preceded by a multitude of signs
Brings message of comfort	Accompanied by a message of judgment
Related to the program of the church	Related to the program for Israel and the world
A mystery revealed in New Testament	Predicted in Old and New Testaments
Believers are judged	Gentiles and Israel are judged
Creation left unchanged	Entails change in creation
Gentiles are unaffected	Gentiles are judged
Israel's covenants unfulfilled	All Israel's covenants fulfilled
No particular relationship to evil	Evil is judged
Takes place before the day of wrath	Follows day of wrath
For believers only	Has its effect on all men
Expectation of the church is "the Lord at hand" (Phil. 4:5)	Expectation of Israel is "the kingdom is at hand" (Mt. 24:14)
Expectation of church is to be taken into the Lord's presence	Expectation of Israel is to be taken into the kingdom

"Back to the Future"
End Times Prophecy, from Genesis to Revelation
Lesson 6 – The Rapture

*** DAY 2: Christ's Return for the Church

1. In John 14:2-3, the first mention of the rapture in the Bible, why did Jesus say he was returning for his own?

2. Read I Thess. 4:13-18, the central passage which describes the rapture.
    a. Where does the Lord come from?

    b. Who does He bring with Him?

    c. What three sounds announce his descent?

    d. After the Lord's descent what first happens?

    e. Then, what happens to those who are still alive?

    f. Where do we actually meet the Lord?

    g. How long will we be with the Lord after that?

3. From Phil. 3:20-21, what will also happen at this time?

4. Read I Cor. 15:51-53
    a. Why does Paul call this a mystery?

    b. How fast will the rapture happen?

    c. What two adjectives describe our resurrected body?

5. On what do we base our hope of being resurrected? I Cor. 15:20-23

ON A PERSONAL NOTE . . .
- What will some of the ramifications be for those left on earth
    1) at that moment?

    2) in the days to follow?

- Will non-Christians in your life wonder where you are? What have you told them concerning your departure plans? How have you encouraged them to come with you?

6-3

"Back to the Future"
End Times Prophecy, from Genesis to Revelation
Lesson 6 – The Rapture

REVIEW:
As we live our lives here on earth we are always looking forward to the *next* event - the next holiday, the next vacation, the next time we see our extended family, the next weekend, the next month, the next year, . . . As members of God's family, Christians rejoice in God's mercy and grace as we look forward to the final stage of our salvation, the resurrection of our bodies (Romans 8:23). This will occur at the supernatural removal of the church called the Rapture.

The term rapture comes from the Latin word *rapturo,* meaning *"caught up."* The Greek verb it is translated from is *harpazo,* denoting a sudden, irresistible act of carrying off by force.[1] The Rapture is not found anywhere in the Old Testament. Appropriately, it was first announced by Jesus Christ our Lord to the disciples in the Upper Room (John 14:2-3). The disciples, beginning to understand the difference between the first and second coming of Christ, were riddled with anxiety and fear. In John 14, Jesus comforts them by revealing more information about their future.

Jesus revealed to the disciples for the first time that believers would be removed from the earth prior to His return to set up His Kingdom. Jesus Himself would come back to take them to the place that He was going to prepare for them in Heaven. And from that time on, they would remain with Christ forever. This promise was not made to mankind in general, but to the disciples, who represent the church. The Rapture will include all believers from the Day of Pentecost to the time of the Rapture.

The central passage on the rapture of the church is found in I Thessalonians 4:13-18. Here we find many details of this important truth. The Thessalonians were clearly looking forward to the return of Christ as the next prophetic event and were grieving that believers who had died would miss it. Paul expounds on the Rapture, assuring them that their departed friends and relatives would be included. Paul tells them that the Rapture was as certain as the death and resurrection of Jesus Christ. At the Rapture, four distinct events will occur.

First we see the *return* of Christ. The Lord Himself will descend from Heaven. Accompanying His return will be three sounds comprising the signal from heaven. There will be a shout of command, probably from the Lord Himself, implying authority and urgency. Next we hear the voice of the archangel. "The only other reference to the archangel is in Jude 9 where he is identified as Michael. He is either the leader of the holy angels or one of the primary leaders. Since he and the other angels have been commissioned to protect the people of God (Dan. 12:1; Heb. 1:14), it may be that he is present to protect the saints of God from Satan and his forces as they pass through his domain... No indication is given as to what is said by Michael, but perhaps it is a word of victory."[2] The third sound will be the sound of a trumpet of God. It is interesting to note that since the days of Moses, trumpets were used to call God's people together for assembly (Num. 10:2). At the Rapture, this trumpet summons all believers together, both the living and the dead, to be taken by Christ to the Father's house. It is probable that unbelievers will hear the sounds, but not understand what is taking place. (See Acts 9:27 and John 12:28-39.)

Next we see a *resurrection*. In I Thessalonians 4:14, we are told that Christ will bring with Him the *spirits* of all Church Age believers who have died since the Day of Pentecost. In v16, we are told that they will be the first to receive their glorified bodies ("*the dead in Christ will rise first*").

Following the resurrection of the dead is the *rapture* of all living believers. While technically only living believers are "raptured," the term *Rapture* applies to the entire event. Paul explains in v. 17 that they will be caught up in the air into the Lord's presence without experiencing physical death. I Corinthians 15:50-53 tells us that their bodies will be made immortal and imperishable. And Phil. 3:20-21 says that their bodies will be like Christ's glorious body.

We also learn in I Corinthians 15 that both the resurrection from the dead and the rapture of the living will happen *"in a moment, in the twinkling of an eye."* The word for "moment" is the same word from which the word "atom" comes. The word means "indivisible," although the atom has now been split. The resurrection of the dead and the translation of the living will occur in an *indivisible* instant of time.[3]

"Back to the Future"
End Times Prophecy, from Genesis to Revelation
Lesson 6 – The Rapture

I Thessalonians 4:17 next describes a *reunion*. There in the clouds all believers since the Day of Pentecost, both those who had died and those still living at the time of the Rapture, will meet victoriously together with Christ.

Finally, in I Thessalonians 4:18 Paul gives us **reassurance** that from that moment on we will *remain* in the presence of the Lord forever!

It is important to note that at the completion of the Rapture:
- Christ's promise to return for His own is fulfilled.
- Our salvation is complete, as our bodies are redeemed from the presence of sin.
- All believers (Church Age) have been united with Christ forever.
- All remaining on earth are unsaved.
- Remaining unresurrected spirits are those of unbelievers in Hades and the Old Testament saints in Paradise of Heaven.
- The next prophetic event will be the Tribulation.

1. Understanding End Times Prophecy, Paul Benware, p. 208.
2. Ibid., Paul Benware, p. 211.
3. Basic Theology, Charles C. Ryrie, p. 538.

"Back to the Future"
End Times Prophecy, from Genesis to Revelation
Lesson 6 – The Rapture

*** DAY 3: The Glorified Body – Equipped for Eternity

1. In Romans 8:23, what is the receiving of our glorified body called?

    Of what is the final stage? *(See Lesson 1, Day 5 Review)*

2. What do both Romans 8:23 and II Cor. 5:2 say?

3. Read I Corinthians 15:35-58
    a. Compare our present body to our future, resurrected body? vv. 42-44

    b. What do vv. 45-49 reveal?

    c. From I Corinthians 15:50-53, why must our bodies be made new?

4. What light is shed in the following verses about our resurrected bodies?

    Phil. 3:20-21; I John 3:2

    John 20:27

    Luke 24:13-18

    Luke 24:35-40

    Luke 24:42-43

    John 20:19, 26; Luke 24:31

    Rev. 1:16

ON A PERSONAL NOTE . . .
- Man is born spiritually dead in sin, but by regeneration the believer is spiritually resurrected (made alive). From Rom. 6:4-6, 13; Eph. 2:5-10; and Eph. 4:21-24, what are some parallels between your spiritual resurrection and your future bodily resurrection?

"Back to the Future"
End Times Prophecy, from Genesis to Revelation
Lesson 6 – The Rapture

REVIEW:

We saw yesterday that at the Rapture, in the twinkling of an eye, all believers in Christ, whether living or dead, will be caught up with Christ in their glorified bodies. Romans 8:29 tells us that the very purpose for which God chose us before the beginning of time was that we may be "conformed to the image of his Son." Ephesians 1:4 tells us that we will be "holy and blameless before Him in love." And Phil. 1:6 tells us that when we meet Christ in the air, our salvation will be complete. We shall be gloriously perfected. Our whole body and soul will be completely new in essence and flawless. It is then that we will be taken to live with Christ in Heaven - the perfect place (John MacArthur, The Glory of Heaven, p. 118).

In Romans 8:23 Paul says that we are waiting eagerly for the redemption of our bodies. And in II Corinthians 5:2 he says that we long to be clothed "with our dwelling for heaven." But what will this glorified (resurrected) body be like?

Paul expounds on the glorified or resurrected body in I Corinthians 15. Paul compares the resurrection of the body to the planting of a seed which produces a plant that is far better. The natural body is sown in death and decay but raised imperishable; it is sown in dishonor but raised in glory; it is sown in weakness but raised in power; and it is sown a natural body but raised a spiritual body (vv. 42-44). Paul goes on to say that just as our earthly body was like Adam's, so our heavenly body will be like Christ's resurrection body (vv. 45-49). It is only in the perfected glorified body that we can live in the presence of God (vv. 50-53).

From Phil. 3:21, we learn two important things concerning our glorified body. First it will not be another body, but will be our earthly body glorified. And second, it will have the same qualities as Christ's resurrected body (see also I John 3:2).

In The Glory of Heaven, p.130, John MacArthur writes,
> "Christ's resurrection body was the same body as before not a whole new one. After He arose, the tomb was empty. The body itself was resurrected - the very same body, but in a glorified state. The wounds from His crucifixion were still visible (John 20:27). He could be touched and handled - He was not merely an apparition or a phantom (Luke 24:39). He looked human in every regard. He conversed a long time with the disciples on the road to Emmaus, and they never once questioned His humanity (Luke 24:13-18). He ate real, earthly food with His friends on another occasion (vv. 42-43). Yet His body had other-worldly properties. He could pass through solid walls (John 20:19). He could appear in different forms so His identity was not immediately obvious (Mark 16:12). He could suddenly appear out of nowhere (Luke 24:36). And He could ascend directly into heaven in bodily form (Luke 24:51; Acts 1:9)."

MacArthur also points out that in Revelation 1:16 Christ's face is shining like the sun. And Daniel 12:3 compares the glorified bodies of the righteous to the brightness of the heaven and the shining of the stars. Not only will our bodies know no pain, tears, sorrow, sickness, or death, but they will shine in brilliant splendor (The Glory of Heaven, p.134).

By becoming spiritually alive, one enters into fellowship with God. The old self is laid aside, or put to death, and the new self is put on. One experiences a newness of life. Likewise, when we receive our resurrected bodies, we will be taken physically by Christ into the presence of God where we will experience an unparalleled life full of joy and peace. No wonder Paul writes in Phil. 3:20 that "our citizenship is in heaven, from which we eagerly wait for a Savior, the Lord Jesus Christ."

"Back to the Future"
End Times Prophecy, from Genesis to Revelation
Lesson 6 – The Rapture

*** DAY 4: The Rapture is Next!

1. In Rev. 3:10, from what does Jesus promise to keep the church?

2. In I Thessalonians 1:9-10, what was the believers' hope?

3. I Thessalonians 5:1-11 - Rapture in relation to the Day of the Lord
   a. What will come as a thief in the night?

   b. To whom do you think the word "they" refers?

   c. From v. 3,
      - What are they saying when this happens?

      - How will destruction come upon them?

      - From what you know about end times, to what period is Paul referring?

   d. In v. 4, who becomes the subject of Paul's writing?

   e. To what does Paul say believers are not destined? v. 9

   f. What does v. 10 tell us?

4. Read II Thessalonians 2:1-8
   a. Which phase of the Lord's coming is Paul discussing? What phrase in v. 1 makes this clear?

   b. By what were the Thessalonian believers not to be shaken? v. 2

   c. What does Paul say must happen before the Day of the Lord comes? v. 3

   d. And what must occur before the man of lawlessness is revealed?

   e. Who do you think the "restrainer" is?

ON A PERSONAL NOTE . . .
Based on the above scriptures, how would you respond to someone who says there is no evidence that the church will escape the Tribulation? (This happened to me recently before writing this lesson, and I failed miserably!)

"Back to the Future"
End Times Prophecy, from Genesis to Revelation
Lesson 6 – The Rapture

REVIEW:
The pretribulation rapture position holds that "the church, the body of Christ in its entirety will, by resurrection and translation, be removed from the earth before any part of the seventieth week of Daniel begins" (Pentecost, Things to Come, p 193). This theory relies on the literal method of interpreting Scripture. A number of arguments support the pretribulation rapture position. The list is long, but some of the main ones are discussed here.

1. Nature and focus of the Tribulation
Let's start by looking at the nature and the scope of the Tribulation. There are many words used in both the Old and New Testaments to describe the *entirety* of this period - wrath, judgment, indignation, punishment, hour of trial, hour of trouble destruction, and darkness. It is obvious that during this time, the wrath of God will be poured out upon the *whole* earth.

However, it is clear from Daniel 9:24 that during this period, God is dealing particularly with the nation of Israel. Jeremiah 30:7 refers to the Tribulation as "the time of Jacob's trouble." The 70 weeks of Daniel are related only to God's program for Israel. A look at Dan. 9:24-27 confirms this, as we see only references to Israel: 1) the Covenant is made with Israel, 2) the Jewish temple is rebuilt, 3) Jewish sacrifices are reinstituted, 4) the Jewish temple is desecrated, and 5) the repentance and blessing of Israel in their land is in view.

Since the church did not exist until after the 69th week of Daniel, it had no part in the first 69 weeks. *It therefore follows that the church will have no part in the 70th week.* In fact, there is no mention of the Church anywhere in passages concerning the Tribulation, Old or New Testament. In Rev. 4-19, believers are referred to as believing Gentiles or believing Jews.

2. Purpose of the Tribulation
Also, we must look at the purposes of the Tribulation. The first purpose, found in Rev. 3:10, is to "test those who dwell on the earth." The description, "those who dwell on the earth," appears seven other times in Revelation and refers not to a geographical position but to a moral classification. The word for dwell is *katoikeo* and has the idea of permanence. These "earth dwellers" are those who consider their citizenship to be on earth and have identified themselves with the earth's commerce and religion. The second thing to notice is the use of the infinitive "to test." In his Greek-English Lexicon of the New Testament, Joseph Henry Thayer states that when God is the subject, the infinitive means, "to inflict evils upon one in order to prove his character and the steadfastness of his faith." Since the true church considers its citizenship to be in Heaven and since the Father never sees the church except perfected in Christ, the Tribulation period clearly is not intended for the church.[4]

In Luke 1:17 (See also Malachi 4:4-5.), we see that the second purpose of Daniel's seventieth week is to "make ready a people prepared for the Lord." As was the ministries of Elijah and John the Baptist, the ministry of "the Elijah of the Tribulation" will be that of preparing a remnant in Israel for the advent of the Lord, the coming of her King. Here again, the church, holy and without blemish, is not in view.

3. The Union of the Church with Christ
The New Testament makes it clear that there is a union between Christ and His church (head and body, bridegroom and bride, vine and branches, etc.). The believer is brought into a oneness with Him. Jesus lives within us.

If the church is in the Tribulation, Christ likewise would be subjected to the wrath and judgment of the period. This is impossible. In addition, scripture makes it clear that the church too has been perfected and delivered from all judgment (Rom. 8:1, John 5:24, I John 4:17). The unity of Christ and His church poses another problem if the church is in the seventieth week. Rev. 13:7 says that in the seventieth week, authority over *all* is given to the beast and to Satan, who is the power behind the beast. If the church were in this period, that would mean that either Christ would lose His place as the Head or that because of his union with the Church, He too would be subjected to Satan's authority. This too is impossible.[5]

4. The Distinction between Rapture and Second Coming
This topic was the subject of Day One's lesson.

"Back to the Future"
End Times Prophecy, from Genesis to Revelation
Lesson 6 – The Rapture

5. The Rapture is an imminent, signless event looked forward to by the early Christians
This subject will be covered tomorrow in Day Five's lesson.

6. There is an interval needed between the Rapture and Christ's Return to Earth
Certain events predicted for the church must occur between the Rapture and the Return. These include 1) the Judgment seat of Christ, 2) the presentation of the church to Christ, 3) the Marriage of Lamb, and 4) there must be time for the salvation of people who will populate the earth during the Millennial Kingdom.

7. Scripture supports it

a. Revelation 3:10 – promise to *keep* the church *from* the *hour* of testing
The word John uses for "from" is the word *"ek,"* which means to escape out of, and not the word *"en,"* which means "to stand firm in." Therefore the promise for the church is that it will be removed from the sphere of testing and not just preserved through it. In addition, it is not the trouble itself that we are kept from, but the very hour itself.

b. I Thessalonians 1:9-10 – the church is promised *rescue* from the wrath to come
Paul clearly indicates that our expectation is the revelation of his Son from heaven who will deliver us from the Tribulation. The word deliver comes from "*rhuomai*" and means "to rescue from something by a forcible act, to exempt from entering into a distress." The word "*ek*" is again used and translated "from" indicating the completeness of our rescue by Christ.

c. I Thessalonians 5:1-11 – the church is of the day, a *different day*
Paul had been discussing the Rapture in I Thess. 4. Paul uses the word "now" (translated from the Greek phrase *"peri de"*) in I Thess. 5:1, indicating that he is talking about a new and contrasting subject. Paul says that the "day of the Lord" will come like a thief in the night. The Rapture closes the Church Age and begins the *"Day of the Lord."* These verses make it clear that we are of *the* day, a different day, and that we are not destined to wrath and darkness. We are destined to the completion of our salvation and to eternal life in the light of Christ.[6]

d. II Thessalonians 2:1-8
Paul wrote this passage to assure early believers that the Rapture (v. 1) would come before the Day of the Lord (v. 2). Evidently some were spreading reports that the suffering the Thessalonians were undergoing was a sign that the Day of the Lord had begun. This was an early appearance of the belief in a post-tribulation rapture. Paul refutes this idea by saying that the first major feature of the Day of the Lord is the revelation of the man of lawlessness (antichrist). He then reminds them of His teaching that the lawless one cannot be revealed until the one who now restrains him is taken out of the way. If the restrainer is God, in the power of the Holy Spirit, then it becomes evident that this restraint cannot be lifted as long as the Holy Spirit indwells the church and is resident on earth. Yes, the Holy Spirit is *omnipresent*, but it is only in the Church Age that the Holy Spirit has been *resident* on earth. This would require that the Rapture occur before the antichrist is revealed.[7]

---

4. J. Dwight Pentecost, Things to Come, pp. 197-198.
5. Ibid., p. 200.
6. Ibid., p. 217.
7. John Walvoord, Major Bible Prophecies, p. 274.

"Back to the Future"
End Times Prophecy, from Genesis to Revelation
Lesson 6 – The Rapture

*** DAY 5: The Rapture is Imminent!

1. What is Webster's definition of "imminent"?

2. What phrases in the following scriptures indicate the imminency of the Rapture?
    a. Romans 13:12

    b. Hebrews 10:24-25, 37

    c. James 5:7-9

    d. I Peter 4:7

    e. I John 2:18

    f. Rev. 1:1

    g. Rev. 3:11; 22:7; 22:20

3. What attitudes and actions should we have as we eagerly await Christ's return for His Church?
    a. I Thess. 1:9-10

    b. Hebrews 10:24-25

    c. James 5:8-9

    d. I Peter 4:7

    e. II Peter 3:11-18

    g. I John 3:2-3

ON A PERSONAL NOTE . . .
- Paul tells us to not forsake assembling together. How do you respond to someone who says you don't have to go to church to be a Christian?

- How does knowing that Christ is coming for you encourage you in your walk with Christ? Ask God for the chance to share this hope with someone today.

"Back to the Future"
End Times Prophecy, from Genesis to Revelation
Lesson 6 – The Rapture

REVIEW:

If you are part of the Body of Christ and you are reading this, then Christ has not returned for His own – the Rapture has not occurred!

However, from the very earliest days of the church, believers had the expectation that Christ would return for them soon. The doctrine of imminence states that the coming of the Lord for the church could happen *at any moment*. Other things *might* happen before the Rapture, but nothing else *must* take place before it happens.

Saying that the Rapture is *imminent* is not the same thing as saying that the rapture is *soon*. Just as in the early days of the church, the Lord's return could be at any moment, but it may not be soon. The doctrine of imminence eliminates the church from any participation in the Tribulation, Israel's 70th week.

The nation of Israel was given many signs to look for as they wait for the 2nd Coming of Christ, but there are no signs or events that must take place before Christ's return for the Church. When looking at passages concerning the return of Christ, we must keep in mind that *passages referring to imminency pertain to the Rapture* and *passages demanding signs pertain to Christ's return to earth*.

Many scriptures in the New Testament exhort the believer to be watching for the Lord Himself and to live in light of this return. James 5:8-9 encourages us to be steadfast and kind, not to grumble. I Peter 4:7 admonishes us to be serious and watchful in our prayers. Hebrews 10:24-25 tells us to be faithful in assembling together and to encourage one another. II Peter 3:11 encourages holy conduct and godliness. I John 3:2-3 ties it all together by saying that "everyone who has this hope in Him purifies himself, just as He is pure."

Taken together, these scriptures embrace every aspect of our sanctification. In <u>The Second Coming,</u> John MacArthur writes, "The hope of Christ's imminent return is a catalyst and an incentive for all these things - every fruit of the Spirit, every Christian virtue, everything that pertains to holiness and Christlikeness, everything that belongs to life and godliness" (p. 67).

"Back to the Future"
End Times Prophecy, from Genesis to Revelation
Lesson 7 – The Judgment Seat of Christ

*** DAY 1: What is the Judgment Seat of Christ?

1. **Christ is our Judge.**
    a. In II Tim. 4:8, what title is given to Jesus?

    b. From John 5:22, 27 who gave Jesus the authority to judge?

    c. According to I Cor. 4:2-5 who is not our judge?

    d. What warning are we given in Romans 14:10-12?

2. **II Corinthians 5:9-10 gives us the purpose of the Judgment Seat.**
    a. What should be our goal as Christians?

    b. Since Paul uses "we" as the subject of these verses, who will stand at this judgment seat - believers or unbelievers?

    c. How do we know it is not a judgment for sin? Heb. 8:12; Col. 1:21-22; Rom. 8:1

    d. What is the purpose of the judgment seat?

    e. Give the meaning of "recompense" (NAS) from a dictionary.

    f. What do you think the term "good or bad" means?

3. **I Corinthians 3:10-15 gives us the result of this examination.**
    a. How will fire be used to test one's work?

    b. From v.14, what two possibilities result?

    c. Can you be as sure as Job about your life and your testimony? Job 23:10

4. **When is The Judgment Seat of Christ?**
    a. When does Christ say we will be rewarded? Luke 14:14

    b. Based on I Cor. 4:5, II Tim. 4:8, and Rev. 22:12, what is associated with the Lord's appearing?

    c. What phrases in James 5:7-9 indicate that this event happens after the Rapture? What instructions are given to us who are waiting for the Lord's return?

    d. In Rev. 19:7-9 John sees the raptured Church in Heaven. What indicates that the Bride of Christ has already been rewarded?

ON A PERSONAL NOTE . . .
- Do you think most Christians know about the Judgment Seat of Christ? What are some erroneous thoughts Christians have concerning their coming judgment?

- In light of the Judgment Seat of Christ, think about how you spend your time – serving the LORD, your family, your job, hobbies, etc. How can you more effectively use your time in light of eternity?

"Back to the Future"
End Times Prophecy, from Genesis to Revelation
Lesson 7 – The Judgment Seat of Christ

REVIEW:

Jesus makes it clear in many passages that believers as well as nonbelievers will be judged after death. For unbelievers it will be a time of condemnation when they are judged for rejecting Jesus Christ. Hebrews 9:27-28 says, "*Just as man is destined to die once, and after that to face judgment, so Christ was sacrificed once to take away the sins of many people; and he will appear a second time, not to bear sin, but to bring salvation to those who are waiting for him.*" It is clear - all will be judged. However, the whole canon of Scripture shows that judgment will be at different places, at different times, for different groups of people. The Judgment Seat of Christ is for all Christians, both those who have died and those who are alive when Jesus comes for His own at the Rapture. Old Testament saints, Tribulation saints, and Millennial saints will be resurrected and judged at later times, as will unbelievers of all the ages.

In II Timothy 4:8 Jesus is called the righteous Judge. And we see in John 5:22, 27 that, in fact, God our Father judges no one but has entrusted **all** judgment to Jesus, the Son of Man. For this reason, the Bible says we should not judge others or ourselves, and we should care little what others think of us. It is only Jesus that knows the secrets and motives of our hearts and can judge righteously. It is Jesus alone that we should live to please. (See also Rom. 14:7-8.)

This judgment is not a judgment relating to sin. It is not a matter of whether we are saved or not. Our salvation has already been secured at the cross by Jesus! Hallelujah! We have put our faith in Him. We know Him as the Son of the Most High God. The very fact that one is standing at the Judgment Seat of Christ is proof that he is part of the Body of Christ and will live forever in His presence.

We, the church saints, will be transformed into his presence with glorified bodies at the Rapture! Now when God the Father looks at us, he sees Jesus' blood covering us; the Father sees Jesus' Robe of Righteousness on us! Don't you love God's heavenly eyesight! I must share another thought from Walvoord, "God sees each believer in the perfection of the person and work of the Son."[1]

So why are we here? We find the answer in II Cor. 5:9-10. The only remaining issue is whether what we have done is worthwhile from God's point of view. This question is whether a work is good, or worthwhile, in the sight of God, or whether it is bad, or worthless."[2]

In I Cor. 3:10-15 we are told that the quality of our works will be tested by fire. Only those works that were done in the Spirit and for God's glory will survive the fire and result in reward. What joy and celebration we will experience as we realize that deeds done on earth have brought Christ glory and honor. Works done in our own strength for our own glory will be destroyed by the fire. This will not bring about judgment on us - our salvation is sure, but we will suffer a loss of reward. We will no doubt feel remorse as we realize that our works were of no eternal value and we realize what could have been!

It is clear that the Judgment Seat of Christ will occur immediately after the Rapture. Luke 4:13-17 clearly associates reward with the resurrection, which for Christians will occur at the Rapture. Many other scriptures support the fact that it will be at His Coming (again, for believers at the Rapture) that we will be judged and rewarded. In Rev. 19:7-9, John sees the Lord ready to return to earth with His bride, the Church. She is clothed in bright, clean linen which represents the righteous acts *(plural)* of the saints. The Church in Heaven has already been judged and rewarded accordingly. Thus we can deduce that the Judgment Seat of Christ occurs between the time of the Rapture and the time of Christ's return. We will receive our wedding garments "in the clouds" prior to our Groom taking us to His Father's house.

Paul was motivated to persevere, knowing that one day he would stand before his Lord and Savior, Jesus Christ, to have his life evaluated. Paul's desire was to hear Jesus say, "Well done, good and faithful servant" (Luke 19:17). Do not we all want to hear Jesus say these words about us as well? Now the questions for us to consider are: "Do we follow Christ like he calls us to do? Are we obedient to His Word? Do we love Him with all of our heart, soul, and mind?" What changes can we make to please God every day?

1. Walvoord, <u>Major Bible Prophecies</u>, p. 306.
2. Ibid.

"Back to the Future"
End Times Prophecy, from Genesis to Revelation
Lesson 7 – The Judgment Seat of Christ

*** DAY 2: Paul's Three Analogies of the Judgment Seat of Christ

1. Life as a *Building.* Look again at I Corinthians 3:10-15.
   a. Who has laid the only or best foundation?

   b. What are the six materials that man or woman can use to build upon this foundation?

   c. Which materials will stand the test of fire? What are some works these three might represent?

2. Life as a *Stewardship.* Read Romans 14:10-12 and I Cor. 4:1-7.
   a. Using a dictionary, what is the meaning of a steward (word used in NIV)? And who is our Master?

   b. How are we as believers described in I Cor. 4:1-7?

   c. What is required of a steward?

   d. What does v. 7 remind us about our gifts and abilities?

   e. What light does Luke 12:47-48 shed on our stewardship?

   f. What talents and abilities have you received from God? For whose glory are you using them? What affairs has Jesus put under your charge?

3. Life as a *Race.* I Cor. 9:24-27
   a. In vv. 24 and 26, how does Paul say we should run?

   b. What do vv. 25 and 27 say about training?

   c. What advice does Hebrews 12:1-2 give concerning running the race?

   d. Write a prayer to Jesus concerning your race.

ON A PERSONAL NOTE …
- On the scale below draw a timeline of your life. Are you being a good builder? Steward? Runner? You can draw above and/or below the line. Put a cross on the line at the age you were saved. Estimate by going close to the line, above the line, or below the line to graph your life and how close you have walked with Jesus (heart / motives / works).

+

_____

Age   0   10   20   30   40   50   60   70 . . .

−

"Back to the Future"
End Times Prophecy, from Genesis to Revelation
Lesson 7 – The Judgment Seat of Christ

REVIEW:

We know that Paul used imagery often in his writings that his readers would be familiar with in their culture. His letters include illustrations of soldiers, athletes, farmers, and workers as teaching tools. Paul uses imagery in several passages to illustrate the Judgment Seat of Christ.

In I Cor. 3:10-15, Paul compares living our life to building a building. These verses show us how Christ will evaluate our lives. We must have Christ as our foundation, the basis for our faith and salvation. The materials used in the building may be interpreted as follows: The gold, silver, and precious stones represent the *lasting quality of the builder's work*; and the wood, hay or straw suggest *work that is temporary and valueless*. As discussed yesterday, the quality of these works will be tested by fire resulting in rewards and losses for the individual.

Walvoord gives us the following insight concerning the materials listed in the passage:
"Though the significance of the materials is not given here, gold in Scripture obviously is used to reflect the glory of God, as in the temple and in the Tabernacle. Anything a Christian may do that will glorify God will survive as gold. Silver is the metal of redemption. The Law required that every firstborn son had to be redeemed with five shekels of silver (Num. 18:15-16). Silver, accordingly, speaks of salvation and winning souls for Christ. The costly stones are not identified because they reflect every other act which, from God's point of view, has eternal value. In contrast, wood, hay, and stubble represent varying degrees of material worth in this world, but each is equally reducible to ashes in the fire of Judgment. Straw is of less worth than hay, and hay is of less worth than wood, but all burn equally. The lesson is clear that at the Judgment Seat of Christ, our lives will be evaluated according to what counts for eternity. Worthy works, however, may include many ordinary tasks, such as a mother caring for her child or a father for his family, as anything that is pleasing to God will be considered 'gold, silver, and precious stone.'"[3]

The phrase "judgment seat" in Romans 14:10 comes from the Greek word *bema* which refers to a raised platform. Originally in Athens, an assembly met on the Pnyx Hill. A bema seat "became known for a tribune, two of which were provided in the law courts of Greece; one for the accuser and one for the defendant. It was applied to a Roman tribune or even translated into a throne."[4] In Romans 14:10-12 and in I Cor. 4:1-7 we get a visual picture of a judge in a courtroom on a throne. Paul is picturing Jesus Christ as King sitting on this impressive decorative throne, passing out rewards to those who have been obedient with right hearts, rights motives, and right usage of their gifts, time, and talents for the glory of God. We are judged for our stewardship of the things God has given us. We are warned in Luke 12:48 that from those who have been given much, much more will be asked. This is when we hope to hear "Well done, good and faithful servant" (I Cor. 9:24-27).

In Paul's last illustration, found in I Cor. 9:24-27, Paul appeals to Christians to prepare like one who was preparing for a race. The city of Corinth was famous for the Isthmian Games, a festival of athletic contests similar to the Olympic Games. In these contests, a judge sat along the finish line on what was also known as the Bema seat (a raised platform) to determine how the runners finished. Winners were given a coveted crown of laurel leaves which faded and died within a couple of days. In order to win a race, a runner must go into strict training. He must be in good physical condition and must also be disciplined. He must run with purpose - to win the prize. A runner must also run within the rules, not aimlessly. Likewise, we as Christians must be spiritually fit and disciplined in order to live victoriously over both Satan and the world. We must fix our eyes on Christ, obeying His Word, as we run straight for the finish line. We live our life in order to win Christ's reward when we have "finished the race." The rewards we will receive will not fade away but will last for all of eternity. We will look at the crowns for believers on Day 5.

---

3. Ibid., p. 309.
4. <u>Vine's Complete Expository Dictionary</u>, p. 337.

"Back to the Future"
End Times Prophecy, from Genesis to Revelation
Lesson 7 – The Judgment Seat of Christ

*** DAY 3: What Will Be Judged?

1. Please look up the following verses and record what will be judged.
   a. II Cor. 5:10

   b. Matt. 12:36-37

   c. I Cor. 4:3-5; Eph. 6:7-8

   d. James 3:1; Heb. 13:17

   e. I Cor. 3:10-15

2. Now look up some "good works" mentioned in scripture.
   a. Matt. 5:16

   b. Matt. 26:7-10

   c. I Tim. 6:18

   d. Matt. 10:40-42

3. What losses might occur? (We will look at the rewards tomorrow.)
   a. I John 2:28

   b. I Cor. 3:15

4. Look again at I Corinthians 3:14-16, Regardless of our outcome at the Bema seat, of what can we be sure?

ON A PERSONAL NOTE . . .
Do you read a passage from the Bible each day and meditate on the meaning of it so that the LORD can "speak" to you? Start a journal and record your thoughts and deepest most joys and hurts, for the Lord cares for you. If a verse seems especially significant, write it down, even write a prayer using that verse. You might not get a verse every day. Each week and then each month look back and look for themes and patterns of how God is "speaking" to you through the verses you recorded. Start recording right here. Pick out a verse from the lesson so far this week that seemed to jump off the page at you or really seemed to speak to your heart. Pray it back to the Father. Write down what thoughts come to your mind: **THIS** is the Holy Spirit using the Living Word to teach, comfort, and admonish you.

"Back to the Future"
End Times Prophecy, from Genesis to Revelation
Lesson 7 – The Judgment Seat of Christ

REVIEW:

If you are like me, the verses we looked at today are a wake-up call; they serve as reminders about everyday living to me. Looking at the first question, the Holy Spirit brings to my mind several examples of things I need to confess. The next question, number two, gives me encouragement. I can say yes, by the grace of God, "I've done that," or "I've started to do that!"

Satan likes to help us forget or think we have not done anything for the LORD. Or he like us to spin our wheels doing things that do not have any eternal value. Sometimes our pride gets in the way – we like the personal recognition and achievement. We even may be doing work <u>for</u> the LORD, but we may not be in His will or in His power. That work will be burned up like the wood, hay, and straw! Some of us even become overcommitted in Christian service in too many places where God has not called us, so that our service becomes futile, reward-less work!

These verses take us down to reality. We don't want to waste our lives by producing works by our own efforts instead of being "God's fellow workers" (1Cor. 3:9). We must be ever humble on our knees before God to keep "self" off of the throne of our heart and keep Jesus Christ in first place on the throne of our heart.

On the other hand, what sorrow it would be to come into Jesus' presence empty-handed! Over and over again we have to check our heart condition. This is why a daily time with Jesus is so important. I know I fail at this sometimes, too. A personal relationship with Jesus **every day** keeps us where we need to be. We must let His Word talk to us daily; it is His fresh, living, breathing Breath. I was petrified to get started with this class. You will not believe the verses God had to use to get me moving because I felt so inadequate! I am sure many of you have a testimony, too, of how God called you to a work, and then confirmed to you with scripture that it was His beckoning.

We all want to hear "the still small voice of God" speak to our mind and heart. That can only happen when we are in His Word daily, meditating on His scriptures, memorizing scriptures, and waiting on Him to speak to us. Real prayer is getting to know God and His desires, not just asking for this or that.

I Corinthians 3:14-16 reminds us that regardless of our outcome at the Bema seat, we are saved, we are there in our glorified and sanctified body, and we will never again be separated from the presence of Lord and Savior Jesus Christ. All praise and glory belong to the Father and to His Son Jesus Christ.

"Back to the Future"
End Times Prophecy, from Genesis to Revelation
Lesson 7 – The Judgment Seat of Christ

*** DAYS 4 & 5: Rewards Given

Let's look at the word for crown used in 1 Cor. 9:25 - "*stephanos*" - The Greek word used here was given to the victor in Greek games. It was called the "victor's crown," the symbol of triumph in the games. The crown was just a wreath made of woven olive leaves! Paul tells us that these athletes did all their training to win the race and their only prize was this perishable crown. However, our crown will be imperishable! This same word, *stephanos*, is used to describe the "crown of thorns" which was put on Christ's head by the Roman soldiers (John 19:2,5). A *diadema*, or "kingly crown," would have been inappropriate for the blasphemous nature of His crucifixion. It is at the Second Coming of Christ in Revelation 19:12 that Jesus is crowned with many diadems or kingly crowns!

1. Using the following scriptures, fill in the chart describing the crowns that will be given.

Scripture	Name of Crown	Reason to Receive It
II Timothy 4:7-8		
I Cor. 9:24-27		
James 1:12; Rev. 2:10		
I Thess. 2:19-20; Phil. 4:1		
I Peter 5:1, 4		

2. What other rewards will believers have in Heaven? Some of these rewards include serving the King! Look up the following verses and record the heavenly rewards or job assignments.

Rev. 20:4; Matt. 19:27-30	
Rev. 2:17; 3:12	
Matt. 25:21	
Matt. 6:20	
Rev. 22:3	

"Back to the Future"
End Times Prophecy, from Genesis to Revelation
Lesson 7 – The Judgment Seat of Christ

ON A PERSONAL NOTE . . .

- In the privacy of your home, pick out a crown that you think you will receive, make a crown out of cardboard and aluminum foil. Wear it around as you do house work or care for your children. Sing praise songs! Worship your King! Cast it at His feet! Make one for your children or grandchildren! Worship together! Commit to serving Him with a loving, caring heart!

- How can you prepare for administrative jobs now so you can serve later?

- What do you need to confess so you will not have any shame at the Judgment Seat?

- How can you start teaching this to your children and grandchildren?

"Back to the Future"
End Times Prophecy, from Genesis to Revelation
Lesson 7 – The Judgment Seat of Christ

REVIEW:
In Revelation 4:10, the 24 elders, who are around God's throne representing the glorified church, are seen casting their crowns at the foot of God's throne, fully aware that He alone is responsible for the rewards they have received. Perhaps these crowns include the ones we have looked at today.

The Greek word for "crown" was used of the wreaths or garlands that were placed on the heads of victorious military officials or athletes. Scripture mentions several "victor's crowns" awarded to believers at the Judgment Seat of Christ. Believers are promised crowns of righteousness, victory, life, rejoicing, and glory. In his study Bible, John MacArthur points out that each crown describes a characteristic of eternal life and, unlike the perishable wreaths of garlands, will be imperishable.

Although we are legally declared righteous (*justified*) and holy (*positionally sanctified*) at the moment of our salvation, the Holy Spirit works in us and through us the rest of our lives to purify us from sin and cleanse us from unrighteousness (*progressive sanctification*). Only when He appears at the Rapture for His own will we receive our glorified bodies and have Christ's righteousness perfected in us (glorification). As believers, we long for the day of His appearing when we will receive the crown of eternal righteousness (II Timothy 4:7-8). This crown is sometimes referred to as the "watcher's crown."

We have already looked at II Cor. 9:24-27 (on Day 2). In this passage, Paul compares living our lives for Christ to running a race. We must exercise self-control, as we discipline our bodies, in order to *run* a victorious life, conquering our old, fleshly nature. We must run faithfully *till the end*, dependent on the power of the Spirit, in order to *win* the imperishable or incorruptible wreath (crown). This crown is often called the "runner's crown."

Sometimes described as the "sufferer's crown," the crown of life is promised in James 1:12 and Rev. 2:10. It is probably the reward referred to in Matthew 5:10-12. This is the crown promised to believers who remain faithful under testing and trial, even to the point of death. The persecution and suffering we face in this life for the sake of Christ pales in comparison to the eternal life we look forward to in His Presence.

As followers of Christ, one of our main desires should be to share Christ with others. Although it is God alone who saves sinners, it is our job to share the gospel with those we know and love. I Thess. 2:19-20 indicates that there awaits a Crown of Rejoicing, or a "soul-winners crown," for those who have shared in bringing others to Christ.

The last crown we looked at today is the crown of glory, sometimes called the "shepherd's crown," which is found in I Peter 5:1-4. In this passage, Peter is exhorting those whom God has appointed to care for His flock in the Chief Shepherd's absence. Shepherds must feed, protect, and lead their sheep in the love of Christ. Here, this crown is reserved for Pastors and elders, whose ministries will be evaluated at the Judgment Seat. Those who have been faithful in their duties will receive an eternal crown of glory. I can't help but think that this crown will also be awarded to those who faithfully shepherd smaller groups within the church today - Sunday school teachers, Bible Study teachers, small group leaders, etc.

The last verses we studied this week looked at the rewards we will have in the Presence of our Lord and Savior. Not only will Jesus give us a new and personal name, which only He knows, but we will be given a new name for Him as well. The intimate, personal relationship we will have with Christ is beyond our comprehension. How exciting it is to think about just sitting and talking with Jesus. We will also reign and serve with Him in many possible capacities. Some of us may be mayors, town leaders, or governors of the regions set up by Jesus. Will these be reserved only for men? We do not know. I heard one woman say that she loves to take care of little children in the nursery. She hopes one of her jobs in heaven will be to care for little ones! How about you? How would you like to serve Christ in heaven? There will be big jobs and little jobs in heaven, but all jobs will be important to Jesus.

Many of us think there will not be tears in heaven. However I imagine that those who realize that they either wasted opportunities or did nothing for Jesus with their lives will shed tears. How sad it would be to come before Jesus to find that we should have done more with our lives or that we lived selfishly for ourselves. Missing what <u>could</u> have been ours – this is not we want to experience in Heaven. We will be disappointed in ourselves and see that we have disappointed our Savior. But He will wipe those tears

"Back to the Future"
End Times Prophecy, from Genesis to Revelation
Lesson 7 – The Judgment Seat of Christ

away (Rev. 7:17, 21:4)! Our wonderful Savior will even show grace upon believers who have nothing to show except their salvation.

Stephen Davey shared a poem about this subject a couple of years ago. John MacArthur had shared with him that his grandfather had written it.

When I stand at the judgment seat of Christ
And He shows me His plan for me
A plan how might my life might have been.
I see how I blocked Him here and I checked Him there
And I would not yield my will.
Will there be grief in my Savior's eyes, grief though He loves me?
He would have me rich, but I stand here now poor,
Stripped of all but His grace.
While memory runs like a hunted thing down a path I can't retrace.
My desolate heart will well nigh break with tears I can not shed.
I will cover my face with empty hands and bow my uncrowned head.[5]

We are challenged each day to live a life of surrender. Paul teaches us that each day, whatever we do, should be an act of worship - an act of service with the right heart, motive, or mind-set: "Whatever you do, do for the glory of God" (1 Cor. 10:31). Should we not wake up each morning and begin each day by asking God, "What can I do for you today? How can I glorify you today in my home, with my husband, at my job, with my family, with my friends?" Stop and think about these questions right now. Write down any ideas the Lord brings to your mind.

We must serve and obey Jesus because <u>we love Him</u>, not just to get rewards. The rewards are an added bonus. Service and obedience are proof of our love. Otherwise, is our love real? Our greatest ambition in life should be to please Jesus, to bring Him honor and glory, and praise. Amen.

---

5. Davey, Stephen, "Paul on Mount Everest, Romans 11:33-36," January 6, 2005.

"Back to the Future"
End Times Prophecy, from Genesis to Revelation
Lesson 8 – Jesus' Letters to the Seven Churches

*** DAY 1: The Revelation of Jesus Christ: Rev. 1

1. **The Revelation: Rev. 1:1-3**
   a. According to the first words of the book, about whom is this revelation?

   b. How did John receive this message?

   c. What must we now do with this message and why?

2. **John's greetings and doxology: Rev. 1:4-6**
   a. To whom is John now writing?

   b. As John offers grace and peace, how does he describe each part of the Trinity?

   c. For what three things does John praise Christ for?

3. **John's prophecy: Rev. 1:7-8**
   a. How does John describe Christ's Second Return to earth?

   b. What titles of our Lord God are given in v. 8?

4. **John's encounter with Christ: Rev. 1:9-20**
   a. Where was John when he had this vision?

   b. To which specific churches was John commanded to send his written scroll?

   c. In v. 12, what did John initially see?

   d. From vv. 13-16, describe the one (Jesus) that John saw "among the lampstands." Draw a picture of what John saw, based on this description.

   e. When John fell at Jesus' feet, what did Jesus do and what did He say about Himself?

   f. Jesus then gives John the meanings of the lampstands and the stars. What were they?

ON A PERSONAL NOTE . . .
- Of all the titles and descriptions of Christ given today, which means the most to you and why?
- Write your own response of praise to Christ.

"Back to the Future"
End Times Prophecy, from Genesis to Revelation
Lesson 8 – Jesus' Letters to the Seven Churches

REVIEW:

The book of Revelation reveals many divine truths. But its most important revelation is that of Jesus Christ. It describes all the events surrounding and following His second coming and reveals His majesty, power and glory. It is a revelation from Jesus Christ and about Jesus Christ. We see that this revelation is the Father's gift to the Son, detailing the Son's inheritance from the Father.[1] The revelation was given to John in a vision by an angel so that true believers would know what *must soon take place*. The word *soon* does not mean *the speed with which things will happen,* but that these events are *imminent*. Believers who read or hear this final word of God to man and take it to heart will be *blessed*.

We see in Rev. 1:4 that John is writing his letter to the seven churches in the Roman province of Asia. He begins by sending them grace and peace from God. He identifies the first Person of the Trinity, God the Father, as *Him who is, and was, and is to come*. Our God is timeless and eternal. The second Person, the Holy Spirit, is described as the *seven spirits before the throne*. The number represents the fullness of the Spirit. Jesus, the third Person of the Trinity, is given a threefold description. First, as the *faithful witness,* Jesus spoke the truth concerning the Word and the will of God. Next, as the *firstborn from the dead*, Jesus is preeminent over all who will be resurrected. Finally, as *ruler of the kings of the earth*, Christ is sovereign over the affairs of men.

Just thinking about Christ causes John to burst out in praise, thanking Him for loving us and for saving us from our sins through His sacrifice on the cross. John also thanks Christ for making us part of His kingdom and for making us His priests (indicating our service and our direct access to God).

Next, the first prophecy in the book of Revelation is given. John says that Christ is coming with the clouds (also, Acts. 1:9-11), that every eye will see Him, and that all peoples of the earth will mourn. We are told in Zechariah 13 that many Jews will turn to Christ when they see Him coming and they will be mourning in repentance. The unsaved Gentiles will mourn out of terror, as they realize that their end is near (Matt. 24:30). John's greeting closes with a reminder of who God (and Christ) is. He is the *Alpha and the Omega*, the One *who is, and who was, and who is to come*, and the *Almighty*. Collectively these titles represent our eternal God's omniscience and omnipotence.

John then gives the churches details of when his vision occurred. John reveals that the vision had occurred while he was on the island of Patmos, on the Lord's Day, and while he was in the Spirit. John further notes that he had specifically heard a voice which told him to write down what he saw and to send it to seven specific churches: Ephesus, Smyrna, Pergamun, Thyatira, Sardis, Philadelphia, and Laodicea. We will be looking at each of these churches as the week unfolds.

The first thing John sees in his vision is a total of seven golden lampstands. These lampstands are identified by Christ in v. 20 as the seven churches. The fact that the lamps are golden symbolizes how precious the church is to Christ. Again, the number seven represents fullness or completeness, so the seven churches symbolize the church as a whole. Yes, they were actual churches, but they are also examples of the kinds of churches that have existed as history has unfolded.

Among the seven lampstands John next sees one "like a son of man." This expression is one used in Daniel 7:13 and refers to Christ. He is walking among the lampstands, or churches. John's description that follows is both awe-inspiring and highly symbolic. Christ's *robe and golden sash* depict Him as our Great High Priest (Heb. 4:14-15, 7:25-26). The *whiteness of Christ's head and hair* is like that of God the Father's in Dan. 7:9 and shows that God the Son is also timeless and pure. Jesus' *eyes were like flames of fire*, portraying His omniscience and His fiery judgment of sin. His feet were like *burnished bronze glowing in a furnace*. In ancient times kings sat on elevated thrones, with those being judged sitting beneath the king's feet. Again, fire relates to judgment; thus Christ is seen as having divine authority to judge and punish. Christ's voice was *like the sound of many waters* (another identification with God the Father, cf. Eze. 43:2). His is the voice of sovereign power and authority. Out of Christ's mouth came a *two-edged sword*, used to strike His enemies and defend His people. His face was *brilliantly shining like the sun,* radiating His unfathomable glory.

"Back to the Future"
End Times Prophecy, from Genesis to Revelation
Lesson 8 – Jesus' Letters to the Seven Churches

In Christ's right hand, He held the seven stars. Christ later explains in Rev. 1:19 that the stars represent the angels of the seven churches. The word for angels, *angeloi*, can also means "messengers." Therefore the seven stars probably represent the leading elders and pastors of each the seven churches. The fact that the stars are in Christ's hand shows that Christ, as Head of the Church, sovereignly rules each church through their leaders.

At this sight of Jesus in all His glory, John fell fearfully at his Lord's feet. Jesus places His right hand on John and comforts him, saying that He is First and the Last (eternal), the Living One who was dead and now alive (conqueror of death and able to save forever), and the One who holds the keys of death and Hades (authority over death). A Christian's death and resurrection are both in Christ's hands.

In Revelation 2-3, John records Christ's letter to each of the aforementioned churches in Asia Minor (modern Turkey today). This was almost 2000 years ago, 30 to 40 years after Christ's death. There were many other churches that Jesus could have selected. However, we shall see the importance and sovereignty of the ones chosen. These letters were written and specialized for each church.

The purpose of writing to the churches proved to be very multifaceted. First, the Lord wanted to address the concerns of the individual congregations in Asia Minor. Second, throughout the history of the church there have been similar types of churches which needed to hear the same approvals and admonitions that Christ gave to the churches of John's time. Any church of the twenty-first century could have similar concerns and could be called a "Pergamum" or a "Sardis." Third, each message can be applied to our individual lives, as personal promises were given to "those who hear."

There are those who see these seven churches as also representing, from a historical viewpoint, the development of the church from the early apostolic church of Christ's time to the church which will exist at Christ's Second Coming. I have filled in the last columns of the chart at the end of this week's lesson to give you a brief look at this idea. Tim Lahaye does an excellent job of expounding upon this view in his book Revelation Unveiled (pp. 33-91). Although there is no scriptural support for this interpretation, many hold to this belief, applying the interpretation only where it fits naturally. Furthermore, it must be noted that the first three eras of church history have come and gone, but the last three or four church "types" can be seen today and will continue to exist concurrently in the last days before the Rapture and the Tribulation.

The title used for Jesus to each church becomes the "perfect and personal Jesus" that the members needed to overcome their struggles. As has always been the case, no matter what our circumstances or trials, JESUS IS THE ANSWER. Jesus looked to see how each church was obeying what it had learned from its pastors. He gives an approval, an admonition, and an appeal to each church. Jesus also encourages each church by giving personal assurances to individuals who "hear and overcome." The "overcomers" to whom Christ makes certain promises encompass genuine believers of all times. I John 5:5 says, "Who is the one who overcomes the world, but he who believes that Jesus is the Son of God?" The promises given to believers describe our future with Christ in Heaven, during the Millennial Kingdom, and for all eternity.

We will look at the seven churches individually this week, noting Jesus' words to each. As Jesus wrote to the churches through John, the cities were already being influenced by the world, false doctrine, and Satan, just like future churches in centuries to come. Using Jesus' words, we will complete the chart at the end of this week's lesson as we continue to study.

---

1. MacArthur, The MacArthur New Testament Commentary, p. 18.

"Back to the Future"
End Times Prophecy, from Genesis to Revelation
Lesson 8 – Jesus' Letters to the Seven Churches

*** DAY 2: The Churches at Ephesus and Smyrna: Revelation 2:1-11

1. **Ephesus: The Church Whose Love Has Grown Cold**
   a. For what did the Lord commend the church at Ephesus?

   b. What was Christ's admonishment to the church?

   c. How did He appeal to the church?

   d. What assurance does Christ give?

   e. What title does Christ use for himself to relate to Ephesus? How would this comfort those in the Church of Ephesus?

   f. Use the passage in Acts 19:11-20 to describe an event in Ephesus. How does it fit with Jesus' directions to the church?

2. **Smyrna: The Suffering Church**
   a. What problems are the Christians struggling with in Smyrna?

   b. Why do you think Jesus says they are "rich"?

   c. What does Jesus exhort the church to do?

   d. What title is used for Jesus from chapter one? How would this title give encouragement to the believers in Smyrna?

   e. What assurances does Jesus give for those who are faithful until death?

3. Fill in the chart on the last page concerning Ephesus and Smyrna, using today's answers.

ON A PERSONAL NOTE . . .
- Why do we need to check the condition of our heart often? What are some specific ways we can "remember" and "renew" our first love for our Lord Jesus?

- One of my favorite questions is, *"Are you being persecuted for Christ's sake? If not, why not?"* What are some of the ways you are being persecuted for Christ's sake (i.e. others put you down and criticize your faith or non-Christian relatives criticize how you do things in your home and make fun of how you raise your children)? How do Christ's words to the church of Smyrna convict or encourage you?

"Back to the Future"
End Times Prophecy, from Genesis to Revelation
Lesson 8 – Jesus' Letters to the Seven Churches

REVIEW:

Ephesus was a prominent city in "Roman" Asia Minor on the Aegean Sea. It was both a religious and commercial center for that part of the world. The Temple of Diana (Artemis to the Greeks), one of the Ancient Seven Wonders of the World, was located here. The temple was the center of immorality, banking, and art.[2] Paul established a church in Ephesus on his second missionary journey and later spent three years there. Paul ordained Timothy to follow him as pastor of the church. Timothy stayed there until a mob murdered him for his adamant preaching against sin. It is thought that John succeeded Timothy as pastor at Ephesus. John was later taken captive and exiled to Patmos from there.[3] Church history indicates that Mary, the mother of the Lord, moved from Jerusalem with John and later died there.[4]

Ephesus was honored by being the first to receive the letters. Ephesus shone brightly among the wickedness all around. God was pleased with her; the church had grown even with all the surrounding sin. Even after a generation, Christian followers in Ephesus were loyal to God's standards. Jesus commended the Ephesians for their deeds, hard work, and perseverance. He applauded the church's intolerance of wicked men and identification of false apostles. Jesus recognized their endurance and steadfastness during hardships. He also gives them credit for hating the Nicolatians, obviously a false sect (Rev. 2:15).

However, Jesus rebuked the Ephesians by saying, "You have forsaken your first love." Although the church had remained faithful in both its doctrine and its service for more than 40 years, the hearts of the members (mostly second generation believers) seemed to be lacking in their devotion to Christ. Jesus urges them to remember how far they've fallen, repent, and return to their first love. It is our love for Christ and our appreciation for all He has done for us that should motivate us to action. *The true Christian walk is a love relationship with Christ, not a works-oriented religion.* As one who "holds the seven stars in his right hand and walks among the seven golden lampstands," Jesus warns the Ephesians that failure to repent will result in their lampstand being "removed from its place."

"The church [at Ephesus] continued and was later the scene of a major church council, but after the 5th century both the church and the city declined. The immediate area has been uninhabited since the 14th century."[5]

Jesus closes his message to the Ephesians by promising that all believers will be given "the right to eat from the tree of life in the paradise of God." The first mention of a tree of life is found in the Garden of Eden (Gen. 3:22). It now appears in the paradise of God (heaven). The tree of life is later seen in the New Jerusalem (Rev. 22) when God makes His dwelling place with man for eternity.

Smyrna was founded around 1000 BC and was destroyed in 600 BC. It was rebuilt many centuries later by one of Alexander the Great's generals. The city was a source of pride for its citizens. Smyrna was considered one of the most beautiful cities the Greeks ever built. Thirty-five miles north of Ephesus, it sat on a hill rising from the sea so that it looked as if the city wore a crown. The nickname, "The Glory of Asia," was given to Smyrna because of its pride and beauty. During the Roman period, Caesar-worship in Asia was centered there.[6]

The meaning of Smyrna gets its name from the resin taken from a thorny tree. This aromatic resin called myrrh was the chief product from this city. To obtain the resin, the tree was hacked by a machete. Therefore myrrh was associated with suffering as the tree was cut and scarred. The Wise Men brought myrrh as one of the gifts to Baby Jesus; it was a foreshadowing of His death and suffering (Matt.2:11). Myrrh was mixed with wine to relieve pain and offered to Christ on the cross (Mark 15:23). Nicodemus used myrrh to anoint Christ's body for burial (John 19:39-40).

The Devil was at work in Smyrna! The Christians were under persecution; life for them was tough and bitter. The Romans thought they could stop the rise of Christianity by persecuting the believers. But the reverse happened. Common Roman citizens became interested in why so many people were willing to die for their faith. In Smyrna an altar was dedicated to the "glorious Emperor God Tiberius" in 24 AD. Each person of the empire had to show his loyalty to the empire by visiting the temple, throwing incense on the fire and getting a certificate proving one's visitation. Most Christians would not follow through with

"Back to the Future"
End Times Prophecy, from Genesis to Revelation
Lesson 8 – Jesus' Letters to the Seven Churches

this ritual because it required one to say "Caesar is Lord." It was not enforced until 94 AD by Domitian, interestingly the same year when the letter was written to Smyrna.

History records that thousands of Christians were killed for their faith. Many were burned at the stake, "thrown to the lions," tortured on the racks, boiled in oil, and roasted over slow fires. Many of the persecutions happened for the amusement of the Romans in the Coliseum and hippodromes around the empire. All of the deaths occurred because Christians would not say "Caesar is Lord" and worship the emperor.

Jesus identified himself with the suffering church. His title, the First and the Last, gave the Christians in Smyrna comfort in their trials and sorrows. Jesus had been victorious over death, and now they would be victorious over death as well. Jesus commends the believers saying that He knows their afflictions and their poverty. Yet He reminds them that they, like us, are rich because of the wonderful promises we have in Christ (II Cor. 6:10, James 2:5).

The believers at Smyrna were then given a time reference for their suffering. Wouldn't we like to know that our problem or suffering is only going to last ten days! Scholars look at this reference in several ways. Some think Jesus may be using these ten days as a symbolic representation of the entire persecution of the church. Others think it refers to persecution under ten evil Roman rulers. Still others think that it anticipates a limited period of time of suffering.[7]

Jesus exhorts the believers at Smyrna to not be afraid of their future sufferings, but to be faithful to the point of death. He then promises them (and believers of all times) a Crown of Life, saying that believers "will not be hurt at all by the second death."

It is interesting to note that of the Seven Churches of Revelation 2 and 3, Smyrna is one of the two that Christ does not rebuke. Smyrna's extreme sufferings had helped to keep them pure, and their faithfulness during this time was like myrrh or sweet perfume to God.[8]

2. Barnett, Living Hope for the End of Days, p.143.
3. David Jeremiah, Escape the Coming Night: Study Guide, Vol.1, p. 49.
4. Barnett, op. cit., p. 144.
5. Walvoord, The Bible Knowledge Commentary: New Testament Edition, p. 94.
6. Jeremiah, op. cit., vol.1, p. 58.
7. Walvoord, op. cit., p. 935.
8. Ibid., pp. 935-936.

"Back to the Future"
End Times Prophecy, from Genesis to Revelation
Lesson 8 – Jesus' Letters to the Seven Churches

*** DAY 3: The Church at Pergamum: Revelation 2:12-17

1. Pergamum: The Worldly Church
   a. What title from Revelation 1 is used to describe Jesus to the church of Pergamum? What does this instrument often symbolize?

   b. What does Jesus say about the city in Revelation 2:13?

   c. What does Christ commend or approve in Pergamum?

   d. What does Christ condemn or admonish in Pergamum?

   e. What appeal and warning does Christ make to the members of this church?

   f. What assurance does Christ give to true believers?

   g. What do you think Jesus meant by the three items He promised in (f)?

   h. How would you describe this church, which was trying to hold on to both their faith and other doctrines? Jesus said we are to live "in the world, but not be of the world."

   i. What lessons can we learn from Christ's words to this church?

2. Fill in your answers concerning Pergamum on the chart on the last page of your lesson.

ON A PERSONAL NOTE . . .
- What worldly practices have we the church allowed to infiltrate and corrupt our beliefs?

- What "worldly habits" are you holding onto that are displeasing to Jesus?

"Back to the Future"
End Times Prophecy, from Genesis to Revelation
Lesson 8 – Jesus' Letters to the Seven Churches

REVIEW:

Pergamum had been the capital of the Roman province of Asia Minor (modern day Turkey) for 300 years. Pergamum looked like a royal city as it sat upon its rocky hill. Its library, second only to the one in Alexandria, Egypt, made it an intellectual center with 200,000 volumes.[9] An altar to Zeus, another one of the Seven Wonders of World, sat 90 feet square and 40 feet tall high on the hill. From a distance, the altar looked like a throne; Jesus called this place "Satan's throne" not only because it was the center for emperor worship but also because it was the center of Satan worship.[10]

The Roman god, Aesculapius, the false god of healing was known as the Pergamite god. The temple was the beginning of an early hospital. The people referred to Aesculapius as their savior.[11] Satan has used false healing as a tool to persuade people that there is divine power coming upon them other than from God. Satan always tries to imitate God. The ancient symbol for Aesculapius, an image of snakes coiled around a rod, is still associated with medicine today.

A definition for Pergamum is "thoroughly married." So in a sense the church "married" the world. This "marriage" was completed when Diocletian, the evil Roman Emperor, died and Constantine took control of the Empire. Constantine declared that the whole Empire would become Christian. During the next few centuries, the Church clearly aligned itself with worldliness and pagan practices. Pagan priests became "Christian priests." Many pagan practices were accepted as Christian practices. Instead of statues and idols of other gods, now there were statues of Christ and saints. Pagan candles, incense burning, and orders of priests and monks became Christian practices. Pagan titles of pontiff, vicar, the queen of heaven (now transferred to Mary)[12] and "most excellent" became Christian titles. The calendar of observances, usage of holy water, and purgatory came directly from pagans whom the early saints tried to convert.[13] Even the name Easter has pagan beginnings from a goddess named Ishtar who had a son, Tammuz. He, according to their legends, supposedly was brought back to life.[14]

Yet God was raising a church right in the midst of this city. Many Pergamite saints had been converted from Satanism, idolatry, and immorality. These young believers flourished for Jesus right where He planted them, even living under the throne of Satan. Jesus commended the church for remaining true to his name and for remaining faithful in this city "where Satan lives."

However Jesus condemned the church at Pergamum for tolerating evil and compromising their Christian beliefs. Some members of the church held to the false teachings of Balaam, and some held to the teachings of the Nicolaitans. Unlike the church at Ephesus, those at Pergamum had allowed false teachings to pollute their doctrine. Worldly habits had seeped into their fellowship.

In Rev. 2:12, Jesus refers to Himself as *the One who has the sharp, two-edged sword*. This sword represents the Word of God which has the ability to separate believers from the world and to condemn the world for its sin (Rev. 1:16; 19:15, 21). Now in Rev. 2:16, Christ warns the Pergamum church to *repent*. Otherwise, He promises to return *soon* and fight against them with the sword of his mouth. It is with the Word of God that all sin is judged. Hebrews 4:12 tells us that the Word of God is sharper than any two-edged sword, dividing even soul and spirit, joint and marrow, and judging the thought and attitudes of the heart.

Christ then promises to give true believers in Rev. 2:17, "some of the *hidden manna*... a *white stone*... and a *new name*..." The "hidden manna" may refer to Christ as the Bread from heaven, the unseen source of the believer's nourishment and strength.[15] In John 6:35, Jesus said, "I am the bread of life." Just as Israel received physical food in the desert, so believers will receive spiritual food.

Scholars differ as to the meaning of the "white stone." Some see it as the admission ticket to the messianic banquet (still in the future for believers), similar to the admission stones for the Greek Olympic banquets that were given to Olympic winners. Barnett believes Christ is referring to our purity. Believers will be washed and made whiter than snow. The important point is that on the stone is a new name, an intimate name known only to the one who receives it. In the Greek Testament, 4:572, Alford tells us that this "new name" indicates acceptance by God and his title of glory. (See also Isaiah 56:5 and 62:2.) We are told in Rev.19:12 that at the Second Coming, Jesus too returns with a name written on Him that no one but himself knows.

"Back to the Future"
End Times Prophecy, from Genesis to Revelation
Lesson 8 – Jesus' Letters to the Seven Churches

Jesus' message to the church at Pergamum is a strong message for us today. Do we test the teachings of preachers we hear and writers we read? Or do we allow beliefs and practices of the world to infiltrate our doctrine and our actions? Have we sided too close to the world? Have we allowed Satan a "foothold" in our church? Have we lost our purity, our intimacy with God, and our nourishment from God's word? Do we have any family resemblance to our Heavenly Father and Holy Brother, Jesus, or do we resemble the world around us? Are we seeking to be like our neighbors who seem to have "it" all, whatever "it" may be? Let us instead seek Jesus with all of our heart, mind, soul, and strength. He calls us to be separate from the world. Just as Jesus called the people of Pergamum to repent, He is calling the people in the compromising churches of today to repent. Let us do so, looking forward to the promises of eternity.

9. Jeremiah, Escape the Coming Night, vol. 1, p. 68.
10. Barnett, op. cit., p.163.
11. Jeremiah, Escape the Coming Night, vol. 1, p. 69.
12. Jeremiah, Escape the Coming Night, vol. 3, p. 117.
13. Barnett, op. cit., p.165.
14. Jeremiah, Escape the Coming Night, vol. 3, p. 114.
15. Walvoord, op. cit., p. 936.

"Back to the Future"
End Times Prophecy, from Genesis to Revelation
Lesson 8 – Jesus' Letters to the Seven Churches

*** DAY 4: The Churches at Thyatira and Sardis: Revelation 2:18 - 3:11

1. **Thyatira: The Church that Tolerates Sin**
    a. What title or description is used for Christ? How is this different from His title in Rev. 1:13?

    b. What praise does Christ have for the church? What does He say about their deeds?

    c. What problem does Christ condemn in Thyatira?

    d. What punishment does Christ promise for Jezebel; for her followers?

    e. What exhortation does Christ give the godly remnant, those not following Jezebel?

    f. What exciting promises does Christ give, assuring all true believers?

2. **Sardis: The Dead Church**
    a. What title is given to the church of Sardis to represent Christ from chapter one?

    b. What does Christ hold against the church?

    c. Christ gives believers at Sardis five instructions to get back on track. What are they?

    d. How do these instructions relate to us as we strive for intimacy with Christ?

    e. What warning is given in v. 3?

    f. How does Christ describe the few true Christians left within the church? v. 4

    g. Christ assures all believers with a threefold promise in v. 5. Write each part here.

3. Fill in information about Thyatira and Sardis on your chart.

ON A PERSONAL NOTE . . .
- What sin(s) of immorality or idolatry are you willingly allowing to remain in your life? Prayerfully repent to the One who searches hearts and minds before He disciplines you with suffering.

- Evaluate your relationship with Christ – not what others would say, but what Christ would say. What steps can you take to "strengthen what remains"?

"Back to the Future"
End Times Prophecy, from Genesis to Revelation
Lesson 8 – Jesus' Letters to the Seven Churches

REVIEW:
Thyatira was located 40 miles southeast of Pergamum and was known for its many artisans, crafts, and guilds. Thyatira was not known for being the biggest or the most beautiful city of Asia Minor. However, it was located on one of the busiest trade routes, and it claimed many trade guilds: bakers, bronze workers, potters, tanners, cobblers, clothiers, weavers, and dyers. These guilds were compulsory; to be able to sell one's goods, one had to be a member. A patron god or goddess was dedicated to each guild. Each guild required paying a tax to that deity. The guilds were known for having huge banquets with sexual immortality as a part of the activities.[16] These banquets were no place for Christians, but to quit the union would be an economic risk or suicide.

The description of Christ given to the church at Thyatira was not a comforting one. It must have created shock and fear when read to the church. Jesus first identifies Himself as the Son of God, emphasizing His deity. This title is different than the title used in Rev.1:13. In Rev. 1, the title "Son of Man" is used to emphasize Jesus' ability to identify with believers and sympathize with their needs, weaknesses, trial, and temptations. Now, however, Christ is emphasizing His *divine power to judge*.

In Rev. 2:18 Jesus' eyes are described as "flames of fire." This image refers to His piercing, revealing gaze that penetrates to the very depths of both the church and the hearts of believers (Matt.10:26, Heb. 10:14). Later in Rev.2:23 Christ declares that He is the One who "searches hearts and minds." As one who *sees all*, Christ is both our Divine and *Righteous* Judge. Rev. 2:18 continues by describing Christ's feet as "like burnished bronze," an alloy which glows brilliantly when polished. This term depicts Christ's purity and holiness as He tramples out sin (Rev. 19:25) in indignation.

As has been His pattern with all the churches, Christ first commends the church at Thyatira before expressing His concerns about it. He assures them that He knows their deeds, their love and faith, their service, and their perseverance. He even notes that, unlike the Ephesians, they are now doing more than before. However the church at Thyatira had a serious problem. A woman referred to as Jezebel who claimed to be a prophetess was leading believers astray, teaching them to take part in the sexual immorality of pagan religions and to eat food sacrificed to idols. Jezebel was probably not her real name but used here to refer to the evil wife of King Ahab who was used by Satan to corrupt Israel (I Kings 16:31-33). Not only was the church allowing a woman to preach in the church (I Tim. 2:12), but they were allowing her to teach false doctrine! Jezebel and her teaching were leading the majority of the Thyatiran believers away from the truth.

Jesus' burning eyes had penetrated and seen the leaders' weak consciences and poor courage to rebuke their "Jezebel." The word "Thyatira" means "continued or perpetual sacrifice." Certainly we can see from Christ's point of view that His Holy Word has been sacrificed and compromised with corrupt, false doctrine. Divine judgment was about to fall on Jezebel, as well as on those "who commit adultery her." Note that the judgment of Jezebel and her followers falls in line with the scriptural principle of Matt. 18:6-7. Jezebel, the one who was leading others astray, was to receive the harshest punishment. Note also the glory Christ would receive as a result of this judgment – all the churches would acknowledge His deity (the one who sees all and is our righteous judge). The churches would also be warned against the evil of tolerating sin.

Not everyone in the church had become a part of this evil imitation. Christ encourages the true believers to hold fast until He comes. To the Thyatiran church, this refers to His coming to them in judgment; but as believers, we are encouraged to hold fast until His return for us at the Rapture.

Christ closes His longest letter to the churches with His promises to all believers. First we are promised "authority over the nations." This refers to our ruling with Christ not only during the Millennial Kingdom but for eternity. We are also promised the "morning star." In Rev. 22:16 Jesus refers to himself as the bright morning star, so perhaps this promise refers to our knowing him fully, not just in part (I Cor.13:12). Walvoord notes that the morning appears just before the dawn and suggests that receiving the morning star "may refer to participation in the Rapture of the church before the dark hours preceding the dawn of the millennial kingdom."[17]

"Back to the Future"
End Times Prophecy, from Genesis to Revelation
Lesson 8 – Jesus' Letters to the Seven Churches

The city of **Sardis** was well known as being the home of the famous Aesop's Fables![18] The city was built high on a hill among cliffs fifteen hundred feet high on three sides with an isthmus (tiny land bridge connecting to a larger land mass) on the fourth side. Through the ages, its rulers were overconfident in their defenses. Because Sardis lacked preparedness, it was conquered twice: by Cyrus the Persian in 549 BC and by Antiochus in 218 BC.[19] Sardis never regained its independence and became under Roman control in 133 BC. The city sat on an important trade route and was a major commercial city. It also was a center of pagan worship, being the site of a temple of Artemis.

Christ describes Himself to the Sardis church as the One who holds the *seven spirits of God and the seven stars.* We know that the term "seven spirits" represents the fullness of the Holy Spirit, who is Christ's Presence in the church. We have seen that the seven stars refer to the seven pastors of the seven churches. Christ is emphasizing His Lordship over the church and its leaders.

What appears at first to be a praise of the church turns out to be a condemnation. Christ says the church at Sardis has a reputation of being alive but in reality they are dead. Spiritual death in the New Testament is always caused by sin (Eph. 2:1). The outward appearance of the Sardis church, that of being alive and vibrant, was a façade for a church "populated by unredeemed people playing church."[20]
They were performing deeds, but Christ in His omniscience knew that their hearts were far from God.

Christ encourages them to wake up and strengthen the few signs of life they had left. They were instructed to remember the truth they had received, obey it, and repent. Otherwise Christ would come and destroy their church. Dead churches at Christ's return can expect the same kind of judgment.

Although the church as a whole was considered dead, Christ recognized the few true believers within the church. He commended them for not soiling their garments. The word for soiled comes from, *moluno*, which means "to defile, stain, or pollute." The faithful believers at Sardis, like all true believers, are promised that they will walk in Christ's presence in white garments. These garments symbolize the perfect holiness and purity of our future, resurrected body.

Christ also promises believers of all time that their name will never be blotted out of the book of life. In John's time, the ruler of a city kept a register of its citizens. If someone died or committed a serious crime, their name was removed from the register. Christ, as ruler of Heaven, promises that our names, written in the Lamb's book of life before the foundation of the world (Rev. 13:8) will never be erased. Furthermore, Christ will acknowledge our name before God and His angels, affirming that we are His.

Outward profession, false confidence, inward deadness – Jesus had names for people like this: "You hypocrites, you white washed tombs" (Matthew 25:28). Think about artificial silk flowers. They can look so real that one has to do a close-up touch test. Jesus, being omniscient, knows where we stand with Him. We have people in our church who are busy and active "for the Lord" but these same people will be unknown by Jesus Christ when He returns (Matt 7:21-23).

Many Americans **profess Christ** but do not **possess Christ**.[21] They do not have the Holy Spirit living within their heart with an ever increasing desire that says, "Not my will, but Yours." If the Holy Spirit lives within our hearts, then we should be becoming more like Jesus every day. A great question to ask oneself once a month or every six months is, "Am I more like Jesus now than six months ago?" Patience? Kindness? Self-control? Thoughtfulness? Integrity? Joy? Peace? Faithfulness? Love? Yes, these are the fruit of the Spirit (Gal. 5:22-23). Is there evidence that we have the Holy Spirit in us? There is no "s" on fruit. <u>All of Jesus' should overflow from us!</u> Christ should be sticking out all over!

---

16. Barnett, op. cit., p.175.
17. Walvoord, op. cit., p. 938.
18. Barnett, op. cit., p. 185.
19. Ibid.
20. MacArthur, op. cit., p. 111.
21. Barnett, op. cit., p. 187.

"Back to the Future"
End Times Prophecy, from Genesis to Revelation
Lesson 8 – Jesus' Letters to the Seven Churches

*** DAY 5: Philadelphia & Laodicea: Revelation 3:7-22

1. **Philadelphia: The Faithful Church**
    a. List the four aspects of the description of Jesus in v. 7.

    b. What does Is. 22:22 tell us about the key of David?

    c. How is Philadelphia commended by Jesus in v. 8-9 and in v. 10?

    d. Based on Acts 14:27, I Cor. 16:9, and Col. 4:3, what does the term "open door" (v.8) mean?

    e. List promises given specifically to the church of Philadelphia in vv. 8-11. (Circle the "I wills.")

    f. Based on what we have studied, to what time period do you think the "Hour of Testing" refers?

    g. What command does Christ give the believers at Philadelphia?

    h. What three promises are made to those who overcome (all believers)? v. 12

2. **Laodicea: The Lukewarm Church**
    a. Give the title used for Christ for this church.

    b. How does the Lord condemn the church in vv. 15-17?

    c. Jesus calls the Laoediceans poor, naked, and blind. What does he mean and what does Jesus call them to do in v. 18?

    d. What other appeal does Jesus make to the Laodicean church in v. 20?

    e. What assurance does Jesus give to those who overcome in v. 21? To what is Jesus referring?

3. Add the information about Laodicea to your chart.

ON A PERSONAL NOTE . . .
- The term "open door" refers to opportunities God gives us for service and witnessing. What open doors are before you at this time? Write a prayer of commitment, asking for Jesus' power.

- What is there "lukewarm" in your relationship with Jesus that He does not like? Are we trying to fit in with the world **and** with the Christian life? Are we making God nauseous? Write a prayer of repentance to the LORD.

"Back to the Future"
End Times Prophecy, from Genesis to Revelation
Lesson 8 – Jesus' Letters to the Seven Churches

REVIEW:

The ancient city of **Philadelphia** was founded in 140 BC by Attalus II, the king of Pergamum. His nickname was Philadelphus because of his loyalty to his brother King Eumenes whom he succeeded. This nickname was similar to the Greek word, *Philadelphia*, meaning "brotherly love."[22] Built at the junction of several important trade routes, the city was founded to be a center of Greek culture and language and was a gateway into central Asia Minor. Therefore, it was an important "key" to the development of the central part of Asia Minor.[23] The citizens of the city would have understood Jesus when He used the term "the wide-open door," knowing how the city had influenced others in the past.

The city of Philadelphia often experienced frequent earthquakes and was even destroyed by quakes several times. Also common were ground cracks, regular tremors, hot mud and volcanic activity in thermal pools. Often, even sometimes weekly, the citizens had to take their tents to live outside the city until the earthquakes and aftershocks had stopped.[24]

Jesus presents Himself to the Church at Philadelphia as the One who is holy and true and who holds the key of David. A *key* in scripture stands for authority and *David* symbolizes the messianic office. The fact that Jesus holds the key of David links Him to His royal kingship to come. The term "key of David" is found in Isaiah 22:22 where King Hezekiah is entrusting Eliakim, a faithful servant, with the key to all the treasures of his kingdom. "As holder of the key of David, Jesus alone has the sovereign authority to determine who enters His messianic kingdom . . . here He is depicted as having the keys to salvation and blessing."[25] Jesus is holding the key to all the *spiritual* treasures of God's kingdom.

Jesus begins His commendation of the believers at Philadelphia by saying in v. 8, "I know your deeds." He next commends them for having a *little power*. John MacArthur explains that this is not a negative comment but a positive one - the church was small in numbers, yet had a powerful impact on its city.[26] Jesus also points out that the church has kept His word and not denied His name. Later in v. 10 Jesus says the believers have kept His command to persevere patiently.

As a result of their faithfulness, Jesus makes several promises to the local church. In v. 8, Christ says He has put an open door before them that no one can shut. By cross-referencing Acts 14:21, I Cor. 16:9, and II Cor. 2:2 we see that Christ was not only guaranteeing the blessings of their salvation and their participation in the Millennial Kingdom, he was also giving this faithful church opportunities to serve and to spread the gospel. In v. 9 Christ promises that the Jewish unbelievers who were persecuting the Philadelphia Christians would come and bow at their feet and acknowledge Christ's love for them (probably indicating their defeat). This picture is similar to Isaiah 45:14 when unbelieving Gentiles will bow down to the remnant of Israel and to Phil. 2:10-11 when every knee in heaven and on earth and under the earth will bow to Jesus and declare Him Lord. Last, but certainly not least, Christ reveals an astounding truth. He promises to keep the church from *the hour of trial that is going to come upon the whole world*. We have already studied this verse when we studied the Rapture. The church at Philadelphia will be kept *from* (not through) Daniel's 70th Week, the Tribulation (as will all believers).

Because Jesus is coming soon, He appeals to the believers at Philadelphia to hold fast to what they have, to persevere to the end (see Matt 10:22), so that no one would take their crown. The words "coming soon" here, unlike in the other churches, refers to the sudden, imminent return of Christ for believers at the Rapture. The crown probably refers to the crown of life (Rev. 2:10) indicating that true believers never need to be afraid of losing their salvation.

As with all the other letters, Christ closes by giving Kingdom promises to all believers. We will be pillars in the temple of God, implying permanence, never to go out from it again. Believers will have an eternal place of honor in heaven. This must have thrilled the believers at Philadelphia who were used to fleeing their city often due to natural disasters. Believers in Christ will also have several names written on him: the name of God, depicting His ownership of us; the name of the New Jerusalem, depicting our eternal citizenship in heaven's capital city; and Christ's new name, depicting His identification with us.

I think we can even say that there are churches dotted across America that fit the description of this Philadelphia church. And we see the efforts of special godly pastors calling their churches not to be influenced by the world-view system, but to commit to a Biblical, God-centered view.

"Back to the Future"
End Times Prophecy, from Genesis to Revelation
Lesson 8 – Jesus' Letters to the Seven Churches

Laodicea was a wealthy city. It was located at the junction of two important roads, one leading east-west from Ephesus into the interior and one leading north-south from Pergamum to the Mediterranean. It was an important commercial center and a strategic banking center. The city was destroyed by an earthquake in 60 AD but had the wealth and ability to rebuild.

To the church at Laodicea Christ introduces Himself as "*the Amen, the faithful and true witness, and the beginning of the creation of God.*" The word "Amen" means "so be it" and is often used in the Bible to affirm that a statement is true. Christ is the Amen - the God of Truth in the flesh. He is also the One through whom all God's promises are confirmed. II Cor. 10:21 says, "For as many as are the promises of God, in Him they are yes. . ." The term "faithful and true Witness" underscores that His assessment of the Laodiceans was accurate. Finally the *beginning* of God's creation means that all things were created through the power of Christ, not that Christ was the first thing God created. John 1:3, Heb. 1:2, and Col. 1:15-16 tell us that Christ existed before God's creation and is sovereign over it.

Do you like to drink lukewarm water? No, neither do I. The Laodiceans knew about lukewarm water. There were hot mineral water springs in nearby Hierapolis and cold water springs in Colosse. There were pipes and aqueducts built to transport the water from both places to Laodicea. But by the time the water got to Laodicea, the hot mineral water had cooled down and the cool spring water had warmed up, so all they got was water that was lukewarm – highly distasteful to drink![27] What was it about the Laodicean Christians that made them as distasteful to Christ as lukewarm water is to us? They were not saved (hot), but they did not openly reject the gospel (cold). They were false Christians, holding to a form of godliness, but denying its power (II Tim. 3:5). Therefore the Laodiceans were useless and lukewarm. Though they thought they were rich and needed nothing, Jesus called them miserable, poor, blind, and naked (v.17).

Instead of pronouncing punishment on this apostate church, Christ offers them true salvation. He begins with a threefold appeal. Jesus tells them to buy *from Him*: gold refined by fire to become rich, white garments to clothe themselves, and eye salve that they may see. Those at Laodicea may have had physical wealth but they were spiritually poor. They would become rich with the spiritual blessings of salvation. A major product of the area was wool, and Laodicea was famous for a black garment made out of black wool. What they needed was the pure, white garments (representing purity) with which Christ clothes true believers. A medical school at Laodicea offered a special salve to heal eye problems. What the Laodiceans needed was not medicine, but spiritual sight. Blindness represents a lack of knowledge and understanding of spiritual truth. They needed Christ to open their eyes and turn them from darkness to light (Acts 26:18). Because Christ loves them, He urges the members to be zealous(hot) and to repent.

Christ follows His call to repentance with the news that *He stands at the door and knocks . . ."* MacArthur explains that "The door on which Christ is knocking is not the door to a single human heart, but to the Laodicean church. Christ was outside this apostate church and wanted to come in - something that could only happen if the people repented." MacArthur goes on the say that "Christ's offer to dine with the repentant church speaks of fellowship, communion, and intimacy."[28]

In other passages we are told that believers will dine and fellowship with Christ at the marriage supper of the Lamb (Rev. 19:9) and in the Millennial Kingdom (Luke 22:20). Here however, in Rev. 3:21, we are told that we will *sit down with Christ on His throne*, indicating that we will one day reign with Him. In Rev. 20:6 we are told that we will reign with Christ during the 1000 year reign of Christ and in Rev. 22:5 we are told we will reign with Him forever and ever!

22. Walvoord, op. cit., p. 939.
23. Jeremiah, op. cit., vol. 1, p. 99.
24. Barnett, op. cit., p. 197.
25. MacArthur, op. cit., p. 119.
26. Ibid.
27. Jeremiah, op. cit., vol. 1, p. 108.
28. MacArthur, op. cit., p. 140.

"Back to the Future"
End Times Prophecy, from Genesis to Revelation
Lesson 8 – Jesus' Letters to the Seven Churches

Rev. 2&3	CHURCHES IN REVELATION					HISTORY OF THE CHURCH[29]	
	Answer – Title of Christ	Approval given by Christ	Admonition given by Christ	Appeal given by Christ	Assurance given by Christ	Historical Period	Approximate Dates
Ephesus 2:1-7						Apostolic church, sowing, organization, evangelism	Pentecost 33 to 60 AD
Smyrna 2:8-11						Persecution, enemy revealed	Nero, Domitian . . . 60 to 300 AD
Pergamum 2:12-17						State church in Roman Empire, wordly alliance, pagan influence,	300 to 800 AD (or to 590 AD)
Thyatira 2:18-29						Papal church, corruption	800 to 1517 AD (or 590 to1517 AD)
Sardis 3:1-6						Reformed church, empty profession, wealth in church	Reformation 1517-1730 AD
Philadelphia 3:7-13						Missionary church, return to Bible truths	Last Days 1730-1900 AD
Laodicea 3:14-22						Apostate church, false teachers, false doctrines	Last Days 1900 AD-?

29. Tim Lahaye, Revelation Unveiled, p. 36.

"Back to the Future"
End Times Prophecy, from Genesis to Revelation
Lesson 9 – This Present Age

*** DAY 1: The Inferred Gap between Christ's 1st and 2nd Comings

1. Upon close inspection the following passages show that the time between Christ's 1st and 2nd Coming, although not seen by the Israelites of the Old Testament, did exist in the mind of God from eternity past. In each passage there is an inferred gap between Christ's two comings. See if you can find this gap which allows for this Present Age in which we live. Write down phrases which relate to His 1st Coming and phrases which relate to His 2nd Coming.

   a. Is. 9:6

   b. Is. 53:10

   c. Zech. 9:9-10

   d. Luke 1:31-32

   e. Is. 61:1-3

2. Read Luke 4:14-21. Why do you think Jesus stopped reading Is. 61:1-3 where He did?

ON A PERSONAL NOTE . . .
God's ways and God's timing are perfect!!! While God promises to answer our prayers which are within His will, there is often a gap in time between when our prayer is made and when it is answered. While we are in the gap, we don't always understand God's purposes and become impatient or even angry. But we must trust that God is working for His greatest glory and our greatest good.
- What unanswered prayer are you struggling with today?

- Ask God if there is a sin in your life that may be hindering your prayer from being answered.

- Read Ps. 42:5-11 and ask God to increase your faith, knowing that all things work for good for those who love the Lord. Keep in mind that God's greatest good for you (and for others) is that you become more like Christ.

"Back to the Future"
End Times Prophecy, from Genesis to Revelation
Lesson 9 – This Present Age

REVIEW:
This Present Age, dating from the rejection of their Messiah by Israel until she turns to Him at the Second Coming, was completely unknown to those in Old Testament times. Just as two separate mountains appear as one from a distance, so the separate comings of Christ appeared as one to readers of the Old Testament scriptures.

Isaiah 9:6
In Isaiah 9:6-7 Isaiah records five things about the Coming Messiah. Only the first part of verse 6 refers to Christ's first coming: He will be born a child into the nation of Israel (*to us*). The rest of this passage will be fulfilled at His second advent. Christ will govern the nation from the Davidic throne with justice and righteousness during the Millennial Kingdom. His rule will then continue *from that time on and forever,* as Christ continues to rule for eternity in the New Jerusalem of the New Earth. Four names describe Christ's character - Wonderful Counselor, Mighty God, Everlasting Father, and Prince of Peace.

Isaiah 53:10
This verse makes it clear that it was the God's will that Christ's first coming should end in suffering and death. Christ's death on the cross satisfied God's righteous demands for judgment against sin. Christ's sacrifice made it possible for not only the nation of Israel but the whole world to come to God in faith for salvation from sin (I John 2:2). Although Christ's death appeared to be the end, we know now that it will be at His second coming that Jesus will rule with His spiritual offspring of all times, doing the will of God forever.

Zechariah 9:9-10
Here again we see an OT prophecy which blends two events into one. In verse 9 we have the prophecy of the first Palm Sunday when Jesus was presented to Israel as their Messiah in His Triumphal Entry. Christ came into Jerusalem riding on a donkey, not on a war stallion, symbolizing that He came in peace. At that time the nation of Israel rejected Him as their King. It will only be after this Present Age (including the Church Age and the Tribulation) that Christ will come again in judgment. It is then that His universal rule will be established.

Luke 1:31-32
In Luke 1:31-32 the angel Gabrielle appears to Mary, foretelling our dear Savior's birth. As this Present Age was unknown at that time, the announcement of Christ's two comings was blended into one. Verse 31 gives us details of His first coming - a son conceived in Mary's womb will be called Jesus, while verse 32 refers to Christ's second coming - the Son of the Most High will rule on the throne of David.

Isaiah 61:1-3 (also Luke 4:18-21)
When Jesus returned to Nazareth after being tempted in the wilderness, He began reading Isaiah 1:1-3, familiar to the Jews as a passage concerning their coming Messiah. Much to their astonishment, Jesus stopped after the phrase, "to proclaim the favorable year of the Lord." Jesus then rolled up the scroll and sat down saying, "Today this scripture is fulfilled in your hearing." Note that "the year of the Lord's favor" refers to the time of God's grace when salvation is offered to all. By this action Jesus himself showed that He was aware of the time gap between His two comings. Christ's mission at His first coming is described in verse 1-2a when He was sent by the Father and anointed by the Spirit to preach the gospel of salvation, freeing those who would receive from the penalty of sin. Christ's mission at His second coming, seen in Isaiah 2b-3, will be different. He will return with vengeance bringing judgment on the unbelievers. But He will also comfort those believers who have survived great persecution during the Tribulation, especially during its last 3 ½ years.

Conclusion
Although the existence of this Present Age, which interrupted God's program with Israel, was unknown in the Old Testament, this age clearly existed in the mind of God from eternity past. The scriptures you have looked at today show that allowance was made for the Present Age without specifically revealing it. Covered during this gap is the time between Israel's *rejection* of their Messiah at His first coming and their *acceptance* of Him at His second coming.

"Back to the Future"
End Times Prophecy, from Genesis to Revelation
Lesson 9 – This Present Age

*** DAY 2: The Mystery Kingdom – During this Age

1. When the word *kingdom* is used in the Bible, there are 3 questions that must be answered to determine which kingdom is being referenced. They are: Who is the ruler? Who are the ruled? When and where is the Kingdom? See if you can fill in the chart below concerning the following kingdoms of God described in the Scriptures.

    a. Universal Kingdom   I Chron. 29:11-12; Ps. 103:19-22; and Ps. 145:13

    b. Spiritual Kingdom   Col. 1:13 and John 3:1-10, Rom. 14:17

    c. Davidic Kingdom   II Sam. 7:12-16

    d. Millennial Kingdom   Matt. 25:34; Rev. 20:1-6

    e. Eternal Kingdom   I Cor. 15:24; Rev. 21:1-22:5

Kingdom	Ruler	Ruled	When	Where
Universal				
Spiritual				
Davidic				
Millennial				
Eternal				

2. After the Jews make it evident that they will not accept Jesus' offer of the Kingdom at His first coming, Jesus begins to reveal a different form of God's kingdom.

    a. What is this mystery form of the kingdom called in Matthew 13:11?

    b. Can you answer the questions above (in question one) concerning this form of God's kingdom?

3. As a member of the Body of Christ, how do you relate to each of the above kingdoms?

ON A PERSONAL NOTE . . .
- How does your life show that Jesus is your King?

- What other people or things sometimes rule your life instead? Is the throne of your life crowded? What actions do you need to take to remove these people or things from the throne of your life?

"Back to the Future"
End Times Prophecy, from Genesis to Revelation
Lesson 9 – This Present Age

REVIEW:
In the Scriptures the word kingdom is used in many different ways. Sometimes a kingdom refers to a Gentile kingdom, sometimes to the kingdoms of Israel and Judah, and sometimes it even refers to the kingdom of Satan. But the most important use of the term kingdom is when it refers to the kingdom of our sovereign God. Even then we must carefully identify which aspect of God's Kingdom is being described.

The **Universal Kingdom** of God refers to God's rule over the entire universe. Nothing can happen outside of the will of God. This sovereign control has existed from eternity past and will continue into eternity future. God has complete control over the hearts of all men, over all elements of nature, and over things created, in both the natural and the supernatural realm. Our omniscient, omnipotent, all-present God is in total control of all things at all times and at all places.

The **Spiritual Kingdom** of God refers to the rule of God over those who are believers, the elect of all times. Anyone who has experienced a new birth by the power of the Holy Spirit has entered into this kingdom. True believers in the Church belong to this kingdom, although the spiritual kingdom of God began long before Pentecost and will continue after the rapture of the Church.

The **Davidic Kingdom** is described in II Samuel 7:16. It is here that God reveals to David that his seed will reign on the throne of David forever, fulfilling the kingdom aspect of the Abrahamic promise. We have previously studied the rule of David's descendants over the house of Judah until the Shekinah Glory departed from the temple (Eze. 10-11) and the Israelites were deported to Babylon. The *time of the Gentiles* (Lk. 21:24) then began while Israel was temporarily set aside. At His second advent, Christ, a seed of David through Mary, will return and rule over both Israel and the world from the Davidic throne.

This coming rule of Christ from David's throne is known as the **Millennial Kingdom**. This is the kingdom that was rejected by the Jews at Christ's first coming. It will be announced again to Israel during the Tribulation and nationally received by Israel. This kingdom is a literal, earthly kingdom to be set up at the second advent of Christ. It will last for 1000 years. As the *Bride of Christ*, believers from the Church Age will return and rule with our Groom.

Actually the Millennial Kingdom is but the first stage of the **Eternal Kingdom of God** - one that will never be destroyed (Dan. 2:44). In the second phase, Jesus reigns from the New Jerusalem over a new heaven and new earth (Rev. 21-22) which is completely void of sin and evil. This kingdom will be free from all opposition to His rule. It will be a restoration of paradise lost. Never again will any created being establish a kingdom and rule anywhere in the universe.[1] The Church will continue its rule with Christ for all eternity!

So, where does that leave us who are living between the two advents of Christ? In Matthew 13, after it becomes apparent that the Jews of that time are rejecting His offer of the kingdom, Christ begins to reveal a **mystery form of the kingdom**, previously unknown in Scripture. He refers to this mystery form of the kingdom as the *kingdom of heaven*. This term is used in Matthew's gospel to describe the character of the kingdom in the present age. Some scholars equate the term *kingdom of God* used in the other New Testament books with the *kingdom of heaven*. However, some say that when Matthew uses the term *kingdom of heaven*, he is referring to the entire sphere of people ruled in the present age (possessors / professors; saved / unsaved; wheat / tares; good fish / bad fish). And when Matthew uses the term *kingdom of God*, it is only the sphere of true believers (part of the spiritual kingdom of God) of this age that he is referencing. Note that although both terms include the Church age, they encompass a slightly longer period of time – the time from Israel's rejection of the kingdom at Christ's first coming until the time of Israel's acceptance of her King at His second coming.

It is also worthy to note that both terms, the *kingdom of heaven* and the *kingdom of God*, are used in scripture to designate the Millennial Kingdom, the Spiritual Kingdom, and the mystery form of the kingdom. We must guard against making the terms absolute. Only the context can determine the meaning intended to be conveyed.[2]

1. Paul Benware, Understanding End Times Prophecy, p. 191.
2. J. Dwight Pentecost, Things to Come, p. 144.

"Back to the Future"
End Times Prophecy, from Genesis to Revelation
Lesson 9 – This Present Age

*** DAY 3: Revealed Mysteries – Character of This Age

1. What is the definition of a New Testament mystery?
    a. I Cor. 2:7

    b. Eph. 3:5

    c. Col. 1:26

2. What new revelation is given in the following New Testament passages?
    a. Matt. 13:11

    b. Rom. 11:25

    c. Eph. 3:3-9 (also Col. 1:26-27; Eph. 1:9; Rom. 16:25)

    d. I Cor. 2:7

    e. Col. 2:2; 4:3

    f. I Tim. 3:16

    g. II Thess. 2:7

    h. Rev. 17:5

    i. I Cor. 15:51

3. What does I Cor. 2:10-14 say about understanding the things of God?

ON A PERSONAL NOTE . . .
- Identify areas of your life where you are doing things in the flesh and not in the Spirit – Bible study, witnessing, prayer, interacting with husband or children or friends, being a steward of your time and money...?

- What have been the results?

- Stop and ask God's Holy Spirit to lead you, give you understanding, and empower you in these areas of your life.

"Back to the Future"
End Times Prophecy, from Genesis to Revelation
Lesson 9 – This Present Age

REVIEW:

This Present Age, from Israel's rejection of the Messiah at His first coming until their acceptance of Him at His second coming, is viewed in Scripture as a mystery. Webster's defines the word ***mystery*** as that which is unknown or puzzling. However, in the New Testament the word is used to refer to something known to God from eternity past which has previously been unknown to man and is now being revealed to the saints by the Holy Spirit. We see in I Cor. 2:7 that God intended these mysteries for our glory since before time began.

In the 27 New Testament usages of the word *mystery*, the body of truth referred to as a *mystery* is particular truth related to this present age. In his book, Things to Come, J. Dwight Pentecost lists the following New Testament *mysteries:*

> "The existence of this present age, which was to interrupt God's established program with Israel was a mystery (Matt.13:11).
>
> That Israel was to be blinded so that Gentiles might be brought into relation to God was a mystery (Rom. 11:25).
>
> The formulation of the church, made up of Jews and Gentiles to form a body, was a mystery (Eph.3:3-9; Col. 1:26-27; Eph. 1:9; Rom. 16:25).
>
> This whole program of God that results in salvation was called a mystery (I Cor. 2:7).
>
> The relation of Christ to men in redemption was called a mystery (Col. 2:2; 4:3).
>
> The incarnation itself is called a mystery (I Tim. 3:16), not as to fact but as to its accomplishment.
>
> The development of evil unto its culmination in the man of sin (II Thess. 2:7) and the development of the great apostate religious system (Rev. 17:5,7) both constitute that which was called a mystery.
>
> That there should be a new method by which God received men into His presence apart from death was a mystery (I Cor. 15:51)."[3]

These mysteries describe the character of this Present Age, which has temporarily interrupted God's program with the nation of Israel. In the New Testament writings, inspired by the Holy Spirit, this entire age and its program is now revealed. As members of the Body of Christ, we have this same Holy Spirit resident within us. It is HE who illuminates the Scriptures for us, who intercedes for us in prayer, and who empowers us to do God's will.

---

3. Pentecost, Things to Come, p. 135.

"Back to the Future"
End Times Prophecy, from Genesis to Revelation
Lesson 9 – This Present Age

*** DAY 4: Kingdom Parables – Course of This Age

1. In Mt. 13:11, what information does Jesus say his parables reveal?

2. Parable of the Sower: (Mt. 13:1-9; Mk.4:1-20; Lk 8:4-15)
    a. Describe the three "unfruitful" soils and what you think they represent.

    b. What does the good soil represent and what results?

3. Tares among the Wheat: (Mt. 13:24-30, 37-43)
    a. Who do you think the owner of the field is?

    b. Who do the wheat, the weeds, and the harvesters represent?

    c. What is the fate of the weeds?

4. Parable of the Mustard Seed: (Mt. 13:31-32; Mk. 4:30-32)
    a. What happens to the mustard seed?

    b. Who do you think the "birds of the air" are?

5. Parable of the Yeast: (Mt. 13:33; Lk. 13:20-21)
    a. What do you think is represented by the yeast? The flour?

    b. What is yeast known for?

6. Parable of the Hidden Treasure: (Mt. 13:44)
    a. What do you think is the meaning of the treasure? The field?

    b. Who do you think the man is?

7. Parable of the Pearl: (Mt. 13:45-46)
    a. How is this parable similar to that of the treasure? What are the differences?

    b. How is a pearl formed?

8. Parable of the Net: (Mt. 13:47-50)
    a. Which parable does this sound like?

    b. When do you think this separation will occur?

"Back to the Future"
End Times Prophecy, from Genesis to Revelation
Lesson 9 – This Present Age

REVIEW:
Up until Matthew 13, Jesus' message has been one of offering God's kingdom to the Jews. Israel's rejection of both the Messiah and His invitation climaxes in chapter 12. Now that Israel has rejected the offered kingdom, Jesus says He is setting aside all natural or physical relationships and establishing a new relationship based on faith. The parables in Matthew 13 answer the question of what would result, in view of Israel's rejection of Him.

Jesus reveals that He is speaking in order to give the "secrets" of *the kingdom of heaven*. The parables in this chapter cover the progress of this kingdom between the two advents of Christ. "Postmillennialism, with its teaching that the world will progressively become more Christian and climax in the return of Christ, has done much to influence the interpretation of the chapter contrary to what it is intended to convey. If anything, Matthew 13 teaches that the world, instead of getting better, will get worse and that evil will triumph until the time of Christ's second coming."[4] Jesus says He is speaking in parables so that the believer will understand these truths, but not the unbeliever.

Parable of the Sower: Mt. 13:1-9; Mk.4:1-20; Lk 8:4-15
In the parable of the sower, this age is characterized by the sowing of seed. The four types of soils represent the four types of hearers. The first type rejects the Word entirely. The second type represents those who superficially receive the Word but fall away under trouble or persecution. The third type represents those who hear the Word but the worries of the world make it unfruitful. The fourth type of soil represents believers - those who receive the Word and produce fruit. This passage tells us that most of the world will reject the gospel message, but there will be those genuinely saved in the present age who will be added to the spiritual kingdom of God. In addition we see that during the course of the age there will be a decreasing response (100 to 60 to 30) to the sowing of the seed.[5]

Tares among the Wheat: Mt. 13:24-30, 37-43
The man in this field represents God, the field represents the world during the present age, and the good seed represents the sons of the kingdom. The weeds are the sons of the evil one, sown by the devil. There will be dual development of good and evil during the age between the first and second coming of Christ. At Christ's return, the angels will "weed out" the evil ones and cast them into Hades, and the righteous, "shining like the sun," will enter the millennial kingdom. Since the Church will have been removed at the time of the Rapture, many feel that this parable has primary reference to Israel during the Tribulation.

Parable of the Mustard Seed: Mt. 13:31-32; Mk. 4:30-32
The kingdom of heaven will grow quickly and extensively. The mustard plant grows from a small seed to a height of twenty to thirty feet in just one year. The Church had a small and seemingly insignificant beginning. Today, however, the *professing church* (both true and professing believers) has become a worldwide institution with millions of people. The birds of air that come to perch in its branches probably represent unbelievers who "lodge" in its branches.

Parable of the Yeast: Mt. 13:33; Lk. 13:20-21
This parable has had several interpretations through the years. Many interpreters, influenced by the postmillennial view, errantly identify the yeast as the Gospel which spreads throughout the world.

Among those in the premillennial camp, there are two different views. One view interprets the yeast as the element of evil which penetrates the Church. Walvoord holds this view and writes that just as yeast enters dough and puffs it up, making it look larger than it actually is, so false doctrine and its followers tend to puff up the Church.[6]

Others, including Pentecost, see the yeast as a positive symbol and focus on the fact that it has been hidden or mixed in the meal. Pentecost writes, "When leaven is introduced into the meal an irreversible process has begun that will continue until it has completed its leavening action. This is intended to stress the way the new form of the kingdom will develop. The power in the kingdom will not be external but internal. . . This new kingdom will flourish, not by military might but by a new principle - the power within.[7]

"Back to the Future"
End Times Prophecy, from Genesis to Revelation
Lesson 9 – This Present Age

Parable of the Hidden Treasure: Mt. 13:44
This parable portrays the relationship of Israel to this present age. In the Old Testament, Israel was regarded as God's treasure (Ex. 19:5, Ps. 135:4). Today, however, she is certainly not seen as a treasure by the majority of the world. It was Jesus who died on the cross (selling all He had and purchasing His treasure with His blood), providing redemption for Israel and assuring her of the many promises God had given her. During the present age Israel is hidden, only to emerge at the end of the age as a major world player as the Second Coming of Christ draws near. *(Wouldn't you say that is happening now?!?)*

Parable of the Pearl: Mt. 13:45-46
Just as the parable of the treasure pictures Christ's dying for Israel, so this parable refers to Christ's dying for His Church. Christ is the merchant and the pearl is the Church. The Church was made possible by Christ's sacrifice. Just as a pearl is a jewel that grows out of an irritation in an oyster, so the Church grew out of the wounded side of Christ. The Church is one of the major purposes of the age between Christ's two comings.

Parable of the Net: Mt. 13:47-50
Similar to the parable of the wheat and the tares, this parable refers to the judgment at the end of the age. The kingdom of heaven is compared to a large fishing net cast into the sea. The fishing net Christ refers to could be up to a half mile long, requiring several boats to drag it. After the nets were drawn to shore, the fish were separated, the bad fish being cast back into the sea and the good fish gathered into the boat. At Christ's return there will be a worldwide judgment. All will be gathered, both Jews and Gentiles, and the angels will separate the wicked from the righteous (Mt. 25:31-46 and Eze. 20:33-38). The wicked Jews and Gentiles will be cast into Hades and the righteous will enter the millennial kingdom. This parable is similar to that of the wheat and the tares. But since the net here is cast into the sea (which typically refers to Gentile nations), some see the emphasis here to be on the judgment of the Gentile nations.

Conclusion:
The parables of Matthew reveal the course of *the kingdom of heaven between the two advents of Christ.* While our King is absent: 1) There will be a sowing of the Word throughout the age. 2) This sowing will be imitated by a false counter-sowing. 3) The kingdom will assume huge outer proportions. 4) However, the kingdom will be marked by inner doctrinal corruption. 5) Yet the Lord will gain for Himself a peculiar treasure from among Israel. 6) The Lord will also gain for Himself a peculiar treasure from the Church. 7) The age will end in judgment, with the unrighteous excluded from the Millennial Kingdom and the righteous taken in to enjoy the blessing of Messiah's reign.[8]

We previously studied the seven letters to the churches found in Revelation 2 - 3 and saw that collectively they depict this present age from the beginning of the Church at Pentecost to the judgment of the apostate church prior to Christ's 2nd coming. They show us the pattern of the development of the Church throughout its history, one of continual growth and increasing apostasy.[9] Although the kingdom of heaven is not the same as the Church, the time period covered by Matt 13 and Rev 2 - 3 is basically the same. Therefore, in these sections of Scripture there is a similarity in the development of the course of the age.[10]

---

4. Walvoord, Major Bible Prophecies, p. 208.
5. Pentecost, Things to Come, p. 146.
6. Walvoord, op. cit., p. 214.
7. Pentecost, op. cit., p. 148.
8. Tim Lahaye & Thomas Ice, <u>Charting the End Times</u>, p. 48.
9. Pentecost, Things to Come, pp. 150-153.
10. Ibid., p.153.

"Back to the Future"
End Times Prophecy, from Genesis to Revelation
Lesson 9 – This Present Age

*** DAY 5: Increased Apostasy Marks the End of the Age (Jude)

1. What three encouraging phrases does Jude use to describe the believers to whom he is writing? v. 1

2. What provisions of God do Christians living among apostasy need? v. 2

3. **The appeal:**
   a. From v. 3 what appeal does Jude make to believers?

   b. Looking at Gal. 1:23, I Tim 4:1, and Heb. 4:14, define "faith."

4. **The apostates:**
   a. How are they described and what are the two errors of their message? v. 4

   b. What additional info do we find about their actions in vv. 8-10 and vv. 16-19?

   c. What will be their fate? vv. 4, 12-15

5. **Strategy for Believers:**
   a. What is the first thing Jude tells his readers? vv17-18

   b. Jude next calls the readers to pursue sanctification. What four commands are given in v. 20? (Look for action verbs.)

   c. Jude's final instructions tell us to reach out to others. In vv. 22-23, what three groups of people are listed and how are we to relate to them?

6. **Security for Believers:**
   a. Of what promise does Jude first remind His readers? (See also John 10:28.)

   b. As opposed to the apostate's future, what does our future hold for us?

ON A PERSONAL NOTE...
- What signs of apostasy do you see around you? . . . In your extended family? . . . Church? . . . Friends? . . . Job outside your home?

- What practical ways can we guard against apostasy's encroachment?

"Back to the Future"
End Times Prophecy, from Genesis to Revelation
Lesson 9 – This Present Age

REVIEW:
From studying the progression of the kingdom of heaven in Matthew 13 and the course of the Church in Revelation 1 - 2, we know that days of apostasy and rebellion will only get worse as this present age comes to a close. The book of Jude warns believers to be on guard against those who try to distort and destroy the gospel and instructs believers how they should live in the midst of such apostasy. It is fitting that the book of Jude is the last book of the Bible before Revelation, which describes Christ's return to establish truth forever.

Although Jude makes no reference to the specific church he is writing, it is clear that he is writing to genuine believers. How encouraging it must have been for the believers to be reminded that they were called, loved by God the Father, and kept secure by Jesus Himself. Jude's prayer for these believers is that they would experience God's mercy, peace, and love as they lived amongst this spiritual battle of truth and error.

Jude makes is plain that he would rather write to them about the blessings of salvation, but instead felt it was urgent to warn his readers of the apostates that had secretly slipped in among them. He appeals to them to *contend for the faith* that these apostates were trying to destroy. The *faith* entrusted to the saints refers to the entire body of truth that had been revealed through the prophets and the apostles. Central to this faith is the truth that salvation is found in Jesus Christ alone.

Jude 4-19 describes these godless apostate men and their actions. Their erroneous teachings perverted God's grace and rejected His Son Jesus Christ as Lord. Jude also writes that these men pollute their bodies, reject authority, and slander celestial beings (v. 8); speak abusively about things they do not understand (v. 10); are grumblers and faultfinders, follow their own evil desires, boast about themselves, and flatter others for their own advantage (v. 16); and are scoffers who are divisive, follow their own natural instincts, and who are without the Spirit (vv. 18-19).

We are told in vv. 4, 12-15 that these apostates were marked for condemnation long ago, that they are twice dead (not bearing fruit in others and without spiritual roots themselves), and that they will face judgment by Christ. We are also told that the blackest darkness of hell has been reserved forever to them. (See also II Peter 4:17.)

In the latter part of his letter Jude give his readers a battle plan for *contending for the faith*. Jude knows it is not enough recognize a problem but it is necessary to combat the problem. Readers are first commanded to remember what the apostles had said about false teachers - that they were present during Old Testament times; they afflicted the early church; they are active today; and they will continue to be a threat in the future.[11]

In verses 20-21, readers are commanded to purse sanctification for themselves. A believer must *build himself up in the faith* (done only by progressing in your knowledge of God's Holy Word). Reading God's Word should always lead one to *pray out of a heart filled with the Holy Spirit*. Jude next commands us to *keep ourselves in the God's love.* This is not a reference to keeping our salvation, but to remain in God's love by obedience to His word and His will (John 15:9-11). Finally we are told that we should live *waiting in expectation for our Lord Jesus Christ to bring us eternal life*. For believers in the Church Age that time will be at the Rapture. Those who come to Christ during the Tribulation will be looking forward to the time of Christ's second coming.

Not only are believers to identify apostates and their false teachings, but we are to reach out to both them and those that are listening to them. Those who become filled with doubt as a result of false teaching need to be encouraged and not criticized. We should deal with them in love and mercy. Those who are following false teaching need to be snatched from the fire of hell and saved. This can only be done by the power of the Holy Spirit as we hold out the Word of Truth. The third category of people we are to reach out to is those deeply entrenched in sin and error. This includes the most committed and corrupted apostates. That we are instructed to show them mercy *mixed with fear* warns us that we must be careful lest we become contaminated by their sin.

"Back to the Future"
End Times Prophecy, from Genesis to Revelation
Lesson 9 – This Present Age

Jude's closing doxology assures us of both the security and the victory we believers have in Christ. We can be sure that Christ will not allow us to fall away from saving faith. He is able to preserve us until the end (John 6:37-40). It is then that Christ will present us before the Father, and we will stand in God's glorious presence holy, blameless, and pure. We will be filled with great joy forever as we live from that time on in perfect fellowship with God, His Son, and believers from all times.[12]

---

11. John MacArthur, The MacArthur New Testament Commentary, II Peter and Jude, p.198.
12. Ibid., p. 212.

"Back to the Future"
End Times Prophecy, from Genesis to Revelation
Lesson 10 – Tribulation: Introduction

*** DAY 1: God's Divine Plan: The Tribulation

Tribulation Begins Day of the Lord

1. When does II Thess. 2:2-8 indicate that the Day of the Lord will begin?

2. The following passages describe the Day of the Lord. Draw a line from each passage below to the time that it references.
   a. Zeph. 1:14-18:   Christ's return at Armageddon
   b. Zech. 14:1-4   Tribulation
   c. II Peter 3:10   Millennial Kingdom

Nature of the Tribulation

3. What word(s) describe this period in the following passages?
   a. Rev. 6:16-17; I Thess. 1:9-10, 5:9; Zeph. 1:15, 18
   b. Rev. 14:7; 16:5-7; 19:1
   c. Is. 26:20-21; 34:1-3   (NAS version)
   d. Is. 13:11; 24:20-21
   e. Rev. 3:10
   f. Jer. 30:7
   g. Joel 2:2; Zeph. 1:14-15

Uniqueness of the Tribulation

4. How does Jesus describe this time in Matt. 24:21?

5. Find phrases from Dan. 12:1; Jer. 30:7; and Joel 2:2 which echo this thought.

6. From Rev. 3:10, how much of the world will be affected?

7. According to Daniel 9:27, how long will the Tribulation last?

8. Who will survive? Matt. 24:13, 22

ON A PERSONAL NOTE . . .
- What are your thoughts about God being a God of Judgment or a God of Wrath?

- How would you explain this to a neighbor?

"Back to the Future"
End Times Prophecy, from Genesis to Revelation
Lesson 10 – Tribulation: Introduction

REVIEW:
Let's look at what we have studied up to this point. We have examined OT scriptures concerning God's purpose, program and promises for His chosen people - the nation of Israel. After the nation of Israel rejected their Messiah at His first coming, God called into effect His *mystery* program, the Church. She too had a distinct purpose and program, as well as distinct promises. We learned that at the Rapture, Christ will return for His Church and take her to the *place He has prepared for her*.

While the Church is in heaven with Christ, God will again turn his attention to Israel during the 70th Week of Daniel – or as it is more commonly known, the Tribulation. Today we will begin a study on the Tribulation, after which we will complete our course by looking at Christ's return to earth, His reign on earth during the Millennial Kingdom, and our life in the new earth and heavens for all eternity.

In the Bible, the phrase *Day of the Lord* is used to describe periods of direct intervention or judgment by God in human history. Referring to a coming time of judgment, some references to the Day of the Lord in the Old Testament deal with periods of judgment that have already occurred. Many, however, refer to a future time of specific judgment when God will intervene in the affairs of men to judge the nations, discipline Israel, and establish His rule on earth. The Jewish day began at midnight with a period of darkness, was followed by a period of light starting at dawn, and ended again in darkness. After the rapture of the Church, the Day of the Lord will begin with the darkness of the Tribulation, be followed by the light of Jesus' reign in the Millennial Kingdom, and end with the darkness of the great white throne judgment and the destruction of our present universe at the close of the Millennium

The scriptures we looked at today show us that the nature of the Tribulation is that of wrath, judgment, indignation, trial, trouble, destruction, darkness, desolation, overturning, and punishment. **No** passage can be found anywhere to lessen the severity of this time that comes upon the earth.[1] Matthew 24:21-22 tells us that such tribulation has not occurred since the beginning of the world, nor will it ever occur again. Except for God's grace and mercy in cutting these days short, no one would be able to survive.

There have been many terrible wars and natural disasters throughout history, but the world has not experienced anything as horrible as the coming Tribulation. Even World War II, with its estimated death toll of 60+ million, cannot match the devastation of this promised time. Some people looked to the Holocaust and called Adolf Hitler <u>an</u> antichrist. The horrible times predicted to come will be like nothing the world has ever seen.

There are several factors that will make the Tribulation unique from any other disastrous time period in history. First, worldwide destruction will take place. It will not be localized to one continent or even two, but every continent will be affected. Secondly, people will act in a unique way, for they will cry out, "mountains fall on us"[2] (Rev. 6:16). The horror and the terror will be so great that people will wish that they were dead! During the Holocaust, Jewish prisoners in the Concentration Camps lost the will to survive or to live. The Great Depression caused many Americans to lose all of their life savings and to lose their jobs overnight. Many company presidents jumped out of office windows to commit suicide when they heard the news of their monetary losses. However, this was not completely worldwide.

Just like in the summer of 2006 when the Israeli War broke out again, Middle East analysts jumped to say, "Is this Armageddon? Is this the end of the world?" No, not at all! The terror and the horror of this time will be world-wide, not just in the Middle East. Think about the destruction of one tsunami or one hurricane or one earthquake, and think about one of these happening worldwide. Remember how many people died in the few minutes that followed the earthquake/tsunami in 2004? Over 118,000 died in 11 countries with 80,000 dying in Indonesia alone. Today we hear increasingly of natural disasters occurring, but they affect a very small corner of the world compared to the Tribulation's coming worldwide devastation. Again, it is going to be worldwide, no part of the earth will be untouched.

During the time of the Tribulation, God will unleash unparalleled wrath and judgment upon the earth and its inhabitants. This is not wrath from men or from Satan, except as God allows. Not only does this period differ from preceding times of trouble in intensity, but in its source - it is from God Himself.

1. J. Dwight Pentecost, <u>Things to Come</u>, p. 235.
2. Charles Ryrie, <u>Basic Theology</u>, p. 540.

"Back to the Future"
End Times Prophecy, from Genesis to Revelation
Lesson 10 – Tribulation: Introduction

*** DAY 2: Purposes of the Tribulation

Purification of the Nation of Israel for their Messiah and His Kingdom

1. In Jeremiah 30:7 what is the Tribulation called? What is the end result of this time?

2. From Jer. 30:11, 15, and 24, what is the "purpose of God's heart" concerning Israel?

3. In the following passages, what is the result of the Tribulation judgment on the nation of Israel?
    a. Dt. 4:30-31

    b. Eze. 20: 37-38 add to this judgment of Israel?

    c. Joel 2:12-13

    d. Zech. 13:7-9

    e. Mal. 4:5-6

Salvation of Many Gentiles

4. What will have happened before the Tribulation comes to an end? Mt. 24:14

5. Who is the great multitude that John sees in Rev. 7:9-14?

Judgment of the Wicked

6. Rev. 3:10 reveals another purpose of the Tribulation? What is it?

7. How do the prophets support this thought?
    a. Jer. 25:30-32

    b. Is. 26:21

8. How does II Thess. 2:12 characterize those who are condemned?

9. What do verses 9, 11, and 21 of Rev. 16 show about the wicked during the Tribulation?

ON A PERSONAL NOTE . . .
- Read about the discipline of God in Heb.12:3-11. Once in Christ, you will never undergo God's wrathful judgment, but you may fall under His discipline. Can you think of a time when that was true of you? What fruit of righteousness was produced in you? Have you thanked God for His love in producing that fruit in you? If you are undergoing His discipline at this time, repent now knowing your Heavenly Father desires you to share in His holiness.

"Back to the Future"
End Times Prophecy, from Genesis to Revelation
Lesson 10 – Tribulation: Introduction

REVIEW:

In Jer. 30:7 the Tribulation is referred to as the time of Jacob's distress. And in Daniel 9:24-27 it is clear that this seventieth week pertains to Daniel's *people* (Israel) and his *holy city* (Jerusalem). The first purpose of God in the Tribulation is to prepare the nation of Israel for her Messiah. As the events of the Tribulation unfold, the Jewish people will suffer terribly at the hands of the antichrist and they will begin to turn to their Messiah. As we shall see, the gospel of Christ's coming kingdom will be preached throughout the world (Mt. 24:14). God will bring about the conversion of 1/3 of the nation (Zech. 13:7-9) who will enter the Millennial Kingdom and experience all the blessings and the promises of the Abrahamic Covenant and its subcovenants.

As a result of the preaching of the King and His coming Kingdom, many Gentiles will also turn to Christ as their Lord and Savior (Rev. 7:9, Matt 25:31-46). This great multitude will also enter the Millennial Kingdom in their natural bodies and experience all its blessings while serving Christ.

A third purpose of the Tribulation is to execute judgment on unbelieving men and nations for their wickedness. Even through the horrors of the Tribulation, humanity will continue to worship the antichrist and curse God. The intensity of judgments is directly linked to the intensity of rejection and hatred of God.

Stephen Davey points out that the Tribulation will expose the true character of Satan – "He will be revealed to care nothing about the human race in spite of generations of masquerading through false teachers his desire to improve mankind and provide prosperity and comfort. Satan's masquerade of light and goodness will be thrown aside and he will become the dragon attempting to destroy the purposes of God. He will spare no one in his quest."[3]

The Tribulation will also reveal God's sovereignty to all of His creation. I am reminded of Psalm 2:2-6:

> *The kings of the earth take their stand*
> *and the rulers gather together*
> *against the LORD*
> *and against his Anointed One.*
> *"Let us break their chains," they say,*
> *"and throw off their fetters."*
> *The One enthroned in heaven laughs;*
> *the Lord scoffs at them.*
> *Then he rebukes them in his anger*
> *and terrifies them in his wrath, saying,*
> *"I have installed my King*
> *on Zion, my holy hill."* NIV

God has had this plan, the Tribulation, in place since the Old Testament days (really, since the beginning of Time). God says that "He wants none to perish" (2 Peter 3:9). Therefore, the Church Age continues and God lingers or waits on sending Jesus for His return (Rapture) so the Tribulation can begin. In the meantime, may we spread the good news of Christ to all we know and serve Him ourselves with all of our hearts. Psalm 2 closes with the following:

> *Therefore, you kings, be wise;*
> *be warned, you rulers of the earth.*
> *Serve the LORD with fear*
> *and rejoice with trembling.*
> *Kiss the Son, lest he be angry*
> *and you be destroyed in your way,*
> *for his wrath can flare up in a moment.*
> *Blessed are all who take refuge in him.* NIV

---

3. Stephen Davey, <u>Four Horsemen and the Coming World Madness - Part I</u>: *A Crash Course on the Coming Tribulation*, Sermon.

"Back to the Future"
End Times Prophecy, from Genesis to Revelation
Lesson 10 – Tribulation: Introduction

*** DAY 3: The Timing for the Tribulation

1. **We have previously studied Daniel's prophetic dream in Daniel 2.**
   a. What power in history has been identified with the fourth kingdom described in Daniel 2:39-43? Was this power ever conquered in history?

   b. Where did the rock, symbolizing God's kingdom on earth, strike the statue? Daniel 2:34

2. **Daniel 7 also describes the four kingdoms represented by the statue of Daniel 2.**
   a. How is the Roman Empire described in Daniel 7:7, 23?

   b. How many horns did Daniel see on this fourth beast; what do they represent? Daniel 7:7, 24

   c. What happened next? Daniel 7:8, 24

3. **We also studied the Seventy Sevens decreed for Israel in Daniel 9.**
   a. Who are the people of the "ruler to come" who destroyed Jerusalem and the temple, the event described in Daniel 9:26?

   b. What does the "ruler to come" (Antichrist) do which signifies that the 70th "seven" has begun? Daniel 9:27

4. **Putting all this information together,**
   a. What must happen politically before the Tribulation can begin?

   b. What actions will signify the start and the middle of the Tribulation?

   c. Whose kingdom will overthrow this fourth beast at the end of the Tribulation?

5. **II Thess. 2 sheds more light on the start of the Tribulation.**
   a. From vv. 2-3, the day of the Lord will not come until who is revealed?

   b. According to vv. 6-7, what must happen before this man of lawlessness is revealed and the Tribulation begins?

ON A PERSONAL NOTE . . .
- Not only does the Holy Spirit restrain evil in the world, but He restrains sin in our personal life as well. As we obey God's Word and yield to God's will, we experience the power of the Holy Spirit in our lives. How have you experienced this life-changing power in recent months? If you have not, what do you think has kept you from doing so?

- Thank the Holy Spirit for His continual presence and His sanctifying power in your life.

"Back to the Future"
End Times Prophecy, from Genesis to Revelation
Lesson 10 – Tribulation: Introduction

REVIEW:
From Daniel's prophecy, we know there remains one last week, the Seventieth Week, for God to deal with Israel. The last week will begin with a covenant being signed between Israel and the "prince who is to come" from the fourth kingdom (Rome).

We have seen that Daniel 2 and Daniel 7 describe the four world empires that will "trample on Jerusalem" before the Lord returns and rules over all the earth from the Holy City. They are 1) Babylon, 2) Medo-Persia, 3) Greece, and 4) Rome.

The Roman Empire was divided into two kingdoms: (remember the prophecy of the two legs?) the Western Empire and the Eastern Empire. Then Germanic tribes, Vandals, Goths, Visigoths, and others started carving up the borders and chiseling away sections of the empire. Different sections were revived in different centuries. One example was the Holy Roman Empire (this was part of Italy, part of France, part of Germany, and parts of Eastern Europe) which lasted from 843 until 1806. During this time, the Roman Catholic Church gained great strength, often acting as a government as it collected taxes and made laws. Even Napoleon tried to reunite much of Europe. Later the countries of Europe began to emerge. Not until after WWII did the idea of reuniting Europe reemerge.

Why do I mention the Roman Empire? We see in Dan. 2:34 that the "stone cut out without hands" (Christ) will strike the statue on its feet of iron and clay and crush them. It is this ten-nation kingdom of the revived Roman Empire that Christ will destroy at His return. The ten horns Daniel sees in Dan. 7:7, 24 are the kings of these ten nations. In Dan. 7:8, 24 we see another horn, or king, arise who is different from the ten kings and who conquers three of the ten kings. This is the beginning of the rise of the antichrist, the "prince who is to come" out of the Roman Empire in Daniel 9:26. After conquering three of the nations, the antichrist will be able to assume leadership over all ten nations of the revived Roman Empire and will enter into a peace covenant with Israel. Daniel 9:27 tells us that the Tribulation begins with the signing of this covenant.

But, when might this be? Scholars today look at the European Union and the European Economic Market to see what might fit this prophecy. Technically, this Ten Nation Kingdom could be formed prior to the Rapture, but the emergence of the leader who will conquer the first three countries/kingdoms and then conquer all ten cannot occur until after the Rapture. His identity most likely will be kept a mystery until after the Rapture. The covenant is probably not a negotiated treaty, but a result of the superior strength of the antichrist. God is still in control. God has a plan, and we know He will execute world events to fit into His plans.

Think about the political and religious upheaval in Israel today. Nothing short of a miracle will bring peace between the Israelis and the Arabs. The power of the antichrist will bring a "false "peace." The covenant will probably include a fixing of Israel's borders, trade relations with neighbors, and protection from outside attacks.[4] Ezekiel 38:11 and I Thessalonians 5:3 mention this "time of peace."

We saw on Day One that the Tribulation starts the Day of the Lord. II Thessalonians 2:2-3 tells us that this day will not come until the man of lawlessness is revealed. II Thessalonians 2:7 tells us that it is the influence of Holy Spirit, resident in the Body of Christ, who is now restraining the coming of the antichrist. Only after the true Church is removed at the Rapture will the antichrist be revealed. This does not mean that the Holy Spirit will no longer be omnipresent or operative in the world, but that He will no longer be resident in men.

---

4. John Walvoord, <u>Major Bible Prophecies</u>, p. 319.

"Back to the Future"
End Times Prophecy, from Genesis to Revelation
Lesson 10 – Tribulation: Introduction

*** DAY 4: Scene in Heaven – Part I

Church Raptured Before the Tribulation: Rev. 4:1

1. What are the first and the last two words of Rev. 4:1? To what do you think "this" refers?

2. Looking back at verses we studied on the Rapture, how does each support that the Church is absent during the Tribulation
   a. Rev. 3:10
   b. I Thess. 5:9
   c. I Thess. 1:10

The Throne Room of God: Rev. 4:1-6a

3. What was John instructed to do in v.1?

4. Where did John find himself "in the Spirit"? See also Ps. 33:13-14

5. How does John describe the One sitting on the throne?

6. What encircled the throne?

7. What surrounded the throne and who was seated on them?

8. Describe the twenty-four elders. Who do you think they are? Read any commentaries you have,

9. What came from the throne?

10. What is the identity of the seven lamps John saw before the throne?

11. What else did John see before the throne?

Worship in Heaven: Rev. 4: 6b-11

12. Describe the four living creatures that John also saw around the throne.

13. What are the words they say unceasingly?

14. What response of worship do the creatures' words evoke from the 24 elders? v11

15. What words of praise do the elders add to the worship of the Lord God Almighty?

ON A PERSONAL NOTE. . .
- Today we have been given a glimpse into the throne room of Heaven. Put yourself in John's place and try to imagine all that he was experiencing.

- Spend time personally worshiping the One sitting on the throne, our Lord God Almighty. (You might want to take your shoes off, as we are on Holy ground!)

"Back to the Future"
End Times Prophecy, from Genesis to Revelation
Lesson 10 – Tribulation: Introduction

REVIEW:

John uses the phrase "*after these things*" in Revelation to mark the beginning of a new vision (7:9, 15:5, 18:1, and 19:1). Prior to this, John has seen the vision of the glorified Christ and received the letters to the seven churches. Here the phrase also marks a transition from matters concerning the Church age to matters concerning Israel in future times - the Tribulation, the Millennial Kingdom, and the eternal state.

When John is commanded to "come up here," many scholars believe that this refers to the church being raptured. The church is not mentioned again from Rev. 6-18. In our study on the Rapture, we saw that scripture supports this thought.

John, in the Spirit, immediately finds himself in the throne room of Heaven. Scripture teaches there are three heavens. The first heaven refers to our atmosphere, the troposphere that surrounds our planet. The second heaven refers to outer space, where planets, stars, and billions of galaxies exist. The heaven John finds himself in is the third heaven, the dwelling place of God, the Sovereign God. Have you ever noticed that the word sovereign has both the words "reign" and "over" in it. John sees God seated on His throne in this third heaven *reigning over all*!

In the throne room of God, John sees many glorious and wondrous things! The light and colors are breathtaking! John describes the One **sitting on the throne** as being like a jasper stone and a sardius in appearance. *Jasper*, described in Rev 2:12 as "crystal-clear," probably refers to a diamond and *sardius* (from which Sardis got its name) refers to a blood-red ruby. Of course, we know how beautifully each stone can reflect light. These two stones express the shining beauty of God's glory and may also symbolize God's blazing wrath. Interestingly, these two stones are the first and last of the twelve gemstones worn on the high priest's "breastpiece of judgment" to represent the twelve tribes of Israel when he entered the Holy of Holies to offer sacrifices (Ex.28:15-21). These two stones may symbolize that even though God's wrath and judgment is about to occur, God's covenant with Israel will remain. John's vision of the throne would not have comforted John but would have reminded him that God is a consuming fire. Balancing these colors of judgment, John sees a rainbow around the throne. John describes it as "like an emerald in appearance" indicating that green was its dominant color. Since the time of Noah the rainbow has been a promise of God's faithfulness, mercy, and grace.[5]

Around the throne of God John sees twenty-four thrones upon which are seated twenty-four elders. The number "24" when used in the Bible speaks of completion and representation, illustrated in the fact that in the Law of Moses there were twenty-four orders of the priesthood. Much discussion has transpired about the twenty-four elders. There are a few clues to help with their identity. First of all they appear to be reigning with Christ. They are clothed in white, and we have seen in our study on the Rapture that judged saints will be clothed in bright, white linen. Also, the gold crowns upon their heads are similar to those given to victors in the Greek games, a *stephanos* crown (not the crown of a sovereign ruler, a *diadem*). This seems to indicate that the elders have been judged and rewarded. Christians will be rewarded at the Judgment Seat of Christ with different crowns for their faithfulness, obedience, and perseverance under persecution. In Rev. 5:8-10, the elders appear to be on thrones, they sing of being purchased by blood for God, they fall down before the Lamb, and they are made to be priests to God. By combining all of these clues together, one can deduce that these twenty-four elders represent the church, raptured before the Tribulation and now in heaven worshiping God before His throne.

After this, John informs us that **from God's throne** come flashes of lightning and peals of thunder. Lightning and thunder are associated with God's presence in the Old Testament (Ex. 19:16; Eze.1:13) and are associated with God's judgment during the Tribulation (Rev. 8:5, 11:19, 16:18). In his series on Revelation, Stephen Davey says, "Do not miss the fact that the redeemed are singing - they are not terrified of His wrath for they have been rescued by faith in Christ."[6]

Before the throne of God John sees seven lamps of fire burning which he tells us **are the seven Spirits of God**. This is a reference to the Holy Spirit. The number seven is the number of perfection or completion and refers to the sevenfold ministry of the Holy Spirit (Is. 11:2). John also sees before the throne something *like* a sea of crystal glass. With this metaphor John is trying to describe the floor of the throne room. Architects will often put a fountain or a pool of water in front of a building. The building's reflection in the water doubles its beauty during the day, and at night the light coming from the building is reflected,

"Back to the Future"
End Times Prophecy, from Genesis to Revelation
Lesson 10 – Tribulation: Introduction

making twice the light. Imagine all the light and color that John has seen reflected by a floor of crystal glass, doubling its splendor and beauty![7]

Finally John sees four living creatures *in the center and around the throne*. Ezekiel 1 gives a more detailed description of these beings and then identifies them as cherubim in Ezekiel 10:15. John's description of them views the cherubim in relation to the created world. MacArthur writes, ". . . the **lion** represents wild creatures, the **calf** domestic animals, the **eagle** flying creatures, and **man** the pinnacle of creation. Symbolically, the **lion** represents strength, the **calf** service, the **man** reason, and the **eagle** speed."[8] Their body and wings are covered with eyes showing that while they are not omniscient, nothing escapes their scrutiny. We know that these angelic beings are involved in announcing the coming judgments of the Tribulation. In Rev. 6 they call the four horsemen into action, and in Rev. 15 they give the seven angels their bowls to pour out on the earth.[9]

Revelation 4 ends with worship of God on the throne. Day and night the four creatures praise the holiness of our eternal God, giving Him glory, honor, and thanks. Perhaps here they are praising God for His holiness demonstrated by judgment. The cherubim's song causes the twenty-four elders around the throne to fall down before the throne, laying their crowns at God's feet, and begin to sing their own song of worship. The elders praise God because of who He is, *our Lord and our God*, and because of what He has done, "*You created all things and because of Your will they existed, and were created.*" Won't you now join these elders in their song?

---

5. John MacArthur, The MacArthur Commentary: Revelation 1-11, pp. 147-148.
6. Stephen Davey, The First Hymns of Heaven - Part II: *True Sightings*, Sermon.
7. Ibid.
8. MacArthur, op. cit., p. 154.
9. Ibid., p. 154.

"Back to the Future"
End Times Prophecy, from Genesis to Revelation
Lesson 10 – Tribulation: Introduction

*** DAY 5: Scene in Heaven – Part II

The Scroll and the Lamb: Rev. 5:1-7

1. Describe the scroll John sees in the right hand of the one on the throne (God the Father)?

2. What does John hear an angel ask?

3. Why does John begin to weep?

4. One of the elders tells John to behold one who is worthy to open the scroll. What titles does the elder use to describe this "worthy one"? Why are these titles significant?

5. Describe what John sees next?

6. What does the Lamb do?

The Celebration in Heaven: Rev. 5:8-13

7. In Rev. 5:8-9 we again see the 24 elders.
    a. What do they, along with the four creatures, do?

    b. They then sing a new song. What does their song say about the Lamb; why is He worthy?

    c. What is in store for those who are followers of the Lamb?

8. Who next joins in the worship of the Lamb? For what seven attributes do they praise the Lamb?

9. Finally who joins in this great hymn of praise?

ON A PERSONAL NOTE . . .
- Jesus shed His blood on the cross, in order that all who confess Him as Savior and Lord may be part of a kingdom and priests to serve God and reign on earth. If you have not settled your future with the Lord, please read Appendix One: The Best Decision of your Life.

- Take your shoes back off, if you haven't already! Our focus today has been on Jesus, the Lamb of God who died in our place to redeem us from sin and death. The "hymns" we have looked at today are wonderful scriptures to store in your memory bank. Use them today to worship the One who is "*worthy to take the book and to break its seals.*" Thank Him for His work on the cross for YOU!

    (Note: On Day 3, we worshipped God the Holy Spirit; on Day 4, God the Father; and today, God the Son. What a privilege and blessing it is to serve such a *MIGHTY* God.)

"Back to the Future"
End Times Prophecy, from Genesis to Revelation
Lesson 10 – Tribulation: Introduction

REVIEW:
Yesterday we left John in the throne room of God, awestruck at what he was seeing and hearing - the majesty of God's throne, the lightning and thunder coming from the throne, the seven flaming lamps before the throne, representing the Holy Spirit, and the 24 elders and the cherubim singing and praising God. As the worship in heaven continues, John notices something in the right hand of GOD. The word for book, *biblion*, used in the text does not refer to a book as we know it, but to a scroll. In John's time, a scroll was a long piece of either papyrus or animal skin, rolled from each end towards the middle. Here God is holding a scroll written inside and on the back, sealed with seven seals.[10]

In the ancient world a will was sealed with seven seals. A Roman will was sealed by seven witnesses who would each put his seal on the will. It could not be opened except in the presence of all seven witnesses. You could see this scroll in Rev. 5 as God's will which was sealed by the seven-fold Spirit.[11]

However, this scroll is best seen as a title deed to the earth. This kind of contract was known all over the Middle East in ancient times. Jeremiah 32 describes this type of document. Jeremiah, instructed by God, bought a piece of land in the territory of Benjamin, although the land was about to be taken over by the Babylonians. This was to be a sign that the Jews would one day return to their land. Two scrolls were written. One was not sealed and became public record. The other was sealed with seven seals and kept in the temple until the owner would later claim his rightful ownership of the land.

This scroll in God's right hand of protection is the title deed to all of creation. What Adam lost with his sin, Christ redeemed at the cross. And one day, God will give the title deed to Christ who will claim his rightful ownership of His land.[12] This scroll does not record what Christ will inherit but how He will regain His inheritance - by means of divine judgment.[13]

John hears an angel ask who was worthy to open the book and break its seals. When no one in all creation (in heaven or on earth or under the earth) was found, John begins to weep. He weeps because there is no one to bring about final redemption of the universe. There is no one to administer the will of the Father. No one can conquer evil, usher in the future kingdom, no one can deliver heaven and clothe mortals with immortality.[14]

But John's weeping was premature! One of the 24 elders tells John to stop weeping and directs his attention to *the Lion from the tribe of Judah, the Root of David*. Both of these titles are Messianic titles which, as shown earlier in this study, point to Christ. Jesus is worthy to open the scroll, not only because of who He is, but because of what He has done. By His death on the cross, Jesus overcame sin (Rom. 8:3), Satan (Col. 2:15), and death (Heb. 2:14-15).

As John looks, he sees not a Lion, but a Lamb! Jesus, the Lamb of God who takes away the sin of the world (John 1:29) is referred to as a Lamb 31 times in the book of Revelation. From John's description of this Lamb, we notice several things. This Lamb is standing (alive) but looking as if He had been slain (His wounds from the crucifixion were visible). The Lamb has seven horns (complete, absolute power) and seven eyes (perfect omniscience, wisdom, and knowledge). John tells us that the eyes represent the seven Spirits of God (Holy Spirit) that are sent out to all the earth (He sees everything concerning both the righteous and the unrighteous).

This scene which began in 5:1 climaxes in v. 7 when the Lamb that John sees comes and takes the scroll out of the right hand of God. Daniel 7:13-14 also describes this time with the words, *"I kept looking in the night visions, And behold, with the clouds of heaven One like a Son of Man was coming, And He came up to the Ancient of Days and was presented before Him. And to Him was given dominion, glory and a kingdom, that all the peoples, nations and men of every language might serve Him. His dominion is an everlasting dominion which will not pass away; and His kingdom is one which will not be destroyed."* Jesus takes the scroll, the title deed to the earth and all creation, to be in His possession forevermore.

At this climatic point, a great chorus of worship and praise spontaneously erupts. Instantly the four living creatures and the twenty-four elders fall down before the Lamb (this is the same response of worship that they gave the Father in Rev. 4:10 - proof of Christ's deity). Remember that John's vision describes a future event which happens at the beginning of the Tribulation. We, as part of the redeemed Church, will

"Back to the Future"
End Times Prophecy, from Genesis to Revelation
Lesson 10 – Tribulation: Introduction

be *present and be participating*. The realization that God's righteous judgment is about to begin and that Jesus will soon return victoriously to establish His kingdom on earth causes a celebration which soon includes every creature in the universe.

The 24 elders, holding harps and golden bowls of incense begin the song. Harps are frequently associated in the Old Testament with both worship and prophecy (I Samuel 10:5, II Kings 3:15). And the bowls, we are told, hold the prayers of the saints. This is not to be seen as the saints in heaven praying for the saints on earth. Instead their prayers are appeals to God for the redemption of the earth. Together the harps and bowls signal that all the prophets' prophecies and all the saints' prayers are about to be fulfilled.[15]

The elders' song begins by affirming that Christ is worthy to take the book and break its seals (to break its seals means to begin the judgments written in the scroll). Christ's worthiness is based on His death on the cross, which purchased men for God from every tribe, tongue, people, and nation (all humanity). By His sacrificial, substitutionary death Christ purchased us from slavery to sin and to Satan and saved us from an eternity in Hell. We, as part of the redeemed of all ages, are part of God's kingdom, are priests to God, and will reign upon the earth with Christ.

At this point John hears myriads of myriads (too many to be counted) of angels join in the praise. Their emphasis is also on Christ's death (the Lamb that was *slain*), the reason for which He is to be praised. They worship Christ for seven of His attributes (seven again being the number of perfection and majesty). The angels praise Christ because of His power, His eternal riches, His wisdom, His might, His honor, His glory and His blessing.

As if the singing is not loud enough, John now sees every creature everywhere (*in heaven, on earth, under earth, on the sea, and all things in them*) join the praise. This universal "choir" cries out, "blessing, honor, glory, and dominion belong to the Lamb." All creation is ecstatic on its coming liberation.

As this great scene of praise and worship comes to a close, we continue to see the four living creatures affirm all that is being said of the Lamb with their continuous "Amens". The stage is set for the Judgment of God and of the Lamb to begin. All of creation acknowledges the holiness, the justice, and the righteousness of this judgment and celebrates the coming Kingdom of Christ.

How about you? Have you acknowledged Christ's worthiness specifically as your Lord and Savior? Philippians 2:10-11 promises that you too will one day bow at His knee and confess Him as Lord. Will you do this as part of God's kingdom, as a priest and co-ruler with Christ, or will you do it still separated from God and as an object of His wrath? If you are not sure, stop right now, read Appendix One, and settle this all-important matter with God. Let us all be able to joyfully join in the hymns of heaven.

---

10. Ibid., p.163.
11. Stephen Davey, The First Hymns of Heaven - Part III: *The Secret Scroll*, Sermon.
12. Ibid.
13. MacArthur, op. cit., p. 164.
14. Davey, op. cit., Sermon.
15. MacArthur, op. cit., pp. 170-171.

"Back to the Future"
End Times Prophecy, from Genesis to Revelation
Lesson 11 – Tribulation: Six Seals

*** DAY 1: The First Seal

1. Remember where we were when we left off last week:
    a. Where is John (in the spirit)?

    b. Who has been deemed worthy to open the sealed scroll?

    c. From where did the scroll come?

    d. Who are the four creatures that summon the actions of the first four seals?

2. First seal: Rev. 6:2
    a. What color is the first horse John sees?

    b. What is in the rider's hand?

    c. What is he given to wear?

    d. What is his mission?

3. **This horseman is not Jesus returning to earth!**
   From the scriptures given and from what we have learned so far, fill in the following chart comparing the rider on a white horse in Rev. 6:2 with the rider on a white horse in Rev. 19:11-16.

Differences in	Rev. 6:2	Rev. 19:11-16
Their weapons		
Their crowns		
Their titles		
Length of peace		
Timing of their coming		

ON A PERSONAL NOTE . . .
- The rider on the white horse introduced by the first seal is the ruler to come of Dan.9:27. He is a deceiver and will offer a false peace to Israel. Deception is one of Satan's main weapons. Deception works because it often appears to be truth. What deceptions does Satan use in your life to rob you of peace?

"Back to the Future"
End Times Prophecy, from Genesis to Revelation
Lesson 11 – Tribulation: Six Seals

REVIEW:
Before we begin our discussion of the seven seals, please look at the chart on Appendix Three. There are two types of passages in Revelation which record events of the Tribulation. The first type, a progressive revelation, reveals events as they progress in time. The second type, called a parenthetical revelation, introduces subjects and events without advancing the order of events. Also note that the seal judgments include **all the judgments** to the end - the seventh seal encompasses the seven trumpets and the seventh trumpet encompasses the seven bowls. It is important that we keep this in mind as we study the events of the Tribulation.

Some would argue that it is unfair for one generation to suffer all of the wrath that God unleashes during the Tribulation. However Stephen Davey offers the following defense (*as if God needs one*):
- This generation will have more knowledge, signs, and opportunity to respond to God's witness than any previous generation
- The intensity of God's judgment will be linked to the intensity of their rebellion
- Every unbeliever in Hades is currently suffering and would gladly trade the torment they are undergoing with the wrath of the Tribulation[1]

The scriptures of Revelation contain many signs and symbols, making it difficult at times to understand. We will take the approach of Ryrie, who states that when interpreting Revelation, always start with what is the clearest.[2]

As Revelation 6 begins, the scene now shifts from the throne room of God to earth. As Christ opens each of the first four seals, we see one of the four living creatures summon a rider on a horse (Rev. 6:1, 3, 5, 7). The judgments of these first four seals are not read but acted out. The four riders have often been called the Four Horsemen of the Apocalypse. Horses in scripture are often associated with military triumph, power, and majesty.[3]

With the opening of the first seal, John sees a white horse, and on it is a rider with a bow. Note that the rider has no arrows. The rider is given a crown and he goes out to conquer the nations. As we have seen, the Tribulation will begin as the antichrist (*the ultimate counterfeit messiah*) arrives on the scene as ruler of a ten-nation kingdom revived from the Roman Empire. Whether the rider on the horse represents the antichrist himself or his worldwide peace is a matter of debate. The absence of an arrow in his bow indicates that He will begin His rise to ascendancy with bloodless, political victories. The peace covenant he makes with Israel will be a peace won by agreement, not by war. Israel's peace and the world's long-sought-after Middle East peace finally arrive as the antichrist promises to protect and defend Israel. Little does the world know what is just around the corner.

Some have tried to identify this rider on the white horse with Christ, who sits on a white horse in Rev. 19. However, by comparing the descriptions of Rev. 6:2 and Rev. 19:11-16 we see that there are several distinct differences in the two riders. They have different weapons. The antichrist weapon is a bow without arrows while Christ's weapon is the sword of His spoken word. The crown worn by the rider on the white horse is a "*stephanos*" - a victor's crown which is temporary, while Christ's crown is a "*diadema*" - a monarch's crown. The peace that the antichrist brings will only last 3 ½ years, but Christ's rule will bring peace on earth for 1000 years. And finally, the arrival of the rider on the white horse occurs at the beginning of the Tribulation, while Christ will return as King of Kings and Lord of Lords at the end of the Tribulation.

Since man's beginnings in the garden, one of Satan's main weapons is deception. The antichrist and his rule will be Satan's grand finale. Meanwhile the father of lies continues to attack us day by day, causing us to turn our eyes away from Christ. It is only as we spend time in God's word and unleash the power of the Holy Spirit in our lives through prayer that we can hear and follow Christ's voice and live the victorious life that God has in store for us.

1. Stephen Davey, Four Horsemen and the Coming World Madness – Part I: *A Crash Course on the Coming Tribulation*, Sermon.
2. Charles Ryrie, Basic Theology, p. 542.
3. John MacArthur, The MacArthur NT Commentary: Revelation 1-11, p. 178.

"Back to the Future"
End Times Prophecy, from Genesis to Revelation
Lesson 11 – Tribulation: Six Seals

*** DAY 2: Seals Two, Three, and Four

1. Second seal: Rev. 6:3-4
   a. What is the color of the second horse John sees?

   b. What is its rider given power to do?

   c. What will become common during this violent time?

   d. What is given to this rider?

2. Third seal: Rev. 6:5-6
   a. The third horse that John sees is what color?

   b. What is in the hand of his third horse's rider?

   c. What three things is John then told?

3. Fourth Seal: Rev. 6:7-8
   a. What color is this fourth and final horse?

   b. What is its rider named?

   c. Who is following close behind?

   d. Why do you think Death and Hades are seen together?

   e. What were the Death and Hades given power to do?

4. Fill in the following table, describing the first 3 ½ years:

Revelation 6	Matthew 24
v. 2	vv. 4-5
v. 4	vv. 6-7a
v. 6	v. 7b
v. 8	v. 7c

5. In Matthew 24:8 what does Jesus call the time covered by Matthew 24:4-8?

ON A PERSONAL NOTE . . .
- Psalm 31:15 tells us that our times are in God's hands. What problem in your life do you need to turn over to our omniscient, omnipotent God, knowing He is in control of your future? His ways and His timing are so much better than ours!

"Back to the Future"
End Times Prophecy, from Genesis to Revelation
Lesson 11 – Tribulation: Six Seals

REVIEW:

Second seal
When Christ opens the second seal the second cherubim commands, "Come!" and a red horse gallops on the scene. Its rider, who is unnamed, is granted the right to take peace from the earth. The red color of the second horse suggests bloodshed and warfare. As the antichrist begins to expand his empire his tactics turn from politics to war. Peace is removed from the earth. Matt 24:6-7 says "You will be hearing of wars and rumors of wars. . . . For nation will rise against nation and kingdom against kingdom . . . ." Times turn into utter chaos and violence. Don't miss the fact that this rider *is given* the right to take peace from the earth. This may appear to be the wrath of Satan or that of man, but in reality it is the ***wrath of God*** that those on earth are experiencing. We are also told that it becomes common for men to slay each other. John tells us that the rider on the red horse is given a great sword. The word used for the sword, *machaira*, refers to a short, stabbing sword that was used by both Roman soldiers and assassins. The wars and the violence of men that begin with the second seal will continue until the end of the Tribulation.

Third seal
As John sees Christ open the third seal and hears the third cherubim call for the third horse and rider, John sees a black horse appear. Its rider is holding a pair of scales in his hand. The color black is associated with famine in Lamentations 5:10. With the outbreak of war, a shortage of food now follows. Jesus foretells this in Matthew 24:7 when he says, "... and in various places there will be famines and earthquakes." The pair of scales the rider is carrying represents the measuring of food and supplies. John then hears a voice from the center (probably God's) saying, "A quart of wheat for a denarius, and three quarts of barley for a denarius..." A denarius represents a day's wages for the average worker and a quart of wheat represents approximately one meal. This would not be enough to feed a normal family. Three quarts of barley could be bought for the same price, but it was of lower nutritional value than wheat and often fed to animals. Starvation and severe famine spread over the entire world. John also hears the voice say, "do not damage the oil and the wine." Both oil and wine are used in the cooking and need to be used carefully.[4]

Fourth seal
In Rev. 6:7-8 Jesus opens the fourth seal and a fourth cherubim summons the last of the four horsemen. An ashen, or sickly pale, yellowish green, horse appears. This color makes us think of gangrene or rotting flesh. This horseman is the only one named, and he is called Death, and he is accompanied by Hades (the grave). The effect of this judgment is the most devastating experienced so far: These two *are given* authority to kill one-fourth of the world's population by sword (war), hunger (famine), pestilence (death), and by wild beasts (many think that this is a reference to wild rats). The Greek word for *war* means death. John MacArthur comments on this word: "Here it may primarily refer to diseases as the cause of death (Rev. 2:23; 18:8), but is broad enough to encompass natural disasters such as the earthquakes predicted by Jesus (Matt. 24:7), floods, and volcanic eruptions. It could also refer to the effects of biological and chemical weapons."[5]

In Matthew 24-25, Jesus addresses His disciples' questions concerning the future in what is known as the Olivet Discourse. There John heard Jesus describe the coming events of the Tribulation. He no doubt recognizes the parallel between what he heard then and what he is now seeing in the opening of the seals. After all, it is Jesus himself that is now opening the seals describing this same time period. In Matthew 24:8, Jesus describes the events of the first four seals as the "beginning of birth pains." As any mother knows, the pains of labor at the beginning only continue to increase in intensity and in frequency as the time for birth draws near!

As previously noted, the riders on the red and the ashen horse have to be given permission to inflict harm on the world. God, by Whom all things were created and have their being, always has been and always will continue to be in control.

---

4. Ibid., pp. 182-183.
5. Ibid., p. 184.

"Back to the Future"
End Times Prophecy, from Genesis to Revelation
Lesson 11 – Tribulation: Six Seals

*** DAY 3: The Seals Continue

1. Fifth seal: Rev. 6:9-11
   a. Who does John see after Jesus opened the fifth seal? Where are they?

   b. What is their cry?

   c. What are they given?

   d. What are they told?

2. In Matthew 24:9, what is *then* mentioned, corresponding to the fifth seal?

3. Based on Matthew 24:9-14, what will happen as the Tribulation unfolds?

4. Sixth seal: Rev. 6:12-17
   a. What happens with the opening of the sixth seal? What are the results?

   b. What do all men do at this time?

   c. What is their cry to the mountains and the rocks?

   d. What do they acknowledge has come? What do they ask?

5. How does Matthew 24:29 parallel this sixth seal?

6. In Matthew 24:21, how does Jesus describe the second half of the Tribulation?

ON A PERSONAL NOTE . . .
- Read Rom. 12:19 and Dt. 32:35-36. Vengeance and vindication are to come from God and not from ourselves. This is an area of weakness for me, as I tend to want justice and payback *now*. How foolish we are to think that our judgment is always right and that we can do God's job better that He can. In your time alone with God today, ask Him to bring to mind any wrongs you are holding on to that you need to confess and turn over to Him. Pray for His strength to overcome evil with good.

"Back to the Future"
End Times Prophecy, from Genesis to Revelation
Lesson 11 – Tribulation: Six Seals

REVIEW:
Fifth seal
As we have seen, each of the seals represents a different judgment of God that strikes the earth sequentially. The seven seals encompass the entire Tribulation, with Christ returning at the end. There is a disagreement among scholars, however, as to which seals occur in the first half and which occur in the second half. Many place the first 6 seals in the first half, while some place the seals and the trumpets in the first half, and the bowls in the second. In many of John Walvoord's writings, he favors placing all of the seals in the second half. However, I agree with both John MacArthur and Stephen Davey that it seems best to see *the first four seals happening in the first half, the fifth stretching from the first into the second, and the sixth and seventh occurring during the second half.*

With the fifth seal we have the first mention of martyrs - people losing their lives because of their testimony and the word of God they shared. John sees underneath the altar the souls of believers killed during the Tribulation because of their faith in Christ. He heard them cry out asking God how long He is going to refrain from judging and avenging their blood on the wicked of the earth. As the seals are judgments not on believers but on unbelievers, this fifth seal does not represent the martyrdom of the saints, but their prayers for God to take vengeance on their killers.

Matthew 24:9 warns that "You will be hated by all nations because of My name." In the first part of the Tribulation, persecution will be allowed by the governments of the nations. Unbelievers, as well as the apostate church, will undoubtedly hate and persecute true believers during this time. This persecution will only intensify after the antichrist sets himself up to be worshiped at the midpoint of the Tribulation. From that time on believers who refuse to worship him and, in fact, oppose him will be seen as blasphemous.

In Rev. 6:11 God responds to the prayers of the martyrs by giving each of them a white robe and telling them to rest a little while longer, until God's predetermined number of those to be killed has been reached. The white robe reminds us of the white garments given to the church at the Judgment Seat of Christ. Here they symbolize "God's gift of eternal righteousness, blessedness, dignity, and honor (cf.3:5)."[6]

Sixth seal
Unlike the first five seals, in which humans are involved, God acts alone in the sixth seal. Along with Christ's breaking of the seventh seal, John sees six natural disasters occur. First to happen is a *great earthquake*. Many earthquakes have occurred in the history of the world, and they will greatly increase in number and intensity as the Tribulation draws near. But this earthquake is more powerful and devastating than any that has occurred in history up to this point. In the aftermath of this great earthquake, *the sun turns as dark as a sackcloth made of hair*. Also *the moon becomes like blood*. Perhaps these effects are a result of volcanic activity which spews ash and smoke into the upper atmosphere. John also writes that *stars fall from the sky*. Since stars are bigger than the earth, this cannot be a reference to literal stars. Instead it probably refers to asteroids and meteor showers. The *sky appears to roll up like a scroll*. This imagery is used several times in the Bible when end time events are being described. This particular passage does not describe the final dissolving of heaven which occurs later in Rev. 21:1 (also in II Pet. 3:10). The last event associated with this sixth seal is that *every mountain and island are moved out of their place*, probably indicating that the crust of the earth begins to move and shift.

The horror and fear caused by the disasters of this seal cause all men from every walk of life to hide in caves and among the rocks, begging for death. Although there is no sign of repentance whatsoever, they do acknowledge in fear that they are experiencing the *great wrath* (indicating that we are now into the second half of the Tribulation) of God and of the Lamb. They foolishly think that by dying they can escape the wrath of God. Blinded by their own sin and the lies of Satan and the antichrist, they still refuse to believe and accept God's free gift of eternal life.

Revelation 6 closes with these unrepentant men asking, "Who is able to stand?" Without God's mercy and grace, the answer would be, "No one."

---

6. Ibid., p. 196.

"Back to the Future"
End Times Prophecy, from Genesis to Revelation
Lesson 11 – Tribulation: Six Seals

*** DAY 4: The 144,000

Introduction: Rev 7:1-8
1. What does John see in Rev. 7:1?

2. What are the four angels doing?

3. John next sees a fifth angel.
    a. What does he have in his hand?

    b. What is his command to the first four angels? Compare this with Rev. 8:7-10.

4. How many were sealed?

5. What is the identity of these sealed?

A More Detailed Description: Rev 14:1-5
6. In this passage, John again sees these 144,000 at the end of the Tribulation. Here we are given more information concerning these sealed witnesses.
    a. How do we know these are the same 144,000? v. 1

    b. What five things do we learn about these 144,000 in vv. 4-5?

ON A PERSONAL NOTE . . .
- Looking at the description of the 144,000 in Rev. 14:4-5 evaluate the witness of your actions, your words, and your service to God.

"Back to the Future"
End Times Prophecy, from Genesis to Revelation
Lesson 11 – Tribulation: Six Seals

REVIEW:

When we come to Chapter 7, we encounter the first of the three parenthetical revelations. Stop now and review Appendix Three, Progression of the Book of Revelation. Chapter 7 forms a parenthesis between the first six seals in Rev 6 and the seventh seal in Rev. 8:1. We left off yesterday in Rev. 6:17 with unbelievers asking, "The great day of wrath has come, and who is able to stand?" Now, in Chapter 7, God answers this question.

John introduces a new vision with the words, "*After this.*" (See also 4:1, 7:9, 15:5, 18:1, 19:1.) In Rev. 7:1 John sees "*four angels standing at the four corners of the world, holding back the four winds of the earth . . . .*" Although John lived around 2000 years ago, he is not indicating that he thinks the earth is flat. The four corners of the world refer to the four points on a compass (N, S, E, and W) from where the four winds blow.

Interestingly enough, scientists have recently proven that Earth does indeed have four corners. In <u>The Revelation Record</u> Dr. Henry M Morris writes, "The earth is not really a perfect sphere, but is slightly flattened at the poles. Its equatorial bulge is presumably caused by the earth's axial rotation, and its four 'corners' protrude from that" (p.126). There are indeed four corners, one at each pole and two at each equatorial bulge. Morris goes on to say that these four corners help in controlling the "atmospheric circulation which governs the wind." Imagine that – the Bible, inspired by our Sovereign Creator God over 2000 years ago, is once again validated by science.

The angles are holding back the wind "*so that no wind would blow on the earth or on the sea or on any tree*". Winds are often associated with judgment and here they are held back for a brief time. Without wind there would also be no waves or movement of clouds. Restraining the wind symbolizes holding back the remaining judgments. Now for a brief time, all will be calm as God seals a special group of witnesses.

John then sees another angel coming from the east (Israel is to the East of the island of Patmos). This angel has the seal of the living God. The word used for seal, *sphragis*, refers to a signet ring and indicates ownership and protection. Remember that Joseph received Pharaoh's ring when he was promoted to second in command over Egypt. This new angel cries to the four angels holding back the winds not to harm the earth or sea or trees until the bond-servants of God have been sealed (note that the first three trumpet judgments of Rev. 8 do in fact destroy 1/3 of the trees, grass, sea, and rivers). Once sealed, these men will have the authority and power of God and will be protected from the judgments to come as they proclaim the good news of Christ and His kingdom. These believing Jews will be saved and sealed during the first half of Tribulation. (Some think they are saved and begin their ministry during the first half, but are not sealed until prior to the trumpet judgments in the second half.)

John next hears that the number of those sealed is 144,000. There are to be 12,000 from each of the twelve tribes of Israel. We learn more about these 144,000 from Rev. 14:1-5 where they meet Christ on Mt. Zion at His return to earth. In Rev 14:1 we are first told that they have the *name of the Lamb and the Father written on their foreheads*. This mark identifies them as God's possession. Later we will see that the antichrist mimics their sealing and has his own followers sealed with his mark. Can't he do anything original?!? We are next told that these bond-servants are morally pure and *have not been defiled by women*. This does not necessarily mean that they are unmarried or virgins, but probably indicates that they have kept themselves away from the sexual promiscuity prevalent during the Tribulation. They are *faithful servants*, following the Lamb wherever He goes. They have been redeemed, set apart for service to God, and are the *firstfruits* of those saved during the Tribulation. These Jewish men are the *firstfruits* of the nation of Israel which God has promised to redeem out of the Tribulation. And in stark contrast to the antichrist and his followers, the 144,000 will speak God's truth *(no lie was found in their mouth)*. Finally these 144,000 are *blameless*, not perfect, but justified. They will be seen as blameless when they stand in God's presence (Jude 1:24).

Israel failed in its mission to be a witness nation for God in the Old Testament. Now it will be a group of 144,000 Jewish men who will be instrumental in bringing more people to Christ than ever before. They will faithfully serve the Lord by proclaiming salvation through faith in Christ alone. Their evangelism will result in the salvation of the nation of Israel, as well as an uncountable number of Gentiles. The believers who survive the judgments of the Tribulation will enter the Millennial Kingdom in their natural bodies along with all of the 144,000 bondservants.

"Back to the Future"
End Times Prophecy, from Genesis to Revelation
Lesson 11 – Tribulation: Six Seals

As followers of Christ in today's world we too have been set apart to spread the good news of Christ to those we encounter. Like the 144,000, we need to be pure and faithful as we hold out the Word of Truth. We must each ask ourselves, "How faithful am I in sharing Jesus with others?" "When others look at my life do they see me or Jesus?" After all we may the only Jesus someone ever sees. Doesn't studying the Tribulation make you want to tell others how to escape the horrors of its judgments? How horrible it would be for someone being tormented in the Lake of Fire to wonder why I never told them about Jesus.

"Back to the Future"
End Times Prophecy, from Genesis to Revelation
Lesson 11 – Tribulation: Six Seals

*** DAY 5: The Great Multitude (*Tribulation Saints*): Rev 7:9-17

1. Starting in v. 9, John next sees a great multitude – so many that no one could count them.
   a. What nationalities comprise this group?

   b. Where are they when John sees them?

   c. What are they wearing? Compare with Rev. 6:9.

   d. What are they holding in their hands?

   e. Of what event does this remind you?

2. What is their cry of worship and what is the result of their cry? vv. 10-12

3. When John is given the identity of these people, what explanation is given? vv. 13-14

4. What is John told the white robes signify? v.14

5. As servants before God's throne, from what three things are they protected? vv.15-16

6. In verse 17, how else will they be taken care of? Compare to Rev. 21:4, 6.

ON A PERSONAL NOTE . . .
- How can knowing that God will always be in the saving business, even during the worst times of the Tribulation, comfort us today?

"Back to the Future"
End Times Prophecy, from Genesis to Revelation
Lesson 11 – Tribulation: Six Seals

REVIEW:
Immediately after John's vision of the 144,000 sealed servants of God, he sees the results of their ministry - *a great multitude of people that no one could count from every nation and all tribes and peoples and tongue.* The Greek used here indicates that these people are from every culture and descent and race and language. (See Rev. 5:9 where Jesus was praised for purchasing men from all humanity.) This would include Gentiles and Jews alike. Let's further look at this group of people, too many to count.

First this group is *standing before the throne and before the Lamb*. So far we have seen the Lamb, the 24 elders sitting on thrones (representing the church), the cherubim, and angels all in the throne room of God. We have also seen the martyrs under the altar (the *firstfruits* of those martyred during the Tribulation) being told to wait until the full number of those to be killed is complete. This group John now sees is clothed with the same *white robes* as the early martyrs, indicating that they too are believers who subsequently die during the Tribulation, primarily during the Great Tribulation (2nd half). Rev. 7:14 confirms this thought by saying *they have washed their robes and made them white in the blood of the Lamb.* This group is mainly made up of those who are martyred by the antichrist and his followers but also includes those who die naturally. They join the group of early Tribulation martyrs in heaven.

John also sees that *they are holding palm branches* in their hands, waving them before the throne of God. In the Bible palm branches are associated with times of celebration, deliverance and joy. It was palm branches that the people waved as Jesus rode into Jerusalem, joyfully declaring He was their Messiah. Waving palm branches was something that was done only for kings. Now palm branches are being waved before God's throne and before the King of Kings and Lord of Lords.

As they wave their branches, John hears this uncountable group of redeemed martyrs *cry out with a loud voice,* worshiping both *God who sits on the throne and the Lamb.* Unlike earlier when the early martyrs were praying for God's judgment and vindication, this great multitude is now worshiping God and the Lamb who have provided them the joy, the deliverance, and the victory of *salvation*. So moved are the angels *standing around the throne and around the elders and the four living creatures* that they *fall down on their faces* and join in the worship. No doubt the elders and the cherubim join in as well. The angels' seven-fold doxology echoes the universal praise that occurred in Rev 5:13. Their song, "*All praise and glory and worship and thanks and honor and power and strength be to our God forever and ever*" is bookended with resounding Amens!

When revealing the identity of the great multitude, the elder says they are those who have "*come out of the great tribulation.*" Stephen Davey explains, "...it can literally be translated, 'these are the ones who are presently coming out of the Great Tribulation.' In other words, the early vision of the 144,000 Jewish evangelists who are preaching on Earth is occurring simultaneously with this vision of all these believers, now literally pouring into heaven, who have just died on Earth.... As John is watching, the number of people entering heaven is actually growing. Like people streaming through the gates into a football stadium, these people keep coming."[7]

Now standing before the throne of God, these Tribulation saints are to serve God day and night in His heavenly temple. We are told that God will *spread His tabernacle over them,* meaning that the sheltering presence of the Lord will protect them. Having suffered terrible persecution by the antichrist and his followers, they are now secure in heaven. With the Lamb as their shepherd, all their needs will be fully satisfied. Everything that they lacked during the Great Tribulation will now be given them. Their physical needs will be met as they will hunger no more, nor thirst anymore, nor will the sun beat down on them (as in Rev. 16:9). Their spiritual needs will be met as well as they will be led to springs *of living water.* And *God will wipe every tear from their eye*s - tears that have been caused by the pain, sorrow, and suffering of the Tribulation. These believers will continue to enjoy the peace, protection, and provision of heaven until they return with Christ to earth to reign with Him during the Millennial Kingdom.

People today are attacking Christianity and predicting that it will soon be part of the past. Isn't it comforting to know that God's Word will stand and that He will victoriously redeem people from all the nations until the end of the ages? This should comfort us, cause us to praise our triune God for His free gift of salvation, and encourage us to continue praying for those we know are lost.

7. Stephen Davey, Four Horsemen and the Coming World Madness - Part VIII: *It Will be Worth it All!*, Sermon.

"Back to the Future"
End Times Prophecy, from Genesis to Revelation
Lesson 12 – Tribulation: First Half

*** DAY 1: The Antichrist

1. Reviewing what we've learned *(by now you probably know these answers by heart)*
   a. Before the antichrist comes onto the scene what has happened in Daniel 7:7, 24?

   b. What happens in Daniel 7:8, 24?

   c. And in Dan. 9:27 what does he do which will be a sign that the Tribulation has begun?

2. What does the prefix *anti* mean?

3. The term *antichrist* is first used in I John 2:18--22. After referring to *the* antichrist how does John describe *an* antichrist, many of whom have appeared?

4. In I John 4:1-3 and II John 7, how does John describe the spirit of the antichrist?

5. What is the difference between an antichrist and a false Christ (Mt. 24:23-24)?

6. What are some other names used for the antichrist in Scripture?
   a. Dan. 7:8

   b. Dan. 9:26

   c. II Thess. 2:3 *(2 different names here)*

   d. Rev. 13:1

7. Referring to Dan. 7:8, 20
   a. How does John describe the eyes of the little horn?

   b. What is coming from his mouth?

   c. What are we told about his appearance?

8. What does Dan. 8:9 say about this ruler's beginning and about the spread of his power?

9. We learn more about the antichrist in Daniel 11.
   a. For whom will he show no regard? v. 37

   b. Who does he worship and how? v. 38

   c. As he attacks other countries (2nd seal), how does he reward those who submit to his authority?

ON A PERSONAL NOTE . . .
- Questions 3 and 4 point out the difference between Christianity and the religious cults of the world - what they believe about the deity of Christ. Can you find scriptures that support that Christ is God in the flesh, that Christ's nature is equal with that of God's? Write these down or, better yet, memorize them to use when cults come knocking at your door. Be ready to share these verses.

"Back to the Future"
End Times Prophecy, from Genesis to Revelation
Lesson 12 – Tribulation: First Half

REVIEW:
What in the world is going on? Last week we looked at events of the Tribulation, mainly the first half, from *heaven's* perspective. This week we are going to look at the first half of the Tribulation from the *world's* perspective.

The antichrist is first mentioned in Daniel 7:8 as the little horn (ruler). Daniel tells us that this ruler arises among the coalition of ten nations that comprise the revived Roman Empire (Dan. 7:7). These nations are also represented by the ten toes of the statue in Nebuchadnezzar's dream in Dan. 2. This ruler who starts out first overthrows three of the ten nations. He then is in a position to bring the entire coalition under his control by a political agreement (mutual consent - Rev. 17:13). As head of this Western confederacy, the antichrist will portray himself as a peacemaker. He will even appear to bring peace to the Middle East by making a seven year covenant of peace with Israel, posing as her protector and defender. Unfortunately this pact is a ruse, but the antichrist is able to convince Israel that he is their best hope for peace and protection.

The Greek preposition *anti* means "*opposed to*" or "*in place of.*" I John 2:22 defines any antichrist as one who denies that Jesus is the Christ, God in the flesh. By denying Jesus, they are also denying God's testimony about the Son. The antichrist, referred to as the man of lawlessness in II Thess. 2:3 and as the "little horn" in Daniel 7:8 is the final antichrist spoken of in I John 2:18 and II John 4:3. He is very much *opposed to* Jesus and His purposes. He is also seen as a false (*in place of*) Christ, as he is Israel's protector in the first half of the Tribulation and then reigns over the world as Satan's substitute messiah in the second half. Other names used for him in scripture include the "prince who is to come," "the man doomed to destruction," and "the beast."

We learn much of what we know about this man from several passages in Daniel. If you haven't already, it would be helpful to put a bookmark at Daniel 2, 7, 8, 9, and 11. We will be referring to these chapters often in our study of the Tribulation.

Antichrist arrives on the scene, not as a villain but as a hero - an instrument of peace. Remember that in the first seal the rider of the first horse had a bow but no arrow. Daniel 7:8, 20 tells us that this little horn has the eyes of a man. This refers to his mental ability or intellect. He will apparently be a political and diplomatic genius. He not only is able to broker peace in the Middle East but will be able to solve massive problems which arise during the Tribulation as he expands his power and control. We are also told that his mouth utters great boasts. This refers to the great speaking ability of the antichrist. He will very eloquently capture and hold the attention of Israel and the rest of the world. Finally in Rev. 7:20 Daniel sees that the little horn now appears to be *larger in appearance than its associates.* Not only does this indicate that is he more powerful than the other horns, but the language of this verse indicates that he has the appearance of a chief or lord. The antichrist will have a commanding appearance.[1]

We saw with the breaking of the second seal that wars begin to break out upon the earth. After making his treaty with Israel, the antichrist's desire for dominance will provoke rebellion. Also, his pact will not keep other nations from the desire to conquer and control Israel. The antichrist's attempts to gain control and destroy his enemies will last throughout the remainder of the Tribulation. Daniel 8:9 indicates that this ruler of the West will grow in power to the south and to the east, toward the Beautiful Land of Israel.

Daniel 11:36-39 reveals that Antichrist's true passion is for war, not peace. Verses 37-38 tell us that he has no regard for the ***gods*** of his fathers, but instead will honor a god of fortresses. Notice that the word *gods* is plural. Some wrongly use the singular form *God*, saying that the antichrist is a Jew. Instead this verse indicates that he has no regard for the pagan gods of his fathers. The term *fortress* is used 5 other times in this chapter and means "a strong place." Therefore, power is the antichrist's god and he spends his treasures to extend his power and control through war. Daniel 11:39 shows that the real power behind his success is Satan, *a foreign god.* As the antichrist expands his control, we are told that he gives honor and roles of authority to those who follow him, and he will also sell them land.[2]

Daniel 11:37 also tells us that the antichrist will show no regard for *the desire of women*. This has been interpreted several ways. It could mean that he is a homosexual or it could mean that he is celibate. Another view which is a little bit of a stretch is that this phrase is indicating his disregard for Christ, as the

"Back to the Future"
End Times Prophecy, from Genesis to Revelation
Lesson 12 – Tribulation: First Half

desire of every Israelite woman was to become the mother of the coming Messiah. Perhaps the best explanation however is that the phrase indicates that he will not have a normal affection for a wife, mother, or sister.

This brief look at the antichrist shows us that he is the ultimate fulfillment of *a wolf in sheep's clothing*. Coming onto the scene as a champion of peace, his ultimate desire is to control the world. Controlled by Satan he will eventually persecute, not protect the nation of Israel during the second half of the Tribulation. We will learn more about the antichrist, Satan's puppet of evil, as we continue our study.

1. David Jeremiah, Escape the Coming Night Volume 3, pp. 45-46.
2. John MacArthur, The MacArthur Study Bible, p. 1222.

"Back to the Future"
End Times Prophecy, from Genesis to Revelation
Lesson 12 – Tribulation: First Half

*** DAY 2: Religion during the 1st Half

Israel

1. In Rev. 11:1 what is John told to measure?

2. In Daniel 9:27, what is stopped by the antichrist?

3. And where does Dan. 9:27 say the antichrist will put up "an abomination that causes desolation"?

4. Therefore what can we conclude has happened either before or during the first half of the Tribulation and the "state of religion" in Israel?

The Great Harlot - *the apostate church:* **Rev. 17:1-7, 18**
Note: Chronologically, Rev.17 probably fits between Rev. 5 and 6

5. What judgment is John now about to see?

6. Later in v15, what does the angel tell John the waters represent?

7. How does the angel describe the harlot's relationship with the kings of the earth? v. 2

8. How is the harlot's relationship with the rest of mankind described? (those who dwell on earth)? v. 2

9. When John sees the vision of the woman, upon whom is she sitting (v. 3)? What does v. 7 add?

10. How is the harlot clothed? What is in her hand?

11. What title is written on her forehead in v. 5?

12. What does John see concerning the woman in v. 6?

13. How does v. 18 further define the woman?

ON A PERSONAL NOTE . . .
- Remembering the apostate church at Laodecia, what signs do you see that indicate increasing apostasy in the church today?

"Back to the Future"
End Times Prophecy, from Genesis to Revelation
Lesson 12 – Tribulation: First Half

REVIEW: (*Today's review is longer than usual. Set aside a little more time to read it.*)
The last standing Jewish temple was destroyed in A.D. 70 by the Romans. However, in Rev. 11:1 John is instructed to measure the temple. We are also told that at the midpoint of the Tribulation the antichrist brings all Jewish sacrifices and offerings to a halt. He will then proceed to defile the temple by setting up the abomination of desolation on a wing of the temple (Dan. 9:27). Therefore we can deduce that the temple has been rebuilt, either before or during the first 3 ½ years of the Tribulation. Israel, living in peace under the protection of the antichrist, is able to reinstitute the Levitical sacrificial system of worship. We know that in Israel today, blueprints exist for the rebuilding of the temple, training of priests has begun, and many of the articles used in temple worship have been made, according to the specifications found in Leviticus.

We have also seen that the gospel will be proclaimed during the entire Tribulation. Many will respond in faith and will suffer persecution and even martyrdom. But what about the rest of the world? Although all the true believers have been raptured, there will be many "left behind" professing Christians who are, in fact, unsaved. An apostate church emerges and grows in power and influence. Walvoord suggests that a this world church movement begins with the three branches of the church that exist today - the Roman Catholic Church, the Greek Orthodox Church, and Protestant Churches.[3] Perhaps even Islam and other cults may join them. Void of the Holy Spirit, this apostate church will be loathsome in its religious practices. This religious harlot is shown to John in chapter 17, after the 7 bowls and by one of the 7 angels which had the bowls. However many scholars agree that chronologically, Rev. 17 probably fits between Rev. 5 and Rev. 6.

In Rev. 17:1 John is summoned to see the *judgment of this great harlot who sits on many waters*. The term *harlot* is used throughout scripture as a metaphor for religious apostasy or idolatry. It never refers to those who do not know God but to those who outwardly profess God while inwardly worshiping and serving other gods. This great harlot on earth is seen in sharp contrast to the true "Bride of Christ" who is in heaven.

False religions of all times will culminate in this *great harlot*. We are told in v. 15 that the many waters that she sits on represent *the peoples and multitudes and nations and tongues* of the world. This harlot will dominate all the unredeemed people of the earth. John is next told that all the kings of the earth will commit immorality with this harlot. As the harlot grows in number and in power, it will be closely aligned with the rulers of the earth. He is also told that not only will kings align themselves with her, but all the *earth-dwellers* (unredeemed*)* will become drunk with her immorality.

John is then carried by the Spirit to the desert where he sees a vision of this great harlot - a woman sitting on a scarlet beast. We will look further at this beast tomorrow, but for now, know that this beast represents the antichrist and his political empire. Just as the beast is supporting the woman, the antichrist will support and use the apostate church's ecclesiastical power to increase his own power. We know that religion has often been a great unifier of peoples and nations. And just as the woman is sitting on the beast, the apostate church will initially have some control over the beast.

This apostate church is not only very influential politically, but she is also very wealthy. Revelation 17:4 tells us that the woman John saw was *clothed in purple and scarlet and was adorned with gold, precious stones, and pearls*. The colors she wears are the colors associated with royalty and wealth and her adornments portray the "trappings of ecclesiastical pomp"[4] that we see in some churches even today.
In this description of the harlot's appearance, many see the garb of high officials in the Roman Catholic and the Greek Orthodox churches. MacArthur comments in his study Bible, "Prostitutes often dress in fine clothes and precious jewels to allure their victims." He goes on to say that likewise the harlot adorns herself to "lure the nations into her grasp." As further indication of the harlot's wealth, John sees a gold cup in her hand, *full of abominations and unclean things*. This immorality is the wine with which the nations become drunk (v. 2), as they participate in her adultery of sin and immorality.

Before we continue in our description of the harlot John sees in his vision, we must stop and look at what many call, "Religious" or "Ecclesiastical" Babylon. The city of Babylon is mentioned over 300 times in the Bible and stands in direct contrast with the city of Jerusalem, mentioned more than 800 times in Scripture.

"Back to the Future"
End Times Prophecy, from Genesis to Revelation
Lesson 12 – Tribulation: First Half

While the city of Jerusalem represents the plans and purposes of God, the city of Babylon represents the plans and purposes of man.[5] Babylon in Scripture is the name for a counterfeit religion - whether a pagan religion or a fake Christianity.

In Genesis 10 and 11 we see that Nimrod, a descendant of Ham, was the founder of Babel (Babylon). It was at Babel that, in direct rebellion of God's decree to multiply and fill the earth, a group led by Nimrod decided to build for *themselves* a city and a tower that reached to the heavens (Gen 11:1-4). This tower was a monument to their pride, as they wished to *make for ourselves a name* and not be *scattered over the face of the earth*. We know that in judging this act, God *confused their language* and scattered them *over the face of the whole earth*. The city's name was later changed to Babylon and had a long history recorded in the Bible and in many other recordings of history. The city and the empire associated with it were conquered by the Medes and the Persians in 539 BC.[6]

Ancient accounts tell us that the wife of Nimrod, Semiramis, became head of the "Babylonian mysteries" and the secret religious rites associated with its worship of idols. She was the first high-priestess of idolatry. Semiramis gave birth to a son, Tammuz, whom she claimed was miraculously conceived. Taking from the promise of Gen. 3:15, Tammuz was supposed to be the savior of his people. This is the first false Messiah mentioned in Scripture. According to legend, Tammuz was said to have been killed by a wild beast and then brought back to life (another satanic imitation of Christ) after 40 days of his mother's weeping. This story of mother and child was incorporated into the religious rites.[7]

Although the rites of this Babylonian worship were secret, this mystery religion and its worship of the mother/child found its way into many pagan religions of the world. Although the names were changed, the story remained the same. In Egypt the mother was called Isis and her son was Osiris. In Greece she was Aphrodite and her son was Eros. And in Italy the mother was Venus and her son was Cupid.[8] In Assyria Tammuz remained the son's name but the mother was Ishtar. In these and many more cases, both the mother and the child were considered divine. The mother was soon called the Queen of Heaven.[9]

The scriptures also allude to this mysterious religion. Jeremiah refers to those making cakes for the queen of heaven and those offering incense to her as well. The worship of Baal was another form. Baal is considered identical to Tammuz. In Zech. 5:1-11 Babylon is portrayed as an evil woman, personifying wickedness.[10]

When the Babylonian empire was conquered by the Medes and the Persians, Babylon as a city and Babylon as a religion remained. However, when the Medes and Persians opposed this religion its leaders moved first to Pergamum. This is why Christ, in His letter to the Church at Pergamum, said they lived *where Satan had his throne*. Eventually the Babylonian religion found its way to Rome where it had influence on the Christian church in Rome. Many of the Babylonian rituals can still be found in the rituals of the Roman Catholic Church.[11]

While many OT prophecies concerning Babylon have been fulfilled, those which foretell its ultimate destruction as a religion and as a city were not. We will see the destruction of Babylon as a religion in the last half of Revelation 17, and later in our study of Revelation 18, we will see the destruction of Babylon as a city.

Now, let's get back to John's vision in Rev. 17. John MacArthur tells us in his study Bible that is was customary for Roman prostitutes to wear a headband with their name on it. The woman John now sees, representing the final apostate church, has a name written across her forehead, a mystery, "BABYLON THE GREAT, THE MOTHER OF HARLOTS AND OF THE ABOMINATIONS OF THE EARTH." Here then is the connection between this universal false church, closely allied with the antichrist, and the mystery Babylon we have just discussed. The source of the harlot's organized rebellion, immorality, and idolatry is ecclesiastical Babylon.

One of the most crucial things we learn about this great harlot is found in v. 6. John sees the woman *drunk with the blood of the saints and with the blood of the witnesses of Jesus*. Like false religions through the centuries, the harlot will be relentless in its persecution of those who hold to true faith in Jesus Christ.

"Back to the Future"
End Times Prophecy, from Genesis to Revelation
Lesson 12 – Tribulation: First Half

The number killed by the apostate church will be second only to the number of martyrs killed in the second half of the Tribulation for refusing to worship the beast.

Rev. 17 closes with the angel saying that the woman is *the great city which reigns over the kings of the earth*. The great city is probably not a reference to a literal city but to the ecclesiastical mystery Babylon of verse 5.

3. John Walvoord, Major Bible Prophecies, p. 323.
4. John Walvoord, The Revelation of Jesus Christ, p. 245.
5. Stephen Davey, Armageddon and the Fall of Babylon - Part III: *The Tale of Two Cities*, Sermon.
6. Walvoord, op. cit., p. 247.
7. J. Dwight Pentecost, Things to Come, p. 365.
8. Ibid., p. 366.
9. Davey, op. cit.
10. Walvoord, op. cit., p. 248.
11. Walvoord, Major Bible Prophecies, p. 321.

"Back to the Future"
End Times Prophecy, from Genesis to Revelation
Lesson 12 – Tribulation: First Half

*** DAY 3: The Fate of the Harlot

The Beast on Which the Harlot Rides: Rev 17:8-14
This is one of the most debated passages in Scripture. Adding to the confusion is the fact that the term "beast" refers at times to Satan, at times to the antichrist, and at other times to his ten nation empire. For now, just answer the questions. We will tackle this passage's meaning in the REVIEW.

1. What do we learn about the beast in v. 8? What is the reaction of the world?

2. How are the seven heads of the beast explained in vv. 9-10?

3. How does the angel divide the seven kings in v. 10?

4. How is the beast described in v. 11?

5. How are the ten horns of the beast described? vv. 12-13

6. What do we know will happen to the antichrist and his ten kings at Christ's return to Earth? v. 14

The Harlot's End: Rev. 17:16-17
7. What will happen to the harlot, probably at the midpoint of the Tribulation? v.16

8. Whose will is carried out by these actions? v. 17

ON A PERSONAL NOTE . . .
- Is there a situation in your life that seems hopeless or out of control? Take comfort knowing that God is in total control and will watch to make sure His purposes stand and His word is fulfilled. Confess any lack of faith and claim his promises (Ps. 11:4; Ps. 103:19; Is. 40:8; Rom. 8:23 are among the many).

"Back to the Future"
End Times Prophecy, from Genesis to Revelation
Lesson 12 – Tribulation: First Half

REVIEW:
Yesterday we saw that during the first half of the Tribulation, with the true church raptured and in heaven, an apostate church rises and grows in number and in power. She is closely aligned with the antichrist, who uses her worldly influence to gain power and control for himself and his empire. The antichrist is represented by the scarlet beast on which the woman rides in Rev. 17:3. Today we look closer at this beast with its seven heads and ten horns.

In John 17:8-14 the angel starts his explanation of the beast by saying that it *"was, and is not, and is about to come up out of the Abyss and go to destruction."* All peoples of the earth, except the elect, will *wonder* or be deceived by this apparent miracle. There are some that see the beast as the political power of the revived Roman Empire which was, was not, and has reappeared. This is the position that Walvoord takes in his commentary on Revelation. It is more probable that the beast represents the antichrist. As we will soon study, there is indication in Scripture that right before the midpoint of the Tribulation, the antichrist will appear to have been resurrected. At that time Satan will indwell the antichrist who will demand that all people worship him throughout the remainder of the Tribulation. This position is taken by both John MacArthur and Stephen Davey in their writings. Either way, both the antichrist and his empire are closely identified with each other, are empowered by Satan, and have been resurrected in power.

The angel identifies the **seven heads** of the beast as *seven mountains on which the woman sits and as seven kings*. Mountains are often used in the Bible to represent rule or power and represent the rulers of the seven Gentile world empires of history. The angel tells John that *five have fallen, one is*, and one *has not yet come*. At the time of John's writing, five world empires had risen and fallen - Egypt, Assyria, Babylon, Medo-Persia and Greece. Rome, represented by the sixth king, was the empire currently in existence. The *one who has not yet come* is the antichrist with his final world empire. Revelation 17:11 goes on to say that the antichrist, *one of the seven*, is *also an eighth*. The antichrist is the seventh king before his resurrection and the eighth after his resurrection when he proclaims himself ruler, not only of the revived Roman Empire, but of the entire world.[12]

Next the angel explains the **ten horns** as the kings who *receive authority with the beast for an hour*. Verses 12-14 probably look ahead to the antichrist's rule as world dictator during the last half of the Tribulation. The ten kings from the revived Roman Empire no doubt continue in authority. Their time is short though as they will be overcome by Jesus at his return.

As the angel returns to the description of the apostate church, it is these same ten horns who, along with the antichrist, will come to hate the harlot. Having used the harlot to gain control of the world, the antichrist will now discard her. This will probably happen near the midpoint of the Tribulation, coinciding with the antichrist's overnight rise to **world** dictator. No longer needing the worldwide influence of the apostate church, he destroys her and sets up the final form of world religion – worship of himself as God.

Revelation 17:17 leaves us with a reassuring thought. This verse will also, no doubt, comfort the true believers alive during the Tribulation. Although Satan seems to succeed as the antichrist and his kings destroy the harlot and set up worship of the antichrist, it is actually God who is in control of world events. *For God has put it into their hearts to accomplish His purpose . . . until God's words are fulfilled.* At the coming of Christ, the antichrist and his one-world government will be judged and destroyed.

As we look around at the rebellion, wickedness, immorality, and idolatry of the world today, we too take comfort knowing that God is reigning over the affairs of men and is watching to see that His word is fulfilled.

---

12. John MacArthur, op. cit., p. 1987.

"Back to the Future"
End Times Prophecy, from Genesis to Revelation
Lesson 12 – Tribulation: First Half

*** DAY 4: Gog / Magog: Ezekiel 38-39

1. Read Ezekiel 38:1-4 (read from NASB if you have it). Who is the prince and where is he from?

2. In Eze. 38:3, over whom are we told Gog rules?

3. On what are the armies riding? Describe their weapons. Eze. 38:4

4. Although the armies are intent on destroying Israel, who is really the instigator of battle? Eze. 38:4

5. What five other countries will join the battle? Eze. 38:5-6

6. Scan Eze. 38:7-12 looking for details from these verses that place Israel in the first half of the Tribulation.

7. What is the purpose of the invaders? Eze. 38:12,13

8. What is God's purpose for the invasion? Eze. 38:16, 23

9. What are the results of the battle? Vv. 18-22; also Eze. 39: 4-5

10. What additional judgment occurs in Eze. 39:6?

11. What happens to the weapons (Eze. 39:9-10) and the bodies (Eze. 39:12-20)?

12. What does their rescue from this battle prove to Israel? (Eze. 39:21-24)

ON A PERSONAL NOTE . . .
- Israel does not have to fight the invading armies of this Russian coalition. Scripture is constantly telling us that God fights for His people. Is there a battle of life that you are currently trying to fight in your own efforts? What is keeping you from resting in the Lord and letting Him fight for you?

"Back to the Future"
End Times Prophecy, from Genesis to Revelation
Lesson 12 – Tribulation: First Half

REVIEW:
Ezekiel 37 describes Israel's restoration as a nation, followed by her turning to the Lord at His Second Coming. Ezekiel 38 and 39 next describe a great battle which occurs during the first half of the Tribulation. This battle is between a Russian-led coalition of nations and Israel.

In vv. 2-3 we are introduced to Gog, a leader who arises in the land of Magog and is the head of Rosh, Mesech, and Tubal. I have read many different interpretations of these names. My best guess is that Magog refers to the territory that made up the former Soviet Union and is some form of the Russian empire. Rosh (Russia), Meshech, and Tubal refer to regions within the land of Magog. It is interesting to note that Moscow is directly north of Jerusalem.

Other members of the coalition include Persia (Iran), Cush (either Ethiopia or Sudan), Put (Libya), and Gomer (either Armenia or Germany) and Beth-to-garmah (Turkey). Again you can find some disagreement among scholars concerning the areas represented by these names. It is safe to say, however, that present day Russia and Iran will be major players in this coalition that comes against Israel and, by default, against their protector (the antichrist and his empire). We know that today Russia and Iran are closely allied and would both dearly love to see Israel brought to her end.

The weapons with which these armies are equipped are weapons of Ezekiel's time, certainly not weapons of today. Some say that Ezekiel is describing war in terms he understood. Others say that there must be a world-wide disarmament before this time. A world-wide shortage of oil could also explain the use of horses. It is interesting to note that Russia still uses mounted troops today.

In Eze. 38:4 we are informed that this battle is really the plan of God. Although this invading coalition thinks they are acting on their own plans, we will see that God is in fact bringing these invaders to the mountains of Israel to be destroyed by Him in judgment. God is seen as leading them by *hooks in their jaws*. Eze. 38:8 says it is God who "*summons*" the troops to the land of Israel.

Scholars also disagree as to the timing of this battle of Gog and Magog. In my reading I have seen it placed before the Tribulation, during the first half of the Tribulation, and at the end of the Tribulation. Eze. 38:8 places this event in the *latter years* and after Israel has been *gathered* to their land. Furthermore Eze. 38:8 says that Israel is living *securely* in their land, and Eze. 38:11 says they are *at rest* (at peace) and living in *unwalled villages* with *no bars* or *gates.* It is these phrases that, to me, pinpoint the time of the battle to be in the first half of the Tribulation. It will probably happen near the end of the 1st half. The destruction of the Russian-led troops will open up the way for the antichrist to declare himself ruler of the entire world.

The purpose of this invasion is seen in Eze. 12-13. In addition to destroying the Jewish people, the invaders plan to carry away the wealth of the land - silver and gold and cattle and goods. However God has a higher purpose in mind. When he destroys the forces coming against Israel, all the nations will know that He is Lord, Sovereign of the world.

We are told that these invaders from *the remote parts of the north* will come *like a cloud and cover the land of Israel* (Eze. 37:15-16). It will appear that Israel is about to be annihilated. But God in His *zeal* and *blazing wrath* will cause a great earthquake to occur in Israel, leveling mountains and causing great panic. The soldiers will turn and use their weapons against each other. Further judgments of pestilence, blood, rain, hailstones, fire and brimstone will completely decimate the troops. God will give their dead bodies to the birds of the air and the beasts of the field. In addition, we are also told that God will send fire upon Magog and on those who inhabit *the coastlands*. All nations will know that the Sovereign Lord has intervened and rescued His people. And the nation of Israel will know that He is the Lord *their* God. (Eze. 39:22).

In the aftermath of the carnage, Eze. 39:9-10 tells us that weapons will be burned, providing fuel for *seven years*. This passage is a key reason why some scholars place this battle either right before or at the beginning of the Tribulation. Others see no problem with weapons being burned into the Millennial Kingdom as people are also beating their swords into plowshares and their spears into pruning hooks (Is. 2:4). Ezekiel 39:11-16 reveals that it will take seven months for the bodies of the dead to be buried.

"Back to the Future"
End Times Prophecy, from Genesis to Revelation
Lesson 12 – Tribulation: First Half

*** DAY 5: As the First Half Comes to a Close

Temple Measured: Rev. 11:1-2
1. Before introducing His two witnesses, God gives John a command.
   a. What is he commanded to measure?

   b. Why is John told not to include the court outside the temple (Court of the Gentiles)?

Two Witnesses of God: Rev. 11:3-6
2. In Rev 11:3 God now introduces two men who will come onto the scene at this time.
   a. What does God call them?

   b. What does He give them authority to do and for how long?

   c. What insight is given in Dt. 19:15 and Matt. 18:16 as to why there are two?

   d. Referring to Gen. 37:34, what emotion is symbolized by the clothing of sackcloth?

   e. How are these two witnesses described in v. 4? (See also Zech. 4:3,11,14)

   f. What happens to anyone wanting to harm these two witnesses? v. 5

   g. What three miracles are the witnesses able to perform, authenticating their message? v. 6

Military Activity of the Antichrist
3. Read Daniel 11:40-45
   a. At the time of the end, who comes against the antichrist?

   b. What is his response?

   c. Finally, where does he set up his headquarters?

4. It is probably then that the event in Dan 9:27 happens. What does the antichrist do?

ON A PERSONAL NOTE . . .
- When God measures something in scripture, it often indicates His ownership of what is being measured. While a believer has all of the Holy Spirit, the Holy Spirit doesn't always have all of us. What area of your life needs to be turned over to the control of the Holy Spirit?

- Do your prayers indicate that God owns you or that you think you own God? How would remembering that it is God who owns you change your prayers?

"Back to the Future"
End Times Prophecy, from Genesis to Revelation
Lesson 12 – Tribulation: First Half

REVIEW:
Temple Measured
In Revelation 11:1-2 John is given an active role in His vision. He was given a measuring rod and was told to measure *the temple of God, the altar, and those who worship in it.* Remember that when John was writing Revelation there was no temple standing. There had been three temples built and destroyed up to this point: the first built by Solomon, the second reconstructed by Zerubbabel after the exile, and the third built by Herod but destroyed by the Romans in 70 A.D. John, no doubt, also knew that Scripture foretold a temple in the Millennial Kingdom. How excited John must have been to learn that a fourth temple would be built. This temple will be rebuilt either prior to or just after the beginning of the Tribulation.

The Greek word used for measuring rod is *kalamos* which refers to a hollow, bamboo-like cane plant that grew in the Jordan Valley. Because it was light, yet rigid, it was often used as a measuring rod. The Greek word *naos* refers only to the inner temple - the Holy Place and the Holy of Holies. The altar to be measured probably refers to the brazen altar located in the courtyard outside the inner temple. As only priests could enter the Holy Place, the worshipers John saw refer to a remnant of believing Jews worshiping God in the rebuilt temple during the Tribulation.

During the last 3 ½ years of the Tribulation, the antichrist, his followers, and Satan's demons will unleash more devastation and oppression than the world and, in particular, Israel has even known. John's measuring of the temple was not done to obtain its dimensions since none are given. "It is best to see it as an indication of God's ownership of Israel, symbolized by her temple, for salvation and for His special protection, preservation, and favor."[13]

In further support of the reason for measuring the temple is the fact that John was told to *leave out the court which is outside the temple and do not measure it.* The court of the Gentiles was outside the courtyard where the brazen altar sat. For a Gentile to proceed past the court of the Gentiles was to defile the temple and would result in his execution. The exclusion of this court in John's measurement symbolized God's rejection of the unbelieving Gentiles of this time who have followed the antichrist and persecuted His people. God explains that the court of the Gentiles *has been given to the nations*, who *will tread underfoot the holy city for forty-two months.* The last 3 ½ years of the Tribulation, known as the Great Tribulation, will bring to a close the "time of the Gentiles" –the period from the time of Babylonian captivity till the return of Christ, during which Gentile nations are in control of the Holy city of Jerusalem.

Two Witnesses
All throughout history, in the darkest of times and in the best of times, God has always raised up servants to faithfully proclaim the gospel and call sinners to repentance. We have already seen the 144,000 who begin preaching the gospel of the kingdom during the first half of the Tribulation. Now, in Rev, 11:3-6, before the darkest days of Earth's history, God empowers two special *witnesses* to testify of His judgment and His free gift of salvation to all who repent and believe.

These two witnesses will prophesy for 1260 days (1260 days = 42 months = 3 ½ years). We learn from Dt. 19:15 and from Mt. 18:16 that Old Testament law required the testimony of two people to confirm a matter. The testimony of these two witnesses will underscore the certainty of God's coming judgments and Christ's coming kingdom. The sackcloth the witnesses are wearing is a symbol of grief, mourning, and distress. There are many instances in the OT of people wearing sackcloth in times of sorrow. The two witnesses are here wearing sackcloth to express their distress over the judgments of the unbelieving world, the desecration of the temple, the rise of the antichrist, and the oppression of Jerusalem.[14]

In Rev. 11:4 John is told that the two witnesses are *the two olive trees and the two lampstands that stand before the Lord of the earth* (imagery taken from Zech. 4). Just as Joshua and Zerubbabel led a spiritual revival in their day, so these two witnesses will lead a great revival during the last half of the Tribulation. God will use the testimony of these two witnesses to cause much of the nation of Israel to return to Him.

Ministering at a time when the antichrist is empowered by Satan, it is God's omnipotent power which enables these two witnesses to overcome their enemies. (We can only imagine how much the antichrist and his followers will hate these two men.) Rev. 11:5 tells us that *fire comes out of their mouth and devours their enemies, miraculously killing anyone who attempts to harm them.* These two also have the

"Back to the Future"
End Times Prophecy, from Genesis to Revelation
Lesson 12 – Tribulation: First Half

power to shut up the sky so that rain will not fall during the days of their prophesying. They have *power over the waters to turn them into blood* and are able to *strike the earth with every plague as often as they desire.* The miracles that these two witnesses perform substantiate the divine origin of their message.

The big question is who are these witnesses? Are they two men who lived previously and have been restored to earth for this ministry? Those who hold the view that these will be men who lived previously, support Elijah and either Moses or Enoch as being the witnesses. There are many verses and reasons to support Elijah, who had the power to deal with his enemies by fire and the power to stop rain from falling. There are some difficulties or debates in deciding between Moses and Enoch. Moses had the power to turn the waters into blood and to strike the earth with plagues. Enoch is suggested by many because he, like Elijah, never experienced death. However we must remember that scripture does not identify these men. Therefore we do not know for sure who these two men are. They are probably two men living during the Tribulation raised up at this special time for this special ministry.

Military Activity of the Antichrist

Although Antichrist comes onto the scene with a message of peace, we see in Daniel 11:39 that he soon turns to warfare, bent on expanding his empire. This warfare is represented by the Red Horse of the second seal (Rev. 6:3-4). In Dan. 11:40-45 we see one of the antichrist's campaigns which occurs as the first half of the Tribulation comes to a close.

Daniel 11:40 tells us that this conflict begins when the *king of the South collides* with the antichrist and the *king of the North storms against him with chariots, horsemen, and many ships.* This joint attack is actually against Israel, but since the antichrist has sworn to protect Israel, they are against him as well.

Who are these two kings? These two kings were mentioned several times in Dan. 11:2-35 and since those verses have already been literally fulfilled in the days of Antiochus Epiphanes we know that the king of the South was the king of Egypt and the king of the North was the king of Syria. Since Daniel was not told that these two kings here are different, we must understand them to be the same.[15]

Therefore when the King of Egypt and the King of Syria attack Israel, the antichrist and his army will rush to the Middle East, invading *countries* on his way (Dan. 11:40). The antichrist's route will be from the north to the south. After conquering Syria, he will march through Israel (*the Beautiful Land*) towards Egypt. Along the way, many *countries will fall,* but Edom, Moab, and Ammon *will be rescued out of his hand* (Dan. 11:41). Antichrist, arriving in Egypt, will enjoy further military success and possess all of the treasures of the land (Dan. 11:42-43). Apparently he will not conquer Libya and Ethiopia for when he turns around to head north they will be *at his heels*, or behind him (Dan. 11:43).

But what causes the antichrist to turn around? We are told that *rumors from the East and from the North will disturb him.* This is probably news of the Gog/Magog invasion (Eze. 38-39) that we studied yesterday. Two of the major armies in this invasion are Russia, *from the North*, and Iran, *from the East.* When the antichrist hears that Israel is being invaded, *he will go forth . . . to destroy and annihilate many.*[16]

But before the antichrist can get to Israel, God will supernaturally destroy the armies coming against Israel, giving him freedom to do what he wants in the Middle East. Daniel 11:45 tells us that at this time, the antichrist sets up his headquarters in Jerusalem.

The destruction of Russia and its allies and the destruction of the southern Muslim coalition against Israel may explain how the antichrist, king of the ten-nation group, can proclaim himself ruler of the world without opposition. Perhaps he even claims credit for the supernatural destruction of his enemies to support his claims to be God. As we know, he breaks his treaty with Israel at this time and begins his 3 ½ year persecution of God's people.

13. John MacArthur, The MacArthur New Testament Commentary: Revelation 1-11, p. 293.
14. Ibid., p. 299.
15. Renald Showers, "The Character and Military Career of the Antichrist", Audio from Friends of Israel's 2007 Prophecy Conference.
16. Ibid.

"Back to the Future"
End Times Prophecy, from Genesis to Revelation
Lesson 13 – Tribulation: 7 trumpets / 7 thunders

*** DAY 1: The Seventh Seal Begins the Seven Trumpet Judgments: Rev. 8:1-6

1. What happens when the Lamb breaks the seventh seal? Why do you think heaven responds this way? v.1

2. John next sees seven angels. vv. 2
   a. How does John describe this group of angels?

   b. According to Luke 1:19 who might one of them be?

   c. What are they given?

3. In the Old Testament, trumpets played a very important part in the lives of the Israelites. How were they used in the following passages of scripture? Can you connect the blowing of the angels' seven trumpets to any of these reasons?
   a. Numbers 10:2

   b. Numbers 10:9; II Chron. 13:12; Eze. 33:3

   c. Numbers 10:10

4. With what time do Zephaniah 1:14-16 and Zech. 9:14 connect the blowing of the trumpet?

5. Describe what John sees happen in vv. 3-4.

6. Do you remember what the prayers of the saints are? Rev. 5:8; 6:9-11

7. What happens after the angel throws fire from the altar to the earth?

ON A PERSONAL NOTE . . .
- In Rev. 8:1, Heaven was silent for thirty minutes. How many minutes do you give the Lord each day? Five? Ten? Thirty? Sixty? If you don't meet with Jesus regularly or meet only for a few minutes, make a commitment now to spend quality time with Him each day. Establish a time and pick a place in your house. Make sure you reserve a chair for Jesus.

    Make a date with Jesus:
    Best time and place to meet _____

    Sign here _____

- May your heart be hushed in His presence and may we be assured that our prayers will be answered according to God's will. Remember, if we don't make it each day, Jesus will be there waiting. Wonder what He would have shared with us?

"Back to the Future"
End Times Prophecy, from Genesis to Revelation
Lesson 13 – Tribulation: 7 trumpets / 7 thunders

REVIEW:
Lesson 13 looked at events leading up to and signaling the midpoint of the Tribulation. This week we pick up with the seventh seal. But first, let's review seals 1-6.

first seal	Rider with bow and crown on *white* horse brings temporary peace
second seal	Rider on *red* horse brings war and bloodshed
third seal	Rider with scales on *black* horse brings global famine
fourth seal	Rider named Death on *pale green* horse brings pestilence and death
fifth seal	Prayers of martyrs for God to judge wicked, avenge their deaths
sixth seal	Total eclipse of sun and moon (sun turns black, moon turns blood red)

Remember that *the first four seals happen in the first half of the Tribulation, the fifth stretches from the first into the second half, and the sixth and seventh occur during the second half.* Also remember that the seventh seal encompasses all of the trumpet judgments and the seventh trumpet encompasses all the bowl judgments.

As the Lamb breaks the seventh seal, the response in heaven is quite different than anything up to now. There is silence in heaven for half an hour. Remember that up till now, John has heard much noise and commotion: lightning and thunder (Rev. 4:5); worship of the four living creatures (Rev. 4:8); songs of praise by the 24 elders (Rev. 4:11); the praise of all of creation (Rev. 5:13); voices of angels (Rev. 5:5-7; 7:2-3); cries of the martyrs (Rev. 6:9-10); and shouts of the great multitude attributing salvation to God and to the Lamb (Rev. 7:9-13). Now, in anticipation of the horror of the coming judgments, all of heaven is hushed. Nearing the Tribulation's end, God's final judgments are set to begin. John MacArthur writes, ". . . saints will be vindicated, sin will be punished, Satan will be vanquished, and Christ will be exalted."[1]

As the suspense mounts, John next sees *the seven angels* who are given seven trumpets. The word "*the*" indicates that this is a group of seven special angels. In fact we are told they are the ones *who stand before God*. The tense of the verb *stand* indicates they have been there for some time. Jewish tradition has long spoken of the "seven archangels of the Presence." Scripture does not name these angels, but it is interesting to note that in Luke 1:9 Gabriel is described as one who *stands in the presence of God*. It is probable that this high ranking group of angels are archangels – Gabriel, Michael, and five others.[2]

In the Old Testament we see that trumpets were the most important musical instruments in the lives of the Israelites. In Numbers 10:2-8 God instructed Moses to use them for summoning the congregation of Israel to the tabernacle and for having the camps set out on a march. The trumpets were also sounded to sound the alarm in time of war, warning people of coming trouble and calling upon God's armies to protect Israel and judge her enemies (Num. 10:9; II Chron. 13:12; Eze. 33:3). In Num. 10:10 God instructs that trumpets are to be blown at feasts, on the first days of the months, and over burnt and peace offerings.

Trumpets also appear in prophecy and are associated with the Day of the Lord (Zeph. 1:14-16). In Zech. 9:14 we are told that the Lord Himself will blow the trumpet as He marches out in wrath to destroy His enemies. Here in Rev. 8-9 and in Rev. 11:15-19 trumpets are sounded with each impending judgment.

Before the trumpet judgments begin, John sees another angel holding a golden censer come to the altar of incense before the throne in heaven. Old Testament priests would twice daily take hot coals from the brazen altar where sacrifices were offered into the Holy Place to the incense altar (Ex. 30:7-8). When the incense was ignited, smoke (symbolizing the prayers of the saints) rose toward heaven as a pleasing aroma to the Lord.[3] Here in the throne room of God it is the prayers of the Tribulation saints against Satan, sin, and their persecutors (Rev. 5:8; 6:9-11) that rise with the smoke of the heavenly incense.

As God is in agreement with their prayers, the angel fills the censer with fire from the altar and throws it to the earth. This censer of fire is symbolic of the divine judgments that God is about to unleash on the earth as Christ's coming draws near. The immediate effects seen on earth include peals of thunder, sounds and flashes of lightning, and another earthquake (probably of greater intensity than that of the sixth seal).

1. John MacArthur, New Testament Commentary on Revelation, p. 238.
2. Stephen Davey, The Trumpets of Seven Archangels - Part I: *Heaven . . . Hushed*, Sermon.
3. MacArthur, op. cit., p. 240.

"Back to the Future"
End Times Prophecy, from Genesis to Revelation
Lesson 13 – Tribulation: 7 trumpets / 7 thunders

*** DAY 2: First Four Trumpet Judgments: Rev. 8:7-13
As you read today's scripture, circle each occurrence of the phrase "a third."

1. First Trumpet Sounded:
   a. What happens as the trumpet is sounded?

   b. What results on earth?

   c. What impact would this have on those living at this time?

2. Second Trumpet Sounded:
   a. What happens with the sounding of the second trumpet?

   b. What results?

   c. How would those on earth be impacted?

3. Third Trumpet Sounded:
   a. What does John see when the third trumpet sounds?

   b. What happens as a result?

   c. What impact would this have on those living at this time?

4. Fourth Trumpet Sounded:
   a. What occurs when the fourth trumpet is blown?

   b. What does this cause?

   c. How might those living on earth be impacted?

5. After the first four trumpets, John hears an ominous announcement.
   a. Who makes the announcement?

   b. What is John told?

6. Fill in the chart on the last page of this week's lesson for the first four seals.

ON A PERSONAL NOTE . . .
- The great star falling from heaven in the third trumpet judgment is named Wormwood, meaning *bitterness*. When people drank from the waters poisoned by this star, they died. What bitterness are you harboring in your life? Is it harming any of your relationships? Won't you confess and release this bitterness to God now before it causes these relationships to die?

"Back to the Future"
End Times Prophecy, from Genesis to Revelation
Lesson 13 – Tribulation: 7 trumpets / 7 thunders

REVIEW:
Today as we look at the first four trumpet judgments it is important to see that all four combine to divinely destroy the earth's ecology. The judgments are literal, physical events that will affect the entire world. Throughout history we have seen people worshiping nature, *the created*, rather than God, *the creator*. We see more and more people today revere "Mother Nature" more than they do Father God. Ironically, with the sounding of the first four trumpet judgments God will use nature to pour out His wrath on the wicked of the earth.

As the first trumpet is sounded, a great storm of hail and fire mixed with blood comes upon the earth. MacArthur suggests that the earthquake caused by the censor of fire hurled to the earth would trigger worldwide volcanic eruptions.[4] However God chooses to do it, the result is that *a third of the earth, a third of the trees, and all of the green grass is burned up*. Land would be burned, crops and fruit trees would be destroyed, animals would die, and there would be a shortage of wood for construction.

With the sounding of the second trumpet something like a great mountain burning with fire is thrown into the sea. This is probably a giant asteroid that ignites as it enters our atmosphere and falls into the sea. As all of the earth's oceans are connected *a third of the sea becomes blood*, probably filled with the blood of the *third of the sea creatures that die*. The ocean will reek with the putrid smell of death. Decay, dead fish and whales will fill the ocean and will come ashore. Seafood will be scarce and those who depend on the seafood industry for their livelihood will be ruined. In addition, a great tidal wave would result from the impact of this "great mountain" which is probably the reason that *a third of the ships are destroyed*. Commercial ships as well as the world's naval fleets will be crippled. Many coastal towns will be devastated.

When the third trumpet is sounded, a great star falls from heaven, burning like a torch. This is possibly a meteor or a comet that breaks apart as it nears the earth, falling on *a third of the rivers and on the springs of waters*. By giving the star a name, Wormwood, it gives the meaning "bitterness" to this plague. Wormwood is a bitter desert herb mentioned only here in the New Testament. However, it is referenced seven times in the Old Testament where it means sorrow and bitter judgment (Deut. 29:18, Prov. 5:4, Jer. 9:15). Probably this large meteor or comet falling to earth will poison a third of the earth's freshwaters so that people, as well as animals, which drink from them die. There will be immediate widespread death as people can survive for a time without food, but not without fresh water.

Next the fourth trumpet sounds and a *third of the sun and a third of the moon and a third of the stars were struck,* causing the intensity of these celestial bodies to be supernaturally reduced by a third. Many other prophets and even Jesus speak of this phenomena (see Joel 2:10, 31; 3:15; Amos 8:9; and Lk. 21:25). Without a third of the sun, a third of the day will be darkened. Imagine what is going to happen to crops that are growing as the sun's light is diminished by one third. Famines will stretch across the globe. Think about going to work or school or soccer games with the sun's light being dim all day long? Many people get depressed without enough sunlight in the winter months. Without a third of the sun's heat, the earth's temperature will drastically plunge. This temperature change will only be temporary as the opening of the fourth bowl increases the intensity of the sun's heat (Rev. 16:8-9). Weather patterns and sea tides will change producing raging storms and floods. Further death will ensue.

Without a third of the moon and the star's light, a third of the night as well will be darkened. Think how this will affect unbelievers who plan their day based on their horoscope and those who worship the sun, moon, and stars? This fourth trumpet demonstrates God's sovereignty over the heavens, and it is He that deserves our praise and worship.

Following the four trumpet judgments, John hears an eagle flying at the height of the midday sun (the midheaven) warning in a loud voice that three more of God's judgments are about to unfold. The word *woe*, used once for each judgment, is used throughout the Bible to express condemnation and destruction – the fate of those dwelling on earth at this time that refuse to repent.

---

4. Ibid., p. 250.

"Back to the Future"
End Times Prophecy, from Genesis to Revelation
Lesson 13 – Tribulation: 7 trumpets / 7 thunders

*** DAY 3: Fifth Trumpet Judgment – The First Woe

Abyss Unlocked: Rev. 9:1-3

1. As the fifth angel sounds his trumpet John sees a star from heaven. v. 1
   a. What has happened to this star?

   b. What phrases in vv. 1-2 indicate that this star is not in inanimate being?

   c. Comparing v. 1 with Isaiah 14:12 and Revelation 12:7-10, who can we conclude this fallen star is?

   d. What is he now given?

   e. Looking at Rev. 8:11, Luke 8:31 and II Peter 2:4, who is being kept in the Abyss?

2. When the Abyss is opened what rises from it and what results? v.2

Locusts (Demons) Unleashed: Rev. 9:4-6

3. What comes out of the smoke and how is their power described? v. 3

4. Although these demonic beings are very powerful, what limits does God put on them? v. 4

5. What are these "locust/scorpion" demons given power to do? What is their sting like? vv. 5, 10

6. What will the torment of these demons cause unbelievers to do? v. 6

Locusts (Demons) Unimaginable: Rev. 9:7-12

7. As these demonic beings are unlike anything we can imagine, John can only attempt to describe their appearance. Circle each occurrence of the word "like" in vv. 7-10, then answer the following:
   a. What did they look *like*?

   b. What was what they wore on their heads *like*?

   c. What were their faces *like*?

   d. What was their hair *like*?

   e. What were their breastplates *like*?

   f. What was the sound of their wings *like*?

   g. What were their tails *like*?

8. Who is the head of this demonic *army*?

9. Fill in the chart on the last page for the fifth seal.

"Back to the Future"
End Times Prophecy, from Genesis to Revelation
Lesson 13 – Tribulation: 7 trumpets / 7 thunders

ON A PERSONAL NOTE . . .

- Again we are struck with the fact that God is in total control – Satan was *given* the key to the Abyss, power was *given* to the locusts, and their power was *restricted* both in time and in scope. Are you in the midst of chaos, suffering, or pain? How does knowing that our Sovereign God is in total control of your situation - the length of time and the depth of the pain - help you? Seek His comfort and His strength today in prayer.

- Believers today are sealed by the Holy Spirit (Eph. 1:13-14) marking us as the Lord's (II Tim. 2:19). Thank God that we are protected from the penalty of sin and death by His Son's shed blood.

"Back to the Future"
End Times Prophecy, from Genesis to Revelation
Lesson 13 – Tribulation: 7 trumpets / 7 thunders

REVIEW:
The judgments of God increase in their terror as the Tribulation unfolds. Each of the first four trumpet judgments has affected the physical universe, but with the fifth trumpet the focus shifts to the spiritual realm. Nothing like the events of the final three trumpets has ever occurred on earth before.

As the fifth angel blows his trumpet the first *woe* begins. John sees a ***star from heaven which had fallen to the earth.*** The personal pronouns used in vv. 1-2, *he* and *him,* show that this is a living being and not an inanimate object. I believe that this star is Satan himself. Isaiah 14:12-15 describes Satan's original fall when he and the angels following him were kicked out of heaven (see also Lk. 10:18). However we know from Job 6 that Satan still has access to God's throne where he often appears to accuse believers. Near the midpoint of the Tribulation Satan and his demons will be defeated in an angelic battle with Michael and his holy angels (Rev. 12). At this point he will be permanently restricted to the earth. We will look further at this battle in Lesson 14.

John next sees the ***key of the bottomless pit*** given to Satan. This bottomless pit (literally, "the pit of the abyss") is referred to seven times in Revelation and always refers to the place occupied by fallen angels. Just as Hades is the preliminary place of suffering for unbelievers, the Abyss is the preliminary place of incarceration for certain wicked fallen angels, awaiting God's final sentencing to the lake of fire. (II Peter 2:4, Jude 6-7).[5] The Abyss is a place that even demons fear. Remember in Luke 8:31 when the demons who left the demonized man begged Jesus not to send them there. In Rev. 9:1-2 Satan receives the key to the horrible place from Jesus (Rev 1:18). As Satan unlocks the pit John sees ***smoke like the smoke of a great furnace*** rise from the pit, so much so that ***the sun and the air were darkened.*** Smoke is often associated with judgment in the Bible.

Out of this vast covering of smoke John sees ***locusts*** with the ***power of scorpions*** emerge upon the earth. These cannot be actual locusts because they have a stinging tail like a scorpion (vv. 3, 5, 10). Instead these locusts are actually demons who, like locusts, are uncountable in number and bring massive destruction. As opposed to real locusts that eat plant life, these demonic creatures are told ***not to hurt the grass of the earth, nor any green thing, nor any tree.*** (Note that in the first trumpet judgment all the grass was burned. Either enough time has elapsed since then for the grass to recover or the grass mentioned here is grass that grows in a different season.)

These demons are given permission to harm ***only the men who do not have the seal of God on their foreheads.*** Certainly this means that God will protect the 144,000 from this plague and may mean that all who have been saved up to this point in the Tribulation will be protected as well. The demons are given permission to torment unbelievers for five months (normal lifespan of a locust), but not allowed to kill anyone. In fact the torment inflicted by the stings of these creatures is so painful that men ***will seek death and will not find it.*** Stephen Davey writes, "In other words, the pistol will not fire, the knife will break . . . poison will not work, they will float when they land the river and they will survive."[6]

Having described the torment of the locusts, John attempts to give a more detailed description of their appearance. As these beings are supernatural beings, John can only describe them with analogies, using words such as "like" and "appeared to be." These locusts were powerful and defiant, *like* horses prepared to charge into battle, and they wore *what appeared to be* victors' crowns like gold on their heads, indicating that they are unstoppable. Their faces were *like* faces of men, indicating that they are intelligent and rational beings. The hair of these locusts was *like* the hair of women, seductive and alluring. They had teeth *like* the teeth of lions, ripping and tearing apart their victims. The breastplates of the locusts were *like* iron, symbolizing invulnerability. The sound of their wings was overpowering, *like* the sound of chariots and many horses rushing to battle. For the third time John says their tails are like those of scorpions, with a sting to torment men for five months. Finally John tells us that that these locusts have a king over them, the angel of the Abyss, He is a high-ranking angel whose names Abaddon (Hebrew) and Apollyon (Greek) both mean destroyer.[7]

5. Stephen Davey, <u>The Trumpets of the Seven Archangels - Part III: The Abyss Unlocked</u>, Sermon.
6. Ibid.
7. MacArthur, op. cit., pp. 262-263.

"Back to the Future"
End Times Prophecy, from Genesis to Revelation
Lesson 13 – Tribulation: 7 trumpets / 7 thunders

*** DAY 4: Sixth Trumpet Judgment – The Second Woe

Demons Released: Rev. 9:13-14

1. As the 6th trumpet is sounded, John hears a voice from the four horns of the golden altar before God. What does this unidentified voice say to the angel with the 6th trumpet? v.14

2. What does the fact that the angels are bound indicate?

Death Results: Rev. 9:15-19

3. What were these angels released to do? v.15

4. How large are the armies of the horsemen? v.16

5. Describe the riders. v.17

6. What do the horses' heads look like? What comes out of their mouths to destroy 1/3 of mankind? vv.17-18

7. Not only is the horses' power in their mouths but in their tails. Describe their tails? v. 19

Defiance Remains: Rev. 9:20-21

8. What is the reaction of the survivors? Of what are their idols made? v. 20

9. Of what other four things does mankind refuse to repent?

10. Fill in the chart on the last page for the sixth seal.

ON A PERSONAL NOTE . . .
- The demonic world is real! What are some ways people today dabble in the supernatural, whether "innocently" or not?

- What sin have you allowed to remain in your life, against God's commands? Will you soften your heart and repent now before you experience God's further judgment?

"Back to the Future"
End Times Prophecy, from Genesis to Revelation
Lesson 13 – Tribulation: 7 trumpets / 7 thunders

REVIEW:
When the sixth angel blows his trumpet, the second "Woe" begins. As the trumpet sounds, John hears a *voice from the four horns of the golden altar which is before God* (altar of incense). This heavenly altar of incense usually is a place of mercy, where God responds to the prayers of his people. Here however, as in the previous trumpet judgment, the altar is an altar of judgment. The voice from the altar commands the angel with the sixth trumpet to *release the four angels bound at the great river Euphrates*. The fact that these angels are bound indicates that they are demons and not holy angels.

The Euphrates is the longest and most important river in the Middle East and is mentioned frequently in the Old Testament. This river ran through the Garden of Eden and was where the first murder occurred. It was also near this river that the tower of Babel was built. Throughout history this area has given rise to many of the world's false religions. It was at the Euphrates that the Israelites lived during their Babylonian exile, and it will be over the Euphrates that armies of the East will cross to battle at Armageddon. The fact that this group of fallen angels is bound here leads some to believe that they are the demons that controlled the four major world empires - Babylon, Medo-Persia, Greece, and Rome.[8]

Whoever these demons are, they are now released under God's sovereignty to *kill a third of mankind.* Although they think they are serving Satan, they are actually carrying out God's purposes. Not only are the four demonic leaders released but John sees with them *armies of horsemen* numbering *two hundred million.* John describes the riders and the horses. The riders had breastplates the color of fire (red) and of hyacinth (dark like smoke), and of brimstone (a sulfurous yellow). These are the colors of hell and are often associated with God's wrath. The horses' heads are like heads of lions and out of their mouths come three plagues of fire, smoke, and brimstone - which kill mankind. However the horses' power not only is in their mouths but is also in their tails. Their tails are like serpents, having heads which do harm as well. What a terrifying picture John portrays. Remember that these are not actual horses, lions, or serpents - these are vile, supernatural demons let loose on mankind.

In the fourth seal, we saw a fourth of the earth's population killed. With an additional third killed by this sixth trumpet, half of the pre-tribulation's population has been killed by these two judgments alone (1/4 + (1/3 x 3/4)). As mind-boggling as it is, we are told that those not killed did not repent! You would think that men experiencing these devastating judgments while at the same time hearing the gospel preached by the 144,000 and the two witnesses would be eager to turn to God. Instead their hearts become harder as they continue in their idolatry, worshiping demons and idols of gold, silver, brass, stone, and wood,

John tells us that the people refuse to repent not only of their idolatry, but of other sins rampant during that time - murder, sorceries, immorality, and thefts. People see death all around them and do not hesitate to take a life, if it is to their benefit. The Greek word for sorceries mentioned in Rev. 9:21 is the root of the word "pharmacy" which we use today. Drugs were used in ancient times (and still continue to be) in pagan rituals and were thought to enhance communication with the gods. MacArthur writes, "Pharmakon can refer to poisons, amulets, charms, séances, witchcraft, incantations, magic spells, contacting mediums, or any object that is tied to pagan idolatry to elicit lust or to seduce."[9] The word used here for immorality, *porneia*, describes any kind of sexual sin or perversion. And theft will be a common occurrence, as the wicked remaining fight to find food, water, clothing, and the other necessities of life.

What a terrifying picture Rev. 9 paints as the fifth and sixth seal unfold. I am reminded of Gen. 6:3 which says that God will not contend with man forever. But for us today, we are still living in a period when God's grace prevails. Is there some sin that you have allowed to remain in your life, despite God's continuing conviction? If so, I urge you to repent today. I put before you the words of Hebrews 3:15 (which quote Ps. 95:7-8) – "Today, if you hear His voice, Do not harden your hearts as when they provoked me."

Revelation 10:1-11:13 makes up one of the parenthetical sections of Revelation. We will delve into that section tomorrow, but Rev. 11:14 ends the discussion of the sixth trumpet by announcing, "The second woe is past; behold the third woe is coming quickly."

8. Ibid., p. 269.
9. Ibid., pp. 273-274.

"Back to the Future"
End Times Prophecy, from Genesis to Revelation
Lesson 13 – Tribulation: 7 trumpets / 7 thunders

*** DAY 5: Seven Thunders; Seventh Trumpet: Rev. 10; 11:15-19

An Angelic Announcement: Rev. 10:1-7

1. Describe the angel John sees in v. 1. What does he have in his hand?

2. What does this strong angel do? What does John hear next? vv. 2-3

3. Why does John not write what the seven peals of thunder utter?   v4

4. What does the angel next do? What is his vow? vv. 5-7

5. John is told to eat the little scroll. What is John told will happen as he does this? Vv. 9-10

6. What is John told he must again do? v. 11

The Seventh Trumpet: Rev 11:15-19

Though the seventh trumpet is sounded in 11:15, its results are not revealed until Rev. 16. Chronologically the time is close to Christ's Second coming.

7. What has been announced in v.14?

8. Describe the reason for the worship that erupts in Heaven as the 7th trumpet is sounded? v. 15

9. In vv. 16 - 18, what coming events are the 24 elders thankfully looking forward to concerning . . .
   a. Christ's Second Coming?

   b. Wicked dead?

   c. OT and Tribulation saints?

10. What does John see happen in heaven? v. 19

11. On earth, what is happening? v. 19

ON A PERSONAL NOTE . . .
- Loud voices were heard in heaven saying, ". . . and He shall reign forever." Sing the chorus, "Our God reigns." What situations do you have in which you would like Jesus to reign supreme? Pray with the truth that Jesus is King over these concerns; He is reigning over them even if there is chaos all around and it seems impossible. Remember, all things are possible with God. (Luke 1:37) Write your prayer here. Then spend some time worshiping our Lord, our Sovereign Creator, and His Christ, our King of Kings and Lord of Lords.

"Back to the Future"
End Times Prophecy, from Genesis to Revelation
Lesson 13 – Tribulation: 7 trumpets / 7 thunders

REVIEW:
Just as Revelation 7 forms a parenthetical section between the sixth and seventh seal, so Rev. 10-11:14 forms a parenthetical section between the sixth and seventh trumpet – giving us additional information without advancing the timetable of the Tribulation.

In Rev. 10:1, John sees *another* (Rev. 5:2, 18:21) strong angel descending from heaven. Though some see this as Jesus, it is clearly not. Although the pre-incarnate Christ was referred to as *the* Angel of the Lord when He appeared to men in the Old Testament, nowhere in the New Testament is He referred to as *an* angel. What's more, our resurrected Lord is always given a title when He appears in Revelation.

This strong angel is *clothed with a cloud*, symbolizing his power and majesty and the fact that he is coming in judgment. The *rainbow upon his head* represents God's mercy in the midst of judgment. His face is *like the sun*, radiating the glory of God, and His feet are *like pillars of fire*, indicating his firm resolve to execute God's judgment. In his hand is *a little book which was open*. Whether this is a different book than that of Rev. 5:1 or whether it is the same book of Rev. 5:1 fully unrolled is debatable. Either way it clearly reveals divine judgment yet to come.[10]

This angel is not only a strong angel but an extremely large one, *as he was able to put his right foot on the sea and his left on the land.* God is the sovereign creator of the land and the sea and has the right to execute judgment on the entire earth. As the angel places his feet on the land and sea, he cries out in a loud voice. Immediately John hears *seven peals of thunder utter their voices* of judgment. But before John can write down what they are saying, a voice from heaven commands him to seal up their messages instead. We are not told why John was not to write the judgments down, but it may be that they are just too awful to be recorded.

At this point, the strong angel lifts *his right hand to heaven*, as if taking a solemn vow, *and swears by Him who lives forever and ever*, the Sovereign Creator of the heavens and the earth and all that is in them, saying "*There will be delay no longer!*" The angel announces that when the coming seventh trumpet is sounded, *the mystery of God is finished*. This *mystery* (preached to prophets in the Old Testament, but details hidden until revealed in the New Testament) refers to the events concluding the Day of the Lord, the judgment of Satan and his followers and Christ's reign on earth for a thousand years.

John is then commanded by the voice from heaven to *take the little book from the angel and eat it*. Just as the angel predicts, the book initially tastes sweet in John's mouth but then turns John's stomach bitter. Even today we can identify with John's response to digesting God's Word – as we rejoice in Christ's coming return and victory, but mourn over the judgments that we know are coming on the earth and its inhabitants. Although John is told not to write down the messages of the seven thunders, he is called to warn *all peoples* of the remaining prophecies that God is about to give him.

The second part of this parenthetical section, Rev. 11:1-14, covers the measuring of the temple and the two witnesses, both of which we have already studied when we looked at the midpoint of the Tribulation. We will look at the end of the two witnesses' ministry next week as we look at the second half of the Tribulation from man's perspective.

"We return now to our regularly scheduled program." With two *woes* down and one to go, the seventh angel now sounds his trumpet in Rev.11:15. This seventh trumpet includes the seven bowl judgments (Rev. 16), the Return of Christ (Rev. 19), and the events leading up to the Millennial Kingdom (Rev. 20). Although the trumpet is sounded here in Rev. 11:15, it is not until chapter 15 that its judgments are described.

For now though, we see a spontaneous celebration of worship and praise in heaven. Loud voices in heaven cry out in joy that *the kingdom of the world has become the kingdom of our Lord and His Christ.* The Greek verb tense used here describes a future event so certain that it is spoken of as having already taken place. Satan's power over the earth will be broken as Jesus returns to defeat Satan and reign on earth for a thousand years. At the end of the 1000 year reign, Jesus will hand over His kingdom to the Father who will, in turn, give Jesus the authority to rule over the eternal kingdom *forever and ever.* Immediately the 24 elders (representing the raptured church) *fell on their faces and worshiped God* for

"Back to the Future"
End Times Prophecy, from Genesis to Revelation
Lesson 13 – Tribulation: 7 trumpets / 7 thunders

His power, His eternal existence, and His sovereignty. The elders rejoice in the events to come that are so certain that they are seen as already happening: the coming rebellion and defeat of the world's armies at Armageddon, the judgment of the wicked and their assignment to the lake of fire, and the resurrection and reward of the Old Testament and Tribulation saints who will remain with Christ forever.

We come to the climax of the vision as John sees the temple of God in heaven open and the ark of God's covenant appear. In the OT, only the high priest could enter the Holy of Holies. The earthly ark in the Holy of Holies symbolized God's presence, atonement, and covenant with the Israelites. The opening of the temple of God in heaven signifies that God will now have unbroken fellowship with His people forever. The ark of His covenant seen now in the throne room of God reminds us of the New Covenant that will take effect as God redeems the nation of Israel and ushers them into the Millennial Kingdom.

Accompanying this opening of God's temple in heaven are terrifying events on earth – flashes of lightning, peals of thunder, an earthquake and a great hailstorm. We will see that these events, all signs of God's wrath and judgment actually occur as part of the seventh bowl, the climax of the seventh trumpet, the climax of the seventh seal. Jesus' return is now at hand!!!

TRUMPET JUDGMENT	ACTION	RESULT
1st		
2nd		
3rd		
4th		
5th		
6th		
7th	7 bowls	Will be studied in Lesson 15

10. Ibid., p. 281.

"Back to the Future"
End Times Prophecy, from Genesis to Revelation
Lesson 14 - Tribulation: Second Half Evil

*** DAY 1: The Woman, the Dragon, and the Son: Rev. 12:1-6

Woman
1. From v. 1 describe the great *sign* which now appears in heaven,

2. There is another place in the Bible where the symbols used to describe the woman are used. Who are the sun, moon, and stars in Gen. 37:9-11?

3. Therefore, what do you think the sign of the woman represents?

4. What else do we learn about the woman in v. 2?

Dragon
5. Describe the next sign that appears in heaven.

6. Later in v. 9 whom does John say the dragon represents?

7. Based on John 8:44, what might the color red represent?

8. What did the dragon's tail do?

9. Where did the dragon position himself and why?

Male Child
10. In v. 5, what does the woman do?

11. Who do you think this male child represents? See also Ps. 2:9.

12. How did Satan try to "devour" Jesus at his birth? Mt. 2:16

13. When was Jesus *caught up to God and to His throne*? Acts 1:9

Flight of the Woman
14. In v. 6 what does John next see the woman do?
    a. Where does she flee and why?

    b. How long will she remain there?

ON A PERSONAL NOTE . . .
- Rev. 12:6 is a wonderful example of God's all-sufficient provision and protection during our temptations and trials. Read I Cor. 10:13 and then think of a time when God has done the same for you. Use God's promise to give you strength and hope in any current situation you are enduring. Praise God who is the same yesterday, today, and tomorrow.

"Back to the Future"
End Times Prophecy, from Genesis to Revelation
Lesson 14 - Tribulation: Second Half Evil

REVIEW:
Last week we looked at the wrathful judgments of God that will unfold during the second half of the Tribulation. The seventh trumpet will be sounded near the end of the Tribulation announcing the triumphant victory of the Lord. Although the seventh trumpet is sounded in Rev. 11, its effects on the earth, the seven bowls, are not recorded until Rev. 16. Next week's lesson will cover these judgments. This week we will be looking at Rev. 12-13, which also describe the second half of the Tribulation, but this time from Satan's viewpoint. During the latter 3 ½ years of the Tribulation, known as the Great Tribulation, Satan's battle against God's purposes and God's people reaches its climax.

We start by looking at the key players of the period. With the start of Rev. 12 John sees a great sign appear in heaven. This sign is the first of seven signs seen in the last half of Revelation. (See 12:1; 12:3; 13:13; 13:14; 15:1; 16:14; and 19:20.) The fact that John calls what he sees a sign clearly shows that it is not to be taken literally but it is a symbol pointing to a reality. Here the woman he sees is not an actual woman but represents something else.

This woman John sees is, by the way, the second of four symbolic women seen in Revelation. In Rev. 2 we saw an actual woman given the symbolic name of Jezebel. She was a false teacher and symbolized paganism. We saw another woman appear as a harlot in Rev. 17, representing the apostate church. And in Rev. 19:7-8 we will see the bride of the Lamb (also in II Cor. 11:2), representing the true Church.[1]

So, the question remains, "Who is this woman?" John first tells us that she is *clothed with the sun*, the *moon* is *under her feet*, and she wears a *crown of twelve stars*. This description immediately takes us back to Joseph's dream in Gen. 37:9-11. This is the only other place in the Bible where these three symbols are found together. Comparing Joseph's dream with the description of the woman in Rev.11, we see that the woman must be Israel - the sun represented Jacob through whom the Abrahamic Covenant would pass, the moon referring to Jacob's wife Rachel, and the 12 stars representing the twelve tribes of Israel.

We are also told that the woman was *with child* and *cried out* in her *labor pains, about to give birth*. The view that the woman is Israel also fits the context here as Christ was born of the seed of Israel. In addition, both Isaiah and Jeremiah refer to Israel as "a woman in labor" (Is. 26:17-18; 66:7-9; and Jer. 4:31; 13:21). The nation of Israel was in pain when the Messiah came the first time, and certainly will be experiencing the intensifying pain of the Tribulation right up to the time of His Second Coming.

John next sees another sign appear in heaven - a *great red dragon*. Later, in v. 9 John tells us that this dragon represents Satan. In fact, Satan appears as a dragon 13 times in the book of Revelation. As John 8:44 identifies Satan as a murderer, the color *red* may represent bloodshed.

This great red dragon has *seven heads and ten horns, and on his heads were seven diadems*. Satan has been ruling the world since man's fall and will do so until Christ's return. Just as we saw in our study of the scarlet beast in Rev. 17, the seven heads with diadems on them represent the seven world empires that Satan will have used to rule the world - Egypt, Assyria, Babylon, Medo-Persia, Greece, Rome, and the future empire of the antichrist. The ten horns represent the ten kings that will rule under the antichrist. This final empire is Satan's masterpiece which he will use to oppose Israel one last time.

We are next told that the dragon's tail *swept away a third of the stars of heaven and threw them to the earth*. Satan's original fall from heaven is recorded in both Isaiah 14 and Ezekiel 28. John now informs us that Satan was able to deceive one third of the angels (stars) into following him in his rebellion and that they fell with him.

The Bible does not tell us how many angels God created, but we do know that at the sounding of the fifth trumpet at least 200 million demonic angels terrify the earth. This demonic force is only part of the one third that fell with Satan. Therefore we can deduce that the number of created angels is over one billion![2]

Finally we are told that John sees this great red dragon stand *before the woman who was about to give birth* (Israel) *that he might devour her child*. Knowing that the Messiah was to come from the nation of Israel, Satan has attempted to destroy them and wipe out the Messianic line. Having failed to do so, he

"Back to the Future"
End Times Prophecy, from Genesis to Revelation
Lesson 14 – Tribulation: Second Half Evil

next turned his efforts towards killing Jesus (the child) himself once He was born, before He could accomplish His saving work on the cross.

In Rev. 12:5, we see the woman give birth to a *son, who is to rule all the nations with a rod of iron.* This is obviously a reference to Jesus, our Lord and Savior who will one day rule the world. John's vision skips everything from the incarnation of Jesus to His ascension as her child was next *caught up to God and to His throne.* We know however that after Jesus' birth, Satan inspired Herod to issue an edict to have all male babies under the age of two killed (Matt. 2). Throughout Jesus' earthly ministry Satan tried unsuccessfully to cut short both Jesus' life and His ministry.

Having failed to kill the Messiah or stop His provision of salvation to those that follow Him, Satan has continued to persecute the nation of Israel to this day. Zech. 12:10-13:1 tells us that during the Tribulation Satan will intensify his efforts to annihilate God's people so that there will be none saved to enter the Millennial Kingdom. It is because of Satan's attempts that John sees the woman flee in v5 to the wilderness where she has a place prepared by God where she will be nourished for 1,260 days, the last half of the Tribulation. In Matthew 24:15-21, Jesus warns of this time when he says, "*Therefore when you see the abomination of desolation . . . then those who are in Judea must flee to the mountains . . . . For then there will be a great tribulation, such as has not occurred since the beginning of the world until now, nor ever will.*" We will study this flight in more detail on Day 3 as we look at the last verses of Rev. 12.

---

1. John MacArthur, The MacArthur New Testament Commentary Rev 12-22, p. 4.
2. Stephen Davey, The Many Faces of Evil - Part 1: *The Relentless Red Dragon*, Sermon.

"Back to the Future"
End Times Prophecy, from Genesis to Revelation
Lesson 14 - Tribulation: Second Half Evil

*** DAY 2: Another War in Heaven: Rev. 12:7-12

1. Read Job 1:6-12. Although Satan and his demons were cast out of heaven at the time of their original rebellion, what three things has Satan been allowed to do since then?
   a. vv. 6-7

   b. vv. 9-11, also Rev. 12:10

   c. v. 12

The Conflict

2. In Rev. 12:7, who does John see waging war with the dragon and his angels?

3. What do we learn about Michael in the following verses?
   a. Dan. 12:1

   b. Dan. 10:12-13, 21

   c. Jude 9

The Conquest

4. What is the result of this battle in heaven? vv. 8-9

5. List all the names and descriptions of the devil found in vv. 9-10. Circles them in your Bible.

The Celebration

6. Looking carefully at v. 10, can you deduce who is celebrating in Heaven?

7. In v.10, to whom does the word "they" refer?

8. Seeing Satan thrown down, what coming time do those in heaven celebrate? v. 10
   ***Note: the verb tense used here indicates future events that are so certain that they are spoken of in past tense*

9. What three things will enable Tribulation believers, as well as believers of all times, to overcome Satan? v. 11

10. Having been thrown down to the earth and the sea, why is the devil filled with great fury? v. 12

ON A PERSONAL NOTE . . .
There are two extremes in people's reactions to the spiritual world - one is to deny its existence altogether and the other is to have an unhealthy interest in it. What truths have you learned about Satan and his demons today? What comfort has today's study given you?

- What lies or accusations does Satan most throw at you? How does God's word refute these lies?

- What burning arrows of guilt does Satan shoot at you? How does the blood of the Lamb extinguish these flames?

"Back to the Future"
End Times Prophecy, from Genesis to Revelation
Lesson 14 - Tribulation: Second Half Evil

REVIEW:
Many people today errantly picture Satan as a little red creature with horns, a long tail, and a pitchfork running around ruling hell. Actually Satan is not cast into hell (Lake of Fire) until after the final battle at the end of the Millennial Kingdom. Even then he will not be the *prince* of hell, but a *prisoner* of hell, suffering the worst of God's wrath forever.

Satan was created by God as the highest of all the angels. Ezekiel 28:12-17 tells us a little about Satan before his fall. He was perfect in wisdom and beauty and he was blameless in all his ways. Anointed by God to cover, or guard, His throne, Satan had continuous, unrestricted access to God's presence. However Satan's pride led to him to rebel and seek to establish his throne above God's. God's judgment on Satan was swift. The devil was stripped of his beauty and holiness and he was cast to the earth, along with the third of the angels who followed him. However since that time, Job 6:1-12 tells us that Satan still has access to heaven.

Although Satan's power and his access to heaven have been restricted, his desires have remained the same - to thwart God and His purposes and to gain worship for himself. His first plan, to cause man to fall thus separating man from God, was overcome by God's promise in Gen. 3:15 of the Messiah who would redeem mankind and rule on earth. As we studied last week, Satan then turned his attention to destroying the Israelites, the people through whom the Messiah was to come. After Christ's birth, he then tried to stop Christ from accomplishing His purposes. But at the cross, which initially looked like a victory for Satan, the penalty for man's sin was paid. And with Jesus' death and resurrection Satan, sin, and death were defeated. Although Satan was defeated and judged at the cross, his sentence has yet to be executed. He and his demons, knowing that they are defeated, are still trying to take as many as they can with them into the lake of fire.

The names used for him in Scripture reveal his true character. The word *devil* is translated from the Greek word *diaballo*, meaning *to slander or defame*. The word *Satan* is a Hebrew word that means *adversary*. In Rev. 12:9 he is also described as *one who deceives the whole world.* This is in keeping with his title, *the father of lies,* given in John 8:44. And in Rev. 12:10 Satan is called *the accuser.* Satan now roams back and forth through the earth, looking for those to devour (I Peter 5:8). And he frequently comes before God's throne, accusing the believers and asking for God's permission to test them (John 1:6-12; Rev. 12:10). His tactics now are twofold: he accuses God, trying to make us doubt His love for us, and he accuses us before God, trying to convince God to take his love away from us. His efforts to turn man away from God sometime succeed, but his efforts to turn God away from His own **will always fail**. We know that *no one can snatch us from the Father's hand* (John 10:28-29), there is *no condemnation for those who are in Christ Jesus*" (Romans 8:1), and *nothing can separate us from the love of God* (Romans 8:38-39).

Since his rebellion and fall, Satan's war against God has not only included attacks on God's people but on God's holy angels as well. In the Old Testament we see Satan and his demons actively oppose the ministry of God's angels to Israel. (See Dan. 10:12-13.) And in the New Testament the devil is called "the prince of the power of the air" (Eph. 2:2) and "the ruler of this world" (John 12:31, 14:30, and 16:11). In Rev. 12:7-9 John now sees a *great war in heaven*. *Michael and his angels* are *waging war with the dragon*. John MacArthur calls this battle *the peak of the war that has been raging between supernatural beings in the heavenly sphere* since Satan's fall. MacArthur even proposes that what triggers this battle may be the passage of raptured believers through the supernatural realm. Perhaps the prince of the power of the air and his demons will oppose this passage, engaging Michael and his holy angels in war.[3]

Whatever the cause, this will be an all-out battle as Satan knows that the time for Christ's Millennial Kingdom is near. As in all other attempts of Satan to oppose God, Satan and his angels are not strong enough to prevail. We are told in v. 8 that *there was no longer a place for them in heaven*. They will no longer have access to God's throne. Instead Satan and his angels are *thrown down to earth*. No longer "*prince of the air,"* Satan will be confined to earth until the end of the Tribulation when he is bound in the abyss for 1000 years. After that time he will be let loose to stage one final rebellion against God before being sent to his eternal destruction in the Lake of Fire.

"Back to the Future"
End Times Prophecy, from Genesis to Revelation
Lesson 14 – Tribulation: Second Half Evil

We are not told when this great angelic battle in heaven begins or how long it lasts, but we do know that the battle comes to a close at the midpoint of the Tribulation. By comparing v. 6 with vv. 13-16, we see that when Satan is thrown down to earth, he persecutes the woman for 1260 days - the second half of the Tribulation.

The defeat of Satan and his permanent expulsion from heaven causes a celebration to erupt in heaven. The loud voice that John now hears in heaven refers to Satan as *the accuser of our brethren*. From that term, we know that those celebrating must be the redeemed saints in heaven. They are rejoicing that the time for deliverance of all creation and the establishment of God's kingdom on earth under Christ's reign has come. How long they have waited!

The saints in heaven then rejoice in the victory of those who have, and *will,* overcome Satan. These overcomers include those killed so far during the Tribulation and those yet to be killed. These overcomers, like all believers, were given victory over Satan solely through God's power. Specific reasons these Tribulation saints were able to stand against Satan include 1) *the blood of the Lamb* - forgiveness is based on Christ's shed blood alone; 2) *the word of their testimony* - they were faithful witnesses, proclaiming God's word during their incredible suffering; and 3) *their refusal to hold onto their life when faced with death* – some were faithful even to death, focusing on their eternal glory.

Concerning these overcomers, John Phillips writes, "What can Satan do with the likes of these? Lock them up in prison and they convert their jailors; torture them and they become partakers of Christ's sufferings and heirs to a greater reward; martyr them and they go straight to be with Christ; turn them loose and they evangelize the world."[4] Oh that we could always have this perspective on life!

The same cause for celebration in heaven causes great concern for the earth and its inhabitants. Satan, defeated, confined to earth, and aware that his time is short, is full of rage. He and his demonic followers turn to unleash their full fury upon the earth and upon God's people during the second half of the Tribulation. Phillips writes, "Satan is now a like a caged lion, enraged beyond words by the limitations now placed upon his freedom. He picks himself up from the dust of the earth, shakes his fist at the sky and glares around choking with fury for ways to vent his hatred and his spite upon humankind. He has been checkmated and mastered by the One he hates most of all."[5]

3. MacArthur, op. cit., pp. 16-17.
4. John Phillips, Exploring Revelation, p. 161.
5. Ibid., p. 150.

"Back to the Future"
End Times Prophecy, from Genesis to Revelation
Lesson 14 – Tribulation: Second Half Evil

*** DAY 3: Woman Persecuted by Dragon, Protected by God: Rev. 12:13-17

1. Seeing that he had been thrown down to earth, what does the dragon do? v. 13

2. How is Israel protected by God from the dragon . . . for how long? v. 14

3. How do the wings of an eagle depict God's care in Ex. 19:4 and in Ps. 91:4?

4. What is the dragon's next plot against the woman (Israel)? v. 15

5. How is Israel spared? v. 16

6. Enraged, what does the dragon now do? v. 17

7. What two phrases describe the true believers of this time?

8. Who do you think the rest of her children include? See also Rev. 14:12

ON A PERSONAL NOTE . . .
- Read John 14:2. Just as God prepared a place for the fleeing Israelites, he has prepared a place for us where we will someday live in His protection and abundant provision. Until then we can expect to be persecuted for faithfulness and obedience to Christ. Maybe you are under attack even now. How does today's lesson comfort you?

- II Tim 4:18 is a great verse to store away in your memory bank: "*The Lord will rescue me from every evil attack and will bring me safely to his heavenly kingdom. To him be glory for ever and ever. Amen.*" (NIV)

"Back to the Future"
End Times Prophecy, from Genesis to Revelation
Lesson 14 - Tribulation: Second Half Evil

REVIEW:
Down through the centuries, the persecution of the Jewish people has been well-documented. They have faced more hatred and hostility than any other people. Much of their persecution has occurred at the hand of God as He has disciplined them in their disobedience. In the Old Testament, God often warns His people of the consequences of their sin, unbelief, and disobedience. As God's people, Israel has also been the target of Satan's attacks. Although Satan's purpose to destroy the Jews is an evil one, we must remember that he can only act as God allows and that he is unknowingly acting as God's instrument of judgment.

Satan's persecution of the Jews has never been as horrific as it was during the Holocaust when Hitler and his Nazi party became obsessed with eliminating the entire Jewish population. However, the suffering that the Israelites will endure during the coming Tribulation will far eclipse anything they have ever experienced. Not only will they endure God's wrath as it is being poured out on the entire world, but during the second half of the Tribulation, Satan, full of rage and knowing his time is short, will also make one last, desperate attempt to prevent the salvation of the nation of Israel and the coming world reign of Christ on the Davidic throne.

We know that Satan's main puppet during the Tribulation is the antichrist. Although this leader poses as Israel's protector during his rise to world power during the first half of the Tribulation, the antichrist shows his true colors when he breaks his covenant at the midpoint and turns against the Jews. It is through the antichrist and his forces that Satan launches an all-out attack against God's people. This all-out attack is the reason for the flight of *the woman* first mentioned in Rev. 12:6.

Jesus warned the Jewish people of Satan's persecution and Israel's flight into the wilderness in Matthew 24:15-22. In this passage, the Lord warns them that when they see the antichrist set up the abomination of desolation in the temple, great tribulation is coming. They must flee to the mountains immediately - without returning home to get anything! This will be especially hard for pregnant and nursing women.

Here in Rev. 12:13-14 John sees that *two wings of the great eagle were given to the woman, so that she could fly into the wilderness . . . away from the presence of the serpent.* Somewhere in my past, I got it into my head that the two wings represented an airplane which would carry the Jewish people to safety. This is not the case. Instead the two wings represent God's direct intervention. We see this same imagery in Ex. 19:4 when God describes His deliverance of the Israelites from bondage in Egypt. *Wings* in Scripture sometimes symbolize strength and speed, but most of all they speak of protection. (See Ps. 17:8; 36:7; 57:1; 61:4; 63:7; and 91:4.) The enormous wingspan of an eagle is a fitting symbol for God's protection and sheltering of Israel.[6]

We are not told where this *place* that Israel flees to is located, but many believe that it will be to the city of Petra in Edom. The term *wilderness* is used in the gospels to describe the mountainous area east of Jerusalem. Also remember that in Dan. 11:41 when the antichrist is carrying out his military conquests, Edom was one of the countries *rescued out of his hand*. Petra, between the Dead Sea and the Gulf of Aqaba, is an ancient city carved into rocky cliffs and approachable only through a narrow gorge. Many of its buildings can only be reached by walking or riding on a camel or donkey between a narrow gap in the sandstone cliffs.

Wherever they are, the Israelites that flee will not only be protected but will be supernaturally sustained. Just as God provided food for the Israelites during their exodus from Egypt, we are told that God will *nourish* those who flee at the midpoint of the Tribulation for the remaining 3 ½ years (*time, times, and half a time*). Perhaps He will keep their clothes and their shoes from wearing out as well (Dt. 29:5).

In Rev. 12:15, John tells us that after the woman's flight, the serpent (Satan) initially pursues her, pouring *water like a river out of his mouth . . . so that he might cause her to be swept away with the flood.* Some scholars interpret this to mean that the antichrist may, through some sort of engineering feat, try to flood the Jewish people out of their hiding place by diverting a river of water. Others say that just as the woman and the serpent are symbols, so the water and the flood represent a great attacking army which the antichrist sends to sweep the Israelites away like a flood (cf. Jer. 46:8; 47:2). Either way, Satan is once again foiled by God who causes the earth to *open its mouth and drink up the river which the dragon poured out of his mouth.* God probably uses an earthquake, as He did in Ex 15 and Num 16, to either drain off the water or to destroy Satan's forces.

Unable to destroy the protected Israelites and even more enraged than before, Satan in Rev. 12:16 turns his attack toward the *rest of her children, who keep the commandments of God and hold to the testimony of Jesus.* This phrase probably includes the remaining Jews in the land of Israel who could not make the trip to Petra as well as all the believing Gentiles. In the evil and perverse times of the Tribulation, obedience to God's commands and adherence to the truths that Jesus taught will clearly identify true believers. Thankfully we know that Satan's renewed attack will also fail to wipe out God's people and that at Jesus' return those who survive will populate the Millennial Kingdom under His reign.

6. MacArthur, op. cit., pp. 30-32.

"Back to the Future"
End Times Prophecy, from Genesis to Revelation
Lesson 14 - Tribulation: Second Half Evil

*** DAY 4: Beast out of the Sea: Rev. 13:1-10

1. In v. 1, how does John describe this beast out of the sea? How is this description similar yet different to that of the red dragon in Rev. 12:3?

2. What did this beast have on his heads instead of crowns?

3. What three animals are used in John's description in v. 2? Does this remind you of anything we have studied? (If not, look back at Dan. 7:3-7.)

4. What three things did the dragon give the beast?

5. What about one of the heads of the beast caused the whole world to follow the beast?

6. Who does John say men worshiped?

7. Circle each occurrence of the word "given" in vv. 5-7.

8. In vv. 5-6, what things come out of the beast's mouth? (Daniel 7:8, 11 told us this as well.)

9. What is he *given* power to do?

10. Over whom is he given authority?

11. Who does not worship the beast?

12. What two things does John warn the saints to expect under the rule of the antichrist?

13. Instead of fighting back, what must these saints exemplify?

ON A PERSONAL NOTE . . .
- Even in the hardest of times of history, the saints will know that God is still in control. Read Ex. 10:1; Job 37:15; Ps. 103:19. How do these verses comfort you today. Can you think of other verses that speak of God's sovereignty over all?

- When we are persecuted, we must not retaliate against our enemies, but entrust ourselves to God for relief, for victory, and for vengeance (Romans 8:37; I Peter 4:19; I Peter 2:23). Are you currently in a situation where you need the Spirit's help in having a godly attitude and godly responses? May we all have the attitude Mary had in Luke 1:38: "Behold the maidservant of the Lord! Let it be to me according to your word." (NKJV)

"Back to the Future"
End Times Prophecy, from Genesis to Revelation
Lesson 14 - Tribulation: Second Half Evil

REVIEW:
Revelation 12, which we looked at last week, reviews Satan's long war against God and His people. At the end of the chapter, we see Satan, the great red dragon, being banned from heaven and confined to the earth. As Rev. 13 opens, John sees the dragon standing on the sand of the seashore (depicting the nations of the world; see Rev. 20:8). Satan, full of rage and knowing his time is short, is ready to take his last stand against God and His people.

Satan, being a spirit being, has always depended on human beings to do his dirty work on earth. Although he controls all unbelievers (John 8:44 and Eph. 2:2), the Bible records several times that Satan and his demons have entered and possessed humans, bringing them under his / their direct control. Luke 22:3, for instance, records Satan entering into Judas. The antichrist will be a man, but at this point he is indwelt by Satan to do his bidding. He will be Satan's ultimate prince of evil.

Note that many believe that the devil, not knowing when the Rapture will occur and trigger the end time events, has always had a man in the wings ready to burst onto the stage. Puppets such as Nero, Napoleon, Hitler, and Stalin would have all gladly stepped forward to rule the world.[7]

Before we delve into today's lesson on the *beast coming out of the sea*, let's review what we have learned so far about the antichrist. Much of what we know about the antichrist is found in Dan. 7:8-26; 8:9-12, 23-25; 9:26-27; and 11:36-45. The antichrist starts out in Dan. 7 as a *little horn* who rises to conquer first *three of the horns* (rulers) of the *fourth beast of Daniel's dream* (the revived Roman Empire). By the beginning of the Tribulation, he has subjugated the remaining rulers and emerged as the head of this Western Empire. Signaling the beginning of the Tribulation, the antichrist and his coalition enter into a peace pact with the nation of Israel in which he promises to protect them for seven years. During the first 3½ years of this period the antichrist will use both warfare and the organized apostate church in his climb to world power. With his military success and the supernatural defeat of the Russian coalition which comes against Israel near the end of the Tribulation's first half, the antichrist positions himself to become ruler of the world.

It is at this point that the antichrist becomes Satanically-controlled. At the midpoint of the Tribulation, he breaks his covenant with Israel, sets up the abomination of desolation in the temple, and moves his military headquarters to Jerusalem. The antichrist and his puppet kings also destroy the apostate church, no longer needing its influence and power.

Now, let's continue with Rev 13. As the dragon stands *on the sand of the seashore*, John sees a *beast coming up out of the sea*. Many see the sea as representing the sea of humanity, or the Gentile nations. Others think it represents the Mediterranean Sea which the antichrist's empire surrounds. MacArthur, however, thinks it represents the abyss where many demons are currently bound. (See Luke 8:31.) John further describes this beast as having *ten horns and seven heads*, This description of the beast is the same as the description of Satan in Rev. 12:3, with the seven heads representing the seven consecutive world empires that were under Satan's control and the ten horns representing the ten kings who will simultaneously rule under the antichrist. Note however that here in Rev. 13, the *ten diadems* are on the beast's ten horns instead of on his seven heads. MacArthur comments on this difference by saying, "This reveals the shift in power from the 7 world empires to the 10 kings under the final antichrist."[8]

This beast represents the antichrist, as he is referred to later with personal pronouns such as "his," "him,", and "he." The beast also represents the antichrist's kingdom, based on this description given in verse 1. This is not unlike today when we use the term Hitler to refer to both the man and his evil empire. As we have discussed, the antichrist's empire starts off as a revived form of the old Roman Empire, but during the second half of the Tribulation, it will expand to cover the entire world.

John sees here that *on his* (the beast's) *heads were blasphemous names*. Down through history, the rulers of the world empires have claimed divinity and blasphemed the true God. We are told in Dan. 11:36 that the antichrist will likewise "*exalt and magnify himself above every god, speaking monstrous things against the God of gods.*"

"Back to the Future"
End Times Prophecy, from Genesis to Revelation
Lesson 14 - Tribulation: Second Half Evil

Next John sees that this beast is *like a leopard*, his *feet are like those of a bear*, and his *mouth is like the mouth of a lion.* Like the fourth beast in Dan. 7:7, the antichrist's final world empire will be a composite of the first three world empires in Daniel's dream. Like Babylon, it will have the power of a lion. Like Medo-Persia, it will have the ferocity and strength of a bear; and like Greece, it will have the speed and viciousness of a leopard. As we have learned, the antichrist's world empire will be Satan's final attempt to stop the reign of Christ.[9]

John goes on to say that the dragon was the source of the beast's *power and throne and great authority.* No one will be able to oppose the antichrist' satanic power, with God's supernatural restraint of the antichrist removed at the Rapture. The antichrist will rule on Satan's throne, just as Christ will one day rule on God's throne over the earth. And this evil prince will have complete authority over the earth, answerable to no one. Dan. 11:36 says he "will do as he pleases." Dan. 7:25 adds that the antichrist will even go so far as to try to change the set times and the laws.

Amazingly John then sees one of the beast's heads *as if it had been slain, and his fatal wound was healed.* This is another one of those much-debated passages. Some see the head whose fatal wound was healed as the revived Roman Empire which was destroyed, yet rises again. But most see this as the antichrist who appears to have been killed and miraculously resurrected. Among this second group, scholars are divided as to whether the antichrist's death is a staged death or a real one. While Satan does not have the power to resurrect, some think that God may allow Satan this power for this specific time.

Whatever the case, the *whole earth* will believe that the antichrist has in fact overcome death and will be *amazed.* This event will cause them to *follow after the beast.* And in following the beast, they will also *worship* the power behind the beast, *the dragon* (Satan). Having seen the antichrist "overcome" death, they will see him as deity, crying out, "*Who is like the beast, and who is able to wage war with him?*" (cf. Ex. 15:11; Ps. 113:5). It is probably this amazing event which allows the antichrist to set up the abomination of desolation, declare to be God, and demand worship by the world.

At this point, John's words remind us that no matter how dark things look, God is still in control. In vv. 5-7, the beast is *given* four things by God. The antichrist is allowed to speak *arrogant words and blasphemies . . . against* not only *God*, but against *His name, His tabernacle, and* against His saints *who dwell in heaven.* He is given *authority to act for forty-two months*, and he is allowed to *make war with the saints and to overcome them.* And he is given *authority over every tribe and people and tongue and nation.* Just as Jesus promised in Matt. 24:21, during this last 3 ½ years there will be *great tribulation* [for God's people] *such as has not occurred since the beginning of the world until now.*

In Rev. 13:8 we are told that while the whole world will worship the antichrist, the exception will be God's elect, chosen from eternity past. These are those whose names are written in the *book of life of the Lamb,* those who have come to Christ during the Tribulation. In vv. 9-10 a charge is given to the Tribulation saints living at that time. They are told to trust God and not to take matters into their own hands. They are to accept God's will for their lives, even if it means *captivity* or being *killed with the sword.* Like other believers that have gone before them, God's people living at this time must exhibit the *faith and the perseverance of the saints.*

No doubt these believers will hold onto the promises in Daniel: that God is in control and has determined what will take place (Dan. 11:36); that Christ will return at the end of 3 ½ years return to destroy both the antichrist and his kingdom (Dan. 7:25-26); and that Christ will then receive His kingdom, both in its earthly and eternal phases (Dan 7:28).

---

7. Stephen Davey, The Many Faces of Evil - Part V: Counterfeit , Sermon.
8. MacArthur, op. cit., p. 7.
9. Ibid., p. 44.

"Back to the Future"
End Times Prophecy, from Genesis to Revelation
Lesson 14 - Tribulation: Second Half Evil

***DAY 5: Beast out of the Earth: Rev. 13:12-18

1. Describe the next beast John sees in Rev. 13:11. From where does this beast come?

2. Describe his actions? v. 12

3. What is this 2nd beast able to do, deceiving those on earth? v. 13-14

4. What does this beast next order the inhabitants of the earth to do? v. 14

5. What happens next in v. 15?

6. Finally, what economic system does this beast establish? vv. 16-17

7. What is this mark? What is the number of the beast? vv.17-18

ON A PERSONAL NOTE . . .
- No believer will have a tougher time than those going through the last half of the Tribulation. Phil 4:13 says, "I can do all things through Christ who strengthens me." How do you need Christ to strengthen you today? What rewards does the Bible promise for obedience to His truths?

- We only have one more lesson on the Tribulation. So I have to ask, are you confident that you have the seal of the Holy Spirit, guaranteeing your inheritance in heaven. Are you looking for Christ' call at the Rapture to take you to heaven, escaping the Tribulation? If you are not looking for Christ, you will be looking for the antichrist. Please turn to Appendix One and *make sure* you belong to Christ.

"Back to the Future"
End Times Prophecy, from Genesis to Revelation
Lesson 14 - Tribulation: Second Half Evil

REVIEW:
II Cor. 11:14 describes Satan as an "*angel of light*," the great deceiver of mankind. Verse 15 continues, "*Therefore it is not surprising if his servants also disguise themselves as servants of righteousness . . . .*" Scripture records many examples of false prophets. They are described as wicked (Jer. 23:11); adulterers (Jer. 23:14); greedy (Eze. 22:25, II Pet. 2:15); self-deceived (Eze. 13:2-3); and idolaters (Jer. 2:8; 23:13).[10]

Just as the antichrist of Rev. 13:1-10 is the ultimate and final false Christ, the false prophet of Rev. 13:11-18 is the final and consummate false prophet. John introduces us to the false prophet by saying, "*I saw another beast coming up out of the earth . . . .*" He, like the antichrist (*another beast*), is a man demonically inspired who will rise to a place of spiritual leadership. Some see the word *earth* here as referring to the Holy Land and believe that the false prophet is a Jew, but this may be a stretch. It is interesting to note, however, that even today overtures are being made between the Pope and Jewish leaders to find common ground. Probably the word *earth* suggests that just as the earth is less terrifying than the sea, so the false prophet will be more subtle and gentle than the antichrist.

John tells us that this beast *had two horns like a lamb and spoke as a dragon*. The horns here do not represent kings as they do on the dragon and the antichrist. Instead the imagery of a lamb reminds us of Matt. 7:15 where false religious leaders are described as a wolf in sheep's clothing - "*Beware of false prophets who come to you in sheep's clothing but inwardly are ravenous wolves.*" Although this "lamb" appears innocent enough, he is demonically inspired and will utter Satan's lies and deceptions. Promising the world a utopia under the antichrist, he will actually lead them into utter destruction.

Now that John has told us who the beast is, he proceeds to describe the false prophet's activities. The false prophet *exercises all authority of the first beast in his presence*. He will have the same demonic power as the antichrist who gives authority to the false prophet to act on his behalf. We see that all the false prophet's efforts will be directed toward one goal – to cause *the earth and those that dwell on it to worship the first beast, whose fatal wound was healed*. In partnership with Satan and the antichrist, he will work to bring about a one-world religion, worship of the antichrist. No doubt the supposed resurrection of the antichrist will go a long way towards achieving this goal.

John Walvoord adds an interesting thought about this false prophet. He says there is some evidence that this second beast is the head of the apostate church during the first half of the Tribulation. After the antichrist rises to a position of worldwide dominance, this apostate church is destroyed. However the false prophet survives and helps assist the antichrist transition to his final form of apostate religion - worship of the antichrist himself.[11]

This transition will begin at the midpoint of the Tribulation when the antichrist sets up the abomination of desolation. Any other religion will not be tolerated and will result in death. Ironically it is those that do worship him that will experience eternal death in the Lake of Fire. This reminds me of Matt 10:28 where Jesus warns those listening not to fear the one who can kill the body but to fear God, the one who can destroy both the body and the soul.

Just as the resurrection of the antichrist mimics the resurrection of Jesus, the false prophet's works will mimic the miracles performed by Jesus, the prophets, and the apostles. *He performs great signs... even makes fire come down out of heaven to the earth in the presence of men*. The miracles of the false prophet will convince the world of his power and deceive the world into worshiping the antichrist. With all the judgments of God raining down upon them, they will be desperately looking for someone that can save them from the carnage and chaos. Perhaps the false prophet's miracles are also done to overshadow the miracles of the Two Witnesses, also on the scene at this time.

As the whole world turns to the antichrist as their Savior, the false prophet orders that an *image of the beast* be made. Amazingly *it was given to him to give breath to the image of the beast* so that it *would even speak*. Somehow the false prophet will animate the image so that it appears to be alive. As technology advances, this becomes more and more imaginable. This image likely will be set up in the Holy of Holies (II Thess. 2:4) and may even be the desolation spoken of in Dan. 11:31. The false prophet will then cause those *who do not worship the image of the beast to be killed*. The world will engage in

"Back to the Future"
End Times Prophecy, from Genesis to Revelation
Lesson 14 - Tribulation: Second Half Evil

the most horrendous form of idolatry ever seen in the history of mankind. This will result in the martyrdom of many of the Tribulation saints. However Satan's plan to extinguish God's people will not succeed and those who survive this unimaginably wicked time will enter into the Millennial Kingdom.

Don't miss the phrase "*it was given*" in verses 14 and 15. In fact, you may want to circle them in your Bible. God is still in control and allowing all of this to happen. The world is deceived not only due to the wicked deception of Satan but because of the judgment of God (II Thess. 2:11-12).

Further exercising the power and authority of the antichrist, Rev. 13:16 tells us that the false prophet will cause all men - the *rich,* the *poor,* the *free men* and the *slaves* to take *a mark on their right hand or on their foreheads*. In the old Roman Empire, slaves were marked, or branded, by their masters to show ownership. Soldiers often branded themselves with the names of their general to show their loyalty. Here the antichrist is placing his mark of ownership on his servants. He is also mimicking God's seal on the foreheads of the 144,000. Notice that the mark is not some chip placed under the skin as some suggest today, but it is *on* the skin.[12]

Without the mark of the beast *no one will be able to buy or sell*. Credit cards and cash will disappear. The mark of the beast will be a "one-world currency." The antichrist and his empire will exercise strict control over the necessities of life, already scarce because of God's judgments and the devastation of war. The tribulation saints who refuse to worship the beast will not only face martyrdom, but also will face extreme poverty and starvation. And midst the rampant illness (plagues), they will also be unable to obtain any needed medicine or medical treatment.

Not only will this tactic give the government sole power of the world's economy, but it will also put immense pressure on the saints to give in to the worship of the antichrist. Resistance can only come through the strength God gives them. Paul's words come to my mind, "*. . . I have learned the secret of being filled and going hungry, both having abundance and suffering need. I can do all things through Christ who strengthens me*" (Phil. 4:12-13).

John goes on to describe this *mark* as either *the name of the beast or the number of his name*. It is not clear just what this number is, but John goes on to say that those with wisdom and understanding will be able to calculate the number, for *the number is that of a man and is six hundred and sixty six*. Volumes have been written speculating how to calculate this number and who it might represent. But it is impossible to figure it out in advance. I believe that it will only be believers with wisdom living at that time who will understand how to identify this number with the antichrist.

We do know, however, that in Scripture "seven" is the number of perfection and is God's number. Since man falls short of perfection, his number is "six.. Repeating this number three times underscores that number is man's number.[13]

As we come to the close of our study of Rev. 12 and 13, let us remember that it is Satan's ultimate goal in opposing God to receive the worship due to God alone. During the last half of the Tribulation, Satan, the antichrist, and the false prophet form a counterfeit trinity, mimicking God the Father, God the Son, and God the Holy Spirit. (For more on this Satanic trinity refer to Appendix Four.) They will deceive most of the world into worshiping Satan and following him into the Lake of Fire. But praise to God, Satan is a defeated foe and his plan to prevent Christ's coming world kingdom will fail. During the seven-year Tribulation many, many more believers will turn to Christ. Many will survive and enter into the Millennial Kingdom. What's more, when Christ returns at the end of the Tribulation, the nation of Israel will finally turn to their Messiah, thus fulfilling the many prophecies that "all Israel will be saved." All honor, praise, and glory go to God the Father and His Son Jesus Christ!

---

10. Ibid., p. 56.
11. John F. Walvoord, The Revelation of Jesus Christ, p. 205.
12. Stephen Davey, The Many Faces of Evil - Part IX: 666, Sermon.
13. MacArthur, op. cit., p. 64.

"Back to the Future"
End Times Prophecy, from Genesis to Revelation
Lesson 15 - Tribulation: Last Days

*** DAY 1: God's Special Witnesses at the End

The Two Witnesses (Rev. 11:7-14)
1. Remember: Rev. 11:3-6
    a. What does He give them power to do and for how long? v. 3

    b. What happens to anyone wanting to harm these two witnesses? v. 5

    c. What three miracles are the witnesses able to perform, authenticating their message? v. 6

2. At the end of their 42 months of testimony, what happens to them?

3. Describe what happens next in vv. 8-10.

4. In vv. 11-12, how does God vindicate His two faithful witnesses?

5. What accompanies their ascension? What are the devastating results?

6. What is the reaction of those left in the city?

The 144,000 (Rev. 14:1-5)
7. Where does John see the Lamb standing? Who is with Him? v.1

8. We looked at vv. 4-5 when we were introduced to these 144,000 in Rev. 7. What did we learn about them from these verses?

9. To what sounds does John compare the voice he hears from heaven? v.2

10. What is being sung? What is this *new song* celebrating? Rev. 5:8-10; 7:10

11. What do we learn about the 144,000 in v. 3?

ON A PERSONAL NOTE . . .
- We are told that the 144,000 follow the Lamb wherever He goes. Is that true of you? Are there some paths you find it hard to follow? Why? What adjustments in your life are needed to clear the path?

- Some say that the hymnal is one of God's greatest missionaries. How does spiritual music play a part in your daily life? How would hearing God's truths in song affect your day? What are some ways you can do this?

"Back to the Future"
End Times Prophecy, from Genesis to Revelation
Lesson 15 - Tribulation: Last Days

REVIEW:
Before we begin with our study in Rev. 14, let's not forget that at the middle of the Tribulation God raises up two special witnesses to prophesy for the 1260 days of the second half (Rev. 11:3-4). Clothed in sackcloth, these two perform miracles to validate their message and are able to kill their enemies with fire flowing out of their mouths (Rev. 11:5-6).

At the end of the Tribulation, we see that an amazing thing will happen. In Rev. 11:7 we see that as the ministry of the two witnesses comes to a close, God will withdraw his protection of them and will allow the antichrist (empowered by Satan) to overcome and kill these two men. Showing great dishonor and contempt for them, the bodies of these two witnesses will be left lying in the streets of Jerusalem (*where also their Lord was crucified*) for all to see. For *three and a half days*, the unbelieving world will celebrate the death of their tormentors, even sending *gifts to one another*.

After three and a half days, our omnipotent God will breathe *the breath of life* into these two dead witnesses, and the men will *stand on their feet*. The world's celebration will come to a sudden end as *great fear* falls upon those watching. At God's command, the two witnesses will then ascend to heaven in a cloud. Within the hour, a great earthquake will occur – destroying a tenth of the city and killing 7000 people, probably all unbelievers. We are told that *the rest, terrified*, will then *give glory to the God of heaven,* the only true God. Some scholars think that the term *the rest* refers to unbelievers who out of fear will acknowledge the power of God but not actually become saved. Others see *the rest* as Jews who will genuinely experience salvation at this time.

Before moving on to the sounding of the seventh trumpet, Rev. 11:14 notes, "*The second woe is past; the third woe is coming quickly.*" This seems to place the resurrection of God's two witnesses immediately before the final bowl judgments which quickly bring the Tribulation to an end.

As we continue our lesson on the last days of the Tribulation, remember that chapters 12-14 form an interlude of parenthetical revelation in the book of Revelation. (Refer to Appendix Three.) At the end of chapter 11, the seventh trumpet is sounded, but the actual bowl judgments are not poured out until chapter 15. Chapters 12 and 13 looked at events of the Tribulation from Satan's perspective, recording Satan's efforts to thwart God's purposes by destroying God's people and recording the activities of the antichrist and the false prophet. Chapter 14 now returns to God's perspective and gives us a preview of the coming judgments that are associated with Christ's return. Specific details of these judgments will be given in the chapters that follow.

By this time in the Tribulation, survivors will have faced the wrath of God in the events of the six seals and the first six trumpets - wars, plagues, famines, and natural disasters. They will also have faced the persecution of Satan, his demons, and his followers as sin and wickedness abounds. Although it seems that no one could survive, we know that some will. Among the believers who survive to enter the Millennial Kingdom is the group of 144,000 Jewish witnesses from the twelve tribes of Israel who have been protected by God, *having* His (Jesus') *name and the name of His Father written on their foreheads*.

We first saw this group being sealed in Rev. 7 at the beginning of the Tribulation. Protected from God's judgments and Satan's fury, they have been faithfully proclaiming the gospel during this horrific time. Here in Rev. 14, John sees them at the end of the Tribulation *standing on Mount Zion* with none other than *the Lamb*, Christ Himself. All 144,000 have survived and are triumphantly standing with Christ on Mount Zion at his return. None have been lost!

This reference is to the earthly Mount Zion, not the heavenly one. Mount Zion is the hill around which David built the city of Jerusalem and is the place from which King Jesus will rule on the Davidic throne during the Millennial Kingdom (Ps. 2:6-9; 48:2). MacArthur writes, "The appearance of the Lamb on Mount Zion is a monumental moment in redemptive history."[1]

As John surveys the scene on earth, he hears *what sounds like* a heavenly choir - many voices (*waters*) being accompanied by harpists. A *new song* was being sung *before the throne and before the four living creatures and the elders*. This song was begun in Rev. 5:9-10 by the four living creatures and the elders, joined by angels in Rev. 5:12, and joined by every created thing in Rev. 5:13. The

"Back to the Future"
End Times Prophecy, from Genesis to Revelation
Lesson 15 - Tribulation: Last Days

Tribulation martyrs join in the singing in Rev. 7:9-10. It is the song of redemption, expressing joy over the accomplishment of God's redemptive work through Christ before His return. Now the 144,000 join the angels, the Old Testament saints, the Church, and the Tribulation martyrs in praising the Father and the Son.[2]

We are told that no one on earth *could learn this song except the 144,000 . . . purchased from the earth*. Obviously unbelievers could not sing this song, but we are not told why others redeemed during the Tribulation cannot. Perhaps they will join the singing after their judgment which will occur before the Millennial Kingdom begins.

Whether a believer is martyred or, like the 144,000, brought safely during the Tribulation period, he will forever be a victor, living with Christ for all eternity. The passages we have studied today reassure us that all believers are eternally secure. Today we are sealed by the Holy Spirit, guaranteeing our protection and His power in our lives. As victors in Christ we can live unafraid of death and can minster with boldness, knowing that no one can snatch us out of His hand (John 10:28-29). Won't you join the heavenly chorus in praising God for His perfect plan of redemption?

1. John MacArthur, The MacArthur New Testament Commentary: Revelation 12-22, p.71.
2. Ibid., p. 75.

"Back to the Future"
End Times Prophecy, from Genesis to Revelation
Lesson 15 - Tribulation: Last Days

*** DAY 2: Three Angels and a Voice from Heaven: Rev. 14:6-13

1. John next sees the *first* of three angels flying in midheaven.
   a. What is the first angel's mission? v. 6

   b. How does this correspond to Mt 24:14

   c. What does this angel first exhort the world to do? Why? v. 7

   d. What does the angel next exhort the world to do and why? v. 7

2. What is the *second* angel's message? v. 8

3. John next sees the *third* angel. This angel's message concerns those who are following the beast (Antichrist). What four things do we learn about their fate? vv. 9-11

4. Rev. 14:12 calls for the perseverance of the saints.
   a. How would the third angel's message help believers to persevere?

   b. What are two traits of the Tribulation saints (and of believers of all times)?

5. John next hears a voice from heaven (God), blessing the Tribulation saints. v. 13
   a. What is John commanded to do?

   b. Who does John next hear agreeing with the Father?

   c. How will the future of believers who die during the Tribulation differ from that of the antichrist's followers? v. 13

   d. What does the phrase, "*their works follow them,*" indicate is waiting for them in heaven?

ON A PERSONAL NOTE . . .
After hearing the gospel, there are only two choices – to confess or to deny Jesus as your Lord and Savior.
- If today's lesson has convicted you of the need to turn to Jesus and secure your eternal future with Him, I implore you to do so NOW! (Read Appendix One.)

- How does the encouragement of the Tribulation saints encourage you as well?

"Back to the Future"
End Times Prophecy, from Genesis to Revelation
Lesson 15 - Tribulation: Last Days

REVIEW:
The Greek word *angelos*, from which we get our word *angel*, means messenger. Throughout the Bible, angels are seen serving as God's messengers. Daniel, Joseph, Mary, and Paul are but a few individuals to whom angels personally appeared. We also see angels involved in the giving of the Mosaic Laws and in announcing the birth of Jesus. And in this study we have repeatedly seen angels involved in the judgments of the end-time events. So far, we have seen them involved in the outpouring of the coming judgments, in controlling nature, and even in releasing demons. In future lessons, we will see angels accompanying Jesus as He returns victoriously to earth, gathering unbelievers for judgment (Mt. 13:42-43, 49-50) and gathering saints for glory (Mt. 24:31).

In Rev. 14:6-12 three of God's messengers appear, each with a final message from heaven. Before the seventh trumpet sounds, pouring the final devastating and rapid-fire bowl judgments on the earth, God makes His last appeal to mankind. These three angels appear flying in midheaven for the entire world to see and hear. Since Satan and his demons have been cast to the earth, no angelic warfare can hinder their mission. The first angel delivers the gospel, the second tells of coming judgment of the antichrist and his world-wide system of evil, and the third warns of condemnation for those who follow the antichrist.

By the time *the first angel* appears, the world will have seen incredible devastation and innumerable deaths, caused by the judgments of God. They will have heard the gospel preached by the 144,000 Jewish evangelists, the two witnesses, and those who have been saved during the Tribulation. They will have also seen the miracles performed by God's two witnesses, validating their message. Sadly though, most of the earth world has rejected God and instead turned to the antichrist (Rev. 9:20-21). God in his unending grace sends this first angel to yet again present the ***eternal gospel*** of Jesus Christ – victory over sin and death through Christ's saving work on the cross. At this point, the gospel would no doubt include the message of the soon-coming Millennial Kingdom.

Because of his message, this first angel then warns *in a loud voice, "Fear God and give Him glory, because the hour of His judgment has come."* Instead of fearing the antichrist who has the ability to kill the body, they should fear God who has the ability to kill both body and soul (Mt. 10:28), However the opportunity for those on earth to turn to God is drawing to a close. The bowl judgments are about to be poured out, followed by the Lord's return in judgment.

One last reason is given by this first angel for worshiping God: He is the One who *made the heaven and the earth and sea and springs of waters*. As the creator of the universe and of each person of all time (John 1:1-3) God is worthy of all *worship* – all glory, praise, and honor, belong to Him and Him alone. As creator of the universe, God alone has the right to judge the created. Furthermore because God reveals Himself in creation, man is without excuse when it comes to acknowledging God's existence and power. (Rom. 1:18-20).

A *second angel* follows the first. Instead of proclaiming the good news of the gospel, this angel is announcing the bad news of the coming judgment on the antichrist's evil empire. This gives the world the answer to their question recorded in Rev. 13:4, "Who is like the beast and who is able to wage war with him?" The second angel cries out from midheaven, "*Fallen, fallen is Babylon the great . . . .*" We saw earlier in our study that the Apostate Church, *mystery* Babylon, was destroyed at the midpoint of the Tribulation by the antichrist when he declares worship of himself the only acceptable form of worship. Here, in Rev. 14:8, the word *Babylon* refers not only to the antichrist's capital city but also to the antichrist's worldwide political, economic, and religious empire. Babylon's fall is so certain that it is spoken of as if it has already happened. We have seen this verb tense before. The fact that the word *fallen* is used twice also emphasizes the certainty of this judgment. Our study of Revelation 18 will shed more light on the actual events of this judgment.

Finally in Rev. 14:9 the third angel appears, revealing the doom of those who follow the antichrist. Many today say that we should never scare unbelievers with the reality of hell. However that is precisely what God is doing in sending this third angel. Stephen Davey writes, "The gospel is not just, 'Believe in Christ and repent of your sin in order to go to heaven;' it is also just as correct to say, 'Believe in Christ and repent of your sin in order to not go to hell.'"[3]

"Back to the Future"
End Times Prophecy, from Genesis to Revelation
Lesson 15 - Tribulation: Last Days

The third angel's message is that anyone who *worships the beast and his image, and receives a mark on his forehead or on his hand* will *drink the wine of the wrath of God, which is mixed in full strength in the cup of His anger.* The angel goes on to reveal the future of all unbelievers of all time. *They will be tormented with fire and brimstone in the presence of the holy angels and . . . the Lamb.* We are also told that *the smoke of their torment will go up forever and ever,* giving them *no rest day and night.* These verses clearly dispute those who today have fallen for Satan's lie that hell is not eternal torment – that those who go to hell will be burned up and cease to exist. As horrible as this punishment appears, we know that God's judgments are holy and just. Even in the Lake of Fire, men will refuse to repent and their hearts will grow harder.

How anyone could hear the messages of these three angels and not repent is beyond my wildest imagination, but scripture is clear that many will not heed God's final warning. We know that sinful man's heart is hardened and his mind is blinded by the god of this world (II Cor. 4:4). Without God's grace and mercy in calling His own, we too would face these unbelievers' fate. Praise to the Father and His Son Jesus Christ who overcame Satan, sin, and death for us!

The message of the third angel closes with a call to the Tribulation saints to persevere. God's judgment on their enemies is coming soon. Furthermore, although the saints are now enduring great persecution and some will even face martyrdom, their suffering is nothing compared to the future torment in store for those who take the easy way out and worship the beast. Here the saints are characterized by their obedience to God's commands and by their continued faith in Jesus Christ. Here, more than ever, faith and works will go hand in hand.[4]

After John's vision of the three flying angels, he next hears a *voice from heaven*. Whenever *a voice from heaven* is heard in the book of Revelation (Rev. 4:1; 10:4, 8; 11:12; 12:10; 14:2, 13; 18:4; 19:1), it is a direct communication from the throne room of God, not a message sent through an angel. Here the voice is probably the voice of God Himself. You can be sure that the words that follow will be extremely important.

In this passage, God orders John to write, "*Blessed are the dead who die in the Lord from now on!*" This is one of the seven beatitudes found in the book of Revelation (1:3; 14:13; 16:15; 19:9; 20:6; 22:7; and 22:14). All martyrs of the Tribulation are blessed, not only because they lived in obedience and trust, but because they *died in the Lord*.[5]

Always in perfect unity with the Father and the Son, the Holy Spirit emphatically agrees by saying, "*Yes.*" He then goes on to add, "*so that they may rest from their labors, for their deeds follow with them.*" This does not mean that those who die will never work, since they will serve Christ during the Millennial Kingdom and for all eternity. Instead it means that they will rest from the difficulties and sorrows of their lives during the tremendous persecution of the Tribulation. Also encouraging to the Tribulation martyrs is the reminder that rewards for their service to the Lord await them in Heaven, as is true for all believers who die in the Lord.

Today's lesson as a whole reminds us that the choice concerning Christ in this life will have eternal consequences. We can deny Christ and live for the pleasures of this world or we can confess Him as Savior and Lord, living for the rest and reward of Heaven.

---

3. Stephen Davey, A Preview of Things to Come – Part III: *The Wine of His Wrath*, Sermon.
4. John Walvoord, The Revelation of Jesus Christ, p. 220.
5. MacArthur, op. cit., p. 104.

"Back to the Future"
End Times Prophecy, from Genesis to Revelation
Lesson 15 – Tribulation: Last Days

*** DAY 3: Final Reaping on Earth; Three More Angels: Rev. 14:14-20

Reaping the Harvest of the Earth
1. In v. 14 John next sees a white cloud with someone sitting on it. What 3 things does John tell us about this person? Based on the description, who do you think he is?

2. John then sees another angel.
   a. To whom does the first angel appeal?

   b. What is his appeal? Why does the angel say it is time?

   c. What happens as a result of the angel's appeal?

Reaping the Grape Clusters
3. From where does a second angel now come and what is in his hand?

4. In v. 18 John sees yet a third angel.
   a. From where did the third angel come and over what does he have power?

   b. In Rev 6:9-10 who had John seen under the altar of the temple and what was their cry?

   c. From Rev 8:3-4 what was burning on the altar?

5. What does this third angel call for the second one to do? Why?

6. After swinging his sickle, what does the second angel do with the clusters he gathers?

7. What results?

8. What similarities and what differences do you see in the two reapings?

ON A PERSONAL NOTE . . .
- Today's study puts a new meaning to the term, "Grim Reaper." Is there someone that you need to share the gospel with before it is too late? What has kept you from doing so? Ask God for the opportunity, the boldness and the words to share Christ's love with them.

"Back to the Future"
End Times Prophecy, from Genesis to Revelation
Lesson 15 - Tribulation: Last Days

REVIEW:
Yesterday we were introduced to three angels, each flying in midheaven with a message from God. The first angel proclaimed the gospel to the whole world, the second angel announced the coming judgment on the antichrist and his world empire, and the third angel announced judgment on those who follow the antichrist. Next a voice from heaven was heard *blessing* those who are martyred for their faith. Today in Rev. 14:14-20 John's vision resumes with a message of judgment – the full fury of God's wrath is unleashed on earth as the Tribulation period comes to a close.

This final wrath of God is pictured in two different ways – first a grain harvest and then a grape harvest. The harvest of grain represents the bowl judgments that are about to fall upon the earth and the harvest of grapes represent the Battle of Armageddon, the final battle being fought as Christ returns to defeat His enemies and establish His reign. Both harvests involve a sickle and both involve reaping.[6]

In the first harvest, the harvest of grain, John first sees *a white cloud and sitting on the cloud was one like a son of man*. This reaper is no doubt Jesus Himself. This description of Christ matches the prophecy in Dan. 7:13 as Christ is presented before God to receive His kingdom. The phrase *like a son of man* also speaks of Christ in Rev. 1:13. The *golden crown on His head* is not the crown worn by a ruler (*diadema*) but is the crown worn by a victor in war or athletic competition, a crown of triumph (*stephanos*). John also sees *a sharp sickle in His hand*. A sickle, used in harvesting grain, had a long wooden handle with a long, curved, sharp iron blade attached to it. When a harvester swung his sickle back and forth the grain stalks were cut off at ground level. So too will Christ cut down His enemies.[7]

Another angel comes out from the God's temple, from before God's throne, crying out to Jesus, *"Put in your sickle and reap, for the hour to reap has come, because the harvest of the earth is ripe."* The term *ripe* means dried up or rotten. It is time for the ungodly to be gathered and burned (judged). We know that ultimately they will be cast into the flames of the Lake of Fire.

We know that the Father has given the Son the authority to execute all judgment (John 5:22, 27). Now, just as the angel requested, Jesus Christ, the One *who sat on the cloud*, swings *His sickle over the earth, and the earth was reaped.* The seven bowl judgments, soon to begin, will kill millions, marking the first phase of the earth's final reaping.

Next follows the vision of the grape harvest which, as noted above, represents the judgment that will take place at the battle of Armageddon. Here the one with the *sharp sickle* is *another angel* who comes *out of the temple which is in heaven.* Following this reaper is yet *another angel, the one who has power over fire* and comes *from the altar.* The altar mentioned here is the heavenly altar of Rev. 8 where the prayers of the saints were offered. This last angel evidently had been ministering there and now comes to make sure that the prayers for judgment and for the coming kingdom are answered.[8] He calls out to the angel holding the sickle to *put in your sharp sickle and gather the clusters form the vine of the earth because her grapes are ripe.* The Greek word used here for *ripe* is different than the one used in v. 15. Here it denotes *bursting with juice*. The armies of the antichrist are bursting with wickedness and ready for judgment.

When the angel swings his sickle to the earth, the clusters are *gathered* and *thrown into the great wine press of the wrath of God*. Similar imagery is found in Rev. 19:15 where at Christ's return He will tread the wine press of the fierce wrath of God. The angel will harvest the grapes, but Christ will be the one who destroys them. In a wine press grapes were smashed in an upper basin and the juice would collect in a lower one. The splattering of juice that would occur represents the blood of Christ's enemies.

We are next told that the *wine press was trodden outside the city* and that blood from the wine press would come *up to the horses' bridles, for a distance of two hundred miles.* Although Jerusalem will be under siege at the time of His return, Christ will battle His enemies outside the city, protecting Jerusalem from further carnage. The second phase of the earth's reaping will occur as the antichrist and his armies are crushed, their blood flowing deep and wide.

6. Stephen Davey, A Preview of Things to Come - Part VI: *The Grim Reaper*, Sermon.
7. MacArthur, op. cit., p. 114.
8. John MacArthur, The MacArthur Study Bible, p. 1983.

"Back to the Future"
End Times Prophecy, from Genesis to Revelation
Lesson 15 - Tribulation: Last Days

*** DAY 4: The Seven Bowl Judgments

Introduction: Rev. 15

1. What is the next great sign in heaven? v. 1

2. What are we told about these seven plagues? v. 1

3. Describe this glimpse into heaven. vv. 2-4

4. From where do the seven angels come? What did the angels receive? vv. 5-8

Bowl Judgments: Rev. 16

5. For each of the following bowls, write where the bowl is poured and what results.
   a. First bowl v. 2

   b. Second bowl v. 3

   c. Third bowl vv. 4-7

   d. Fourth bowl; what is man's reaction to the judgment? vv. 8-9

   e. Fifth bowl; what is man's reaction to the judgment? vv. 10-11

   f. Sixth bowl judgment v. 12

6. When the sixth bowl is poured out, what does John see; what is the purpose of the frog-like demons; and what battle is being prepared for? vv. 13-16

7. The seventh bowl judgment vv. 17-21
   a. Where does the seventh angel pour his bowl?

   b. What does, "It is done," mean? What does it remind you of?

   c. The destruction is worldwide, as never before. List all the natural disasters that occur.

   d. What happens to Jerusalem, the great city?

   e. What other city specifically receives the cup of God's wrath?

   f. Unbelievably, how do men continue to respond?

ON A PERSONAL NOTE . . .
Life has a lot of things that can go wrong: someone loses a job, someone gets sick or has cancer, someone is in a fatal car wreck, a child is born with a disability, a teenager rebels or gets addicted to drugs, a husband is an alcoholic . . . . The list can go on and on. Unbelievers want to curse God and believers sometimes say, "Why me?" After the seal, trumpet, and bowl judgments, people blaspheme the name of God and refuse to repent of their wicked ways.

- What is a better way to respond to these types of hurts in our fallen world? We must be careful not to waste the suffering by missing the blessing.

- How can we help others see Jesus in the midst of pain and suffering?

"Back to the Future"
End Times Prophecy, from Genesis to Revelation
Lesson 15 - Tribulation: Last Days

REVIEW:
Having concluded the parenthetical revelation of Chapters 12-14, our study returns to the chronological revelation, picking up after the opening of the seventh trumpet. The seven bowls described in Rev. 15-16 occur as part of the seventh trumpet, just as the seven trumpets are part of the seventh seal.

As Rev. 15 opens, John sees a third sign in heaven described as great and marvelous. (See Rev. 12: 1, 3 for the other two signs.) He sees *seven angels* with *seven plagues*. These plagues are described as the *last, because in them the wrath of God is finished*. This description refutes the "pre-wrath" view – God's wrath begins with these plagues so the Rapture does not happen until just prior to the bowl judgments. Clearly these bowls are described as *the last*, not the first, of God's wrath. And with the bowl judgments, God's wrath is *finished*, not begun. The bowl judgments *finish* what began with the seal and trumpet judgments.

Next John sees *a sea of glass mixed with fire*. We previously saw this sea of glass before God's throne in Rev 4:6, but here it is different - it is mixed with the fire of God's judgment. Standing on this sea are the Tribulation martyrs, *those who had been victorious over the beast and his image and the number of his name*. The martyrs are now holding harps, frequently associated with praise in the Bible. And they are singing *the song of Moses* and *the song of the Lamb*.

Although the words sung here do not exactly match those of the two songs mentioned, the themes and many of the terms are similar. The *song of Moses* is the song of victory and deliverance that the Israelites sang after God led them out of Egypt (Ex. 15:1-18). It also celebrates God's judgment and wrath on His enemies. The *song of the Lamb* is found in Rev. 5:8-14 where the redeemed saints are singing before God's throne. They are celebrating Christ's victory over sin and the deliverance of His people from slavery to sin. The Tribulation martyrs, having been delivered from the antichrist's persecution, add praise to God for His character, His works, and His ways. God will judge the wicked, and in the Millennial Kingdom *all the nations will come and worship before* Him (Ps. 66:4; Is. 66:23).[9]

John then sees the *temple of the tabernacle of testimony in heaven ... opened.* In both the OT tabernacle and temple, the Ark of the Covenant (with Moses' two stone tablets) was located in the Holy of Holies. This inner place was sometimes referred to as *the tabernacle of testimony.* John is now seeing the Holy of Holies in the heavenly temple. In our study of the seventh trumpet, we also saw this Holy of Holies opened, accompanied by lightning, thunder, an earthquake, and a great hailstorm.

From God's heavenly throne, the seven angels with the seven plagues now emerge. These angels are *clothed in linen, clean and bright* with *golden sashes around their chests*. These angels are representing Christ in judgment, so it is not surprising that their robes and sashes are like that of Jesus Christ in Rev. 1.[10] *One of the four living creatures* from around the throne of God gives *the seven angels seven golden bowls, full of the wrath of God.* The Greek word for *bowls, Phialas*, refers to *shallow saucers*. They are not containers from which a steady stream would flow. Instead the wrath coming from one of these bowls would be emptied out all at once.

Chapter 16 details each of the seven bowl judgments. Unlike the trumpet judgments which afflicted a third of the earth and heaven, the bowl judgments are much more severe and will devastate the entire world. The bowl judgments are intense, rapid-fire judgments which will culminate with the return of Christ. Remember that by the time these seven final judgments are poured out, the wicked will have been warned repeatedly to repent by the 144,000, God's two prophets, those saved during the Tribulation, and the flying angel. By this time, unbelievers will acknowledge that the judgments are from God (Rev. 6:16-17), but love their sin too much to repent.

The bowl judgments begin as John hears a loud voice, undoubtedly God's, command the seven angels, "*Go and pour out on the earth the seven bowls of the wrath of God.*" Immediately the *first angel* pours out his bowl on the earth. As a result, *loathsome and malignant sores* appear on the followers of the antichrist. The Greek words used to describe these sores indicate that inflamed, oozing, ulcer-like sores will torment all who have *the mark of the beast and worship his image*.[11]

Before the sores of the wicked have had time to heal, the *second angel* pours *his bowl into the sea.* This causes the sea to *become blood, like that of a dead man.* The oceans will no longer be fluid, but

"Back to the Future"
End Times Prophecy, from Genesis to Revelation
Lesson 15 - Tribulation: Last Days

will become thick, dark, and coagulated. *Every living thing in the sea* will die, causing an unbelievable stench. Dead sea plants and animals will wash ashore, contaminating all the world's beaches. The ocean's food chain will be destroyed.

Almost without the blink of an eye, the *third angel* pours his *bowl into the rivers and the springs of waters*. Like the ocean, they become blood as well. Drinking water, already scarce, becomes non-existent. There will also be no clean water to wash the unbeliever's oozing sores. As the nightmare of thirsting to death faces the entire planet, people will certainly question God's mercy, love, and grace, As if to answer their questions, *the angel of the waters* reminds us in vv. 5-7 that God's judgments are true and righteous. *Just as the wicked poured out the blood of saints and prophets*, God has now *given them blood to drink. They deserve it.*

The *fourth angel* pours his bowl *on the sun* causing it to give out such *fierce heat* that it *scorches men with fire*. I have read that even a slight increase in the sun's heat could raise the temperature on earth by 100 degrees. Remember too that there will be no oceans or fresh water to help cool the earth. Forest fires will break out all over the world. The sun's intense heat will also melt the polar ice caps, causing worldwide flooding. Unbelievers who are affected not only refuse to repent but begin to blaspheme the name of God. Up until this point, only the antichrist has been seen blaspheming God.

Next, *the fifth angel pours out his bowl on the throne of the beast, and his kingdom became darkened*. Stephen Davey writes of this judgment, "What irony this is – unbelievers have loved the darkness because their deeds were evil, and God will give them a taste of it."[12] How horrible that time will be. We are told that unbelievers *gnaw their tongues because of pain*. It is unfathomable that unbelievers plagued with sores, having no water to drink, scorched with heat, and now in total darkness continue to blaspheme the name of God, still refusing to repent.

In the sixth bowl judgment, *the sixth angel* pours his bowl on the *Euphrates* River drying it up to prepare the way *for the kings from the east*. A survey of one hundred commentaries of the book of Revelation reveals at least fifty interpretations of the identity of these kings.[13] The simplest and best explanation is that these kings refer to the Kings of the Orient who will gather for the final world conflict. The Euphrates River is the water boundary on the east between the Holy Land and Asia. It is the longest river in western Asia, stretching 1800 miles from Syria to Babylon and emptying into the Persian Gulf.[14] The Euphrates' source, found in the snowfields and ice cap on Mt. Ararat, will have melted in the heat of the fourth bowl.[15] At this point John sees *three unclean spirits like frogs* coming out of the mouths of the dragon, the beast, and the false prophet. Unleashed by the unholy trinity, these demons perform signs, deceiving not only the kings of the East but the *kings of the whole world*, and *gather them* together *for the war of the great day of God*. They will gather 60 miles north of Jerusalem in a valley by Mount Megiddo for what is known as the Battle of Armageddon. We will study this battle next week.

As the *seventh angel* pours out his bowl *upon the air* great signs occur in nature. God's voice comes from the His throne saying, "It is done," reminding us of Jesus' final words on the cross. With this bowl, God's wrath is complete. With *flashes of lightning* and *peals of thunder, a great earthquake* occurs, unlike any other in history. The whole world shakes. Jerusalem, *the great city*, is split into three parts and cities of the nations fall. The antichrist's capital city, *Babylon*, is given a special drink of God's *fierce wrath*. Every island and every mountain disappear. (Also see Is. 40:4.) What's more, 100 pound *hailstones* fall *down from heaven upon men*, causing men to blaspheme God (Rev. 16:21).

As I study these bowls, Jesus' words in Mt. 24:22 keep ringing in my ears: "Unless those days had been cut short, no life would have been saved; but for the sake of the elect those days will be cut short." Praise to God who remembers His own! For those who survive, Jesus' return is now imminent.

9. John MacArthur, The MacArthur New Testament Commentary: Revelation 12-22, pp. 127-132.
10. Stephen Davey, A Preview of Things to Come - Part VII: *A Pause in the Mercy of God*, Sermon.
11. MacArthur, op. cit., p. 139.
12. Davey, op. cit., Sermon.
13. John Walvoord, The Bible Knowledge Commentary Old Testament, p. 967.
14. Sam Gordon, Revelation: Worthy is the Lamb, p. 332.
15. MacArthur, op. cit., p. 146.

"Back to the Future"
End Times Prophecy, from Genesis to Revelation
Lesson 15 - Tribulation: Last Days

*** DAY 5: Political, Commercial Babylon Destroyed: Rev 18

Mark Hitchcock, in *The Second Coming of Babylon,* writes:
"Babylon must rise again and be totally wiped out in the final day of the Lord... at the end of the Tribulation in conjunction with the second coming of Jesus Christ. And I believe that what we see happening before our very eyes in Iraq and in the Middle East is setting the stage for the rapid rise and fall of Babylon."

1. What is the final fate of Babylon, according to Jeremiah 50:12-13, 25-26, 39-40?

2. Read Isaiah 13:19-22.
   a. How is Babylon described?

   b. Describe Babylon's future?

3. Read Revelation 18:1-8.
   a. What does the angel declare about Babylon?

   b. What does the angel declare about nations, kings, and merchants of the earth?

   c. What does God call His people in the city to do?

   d. What sins of the wicked in Babylon are mentioned? What is her boasts?

   e. What plagues will she experience in one day? What will God use to destroy Babylon?

4. Read Revelation 18:9–24.
   a. What three groups of people are seen lamenting the burning of Babylon? vv. 9, 11, 19

   b. How fast will the destruction occur? vv. 10, 17, 19

   c. What unusual cargo is mentioned in v. 13?

   d. Who is rejoicing? v. 20

   e. What does the throwing of the millstone into the sea represent? v. 21

   f. What was found in her? v. 24

ON A PERSONAL NOTE . . .
- Rev. 18:5-7 depicts *Babylon as living luxuriously, glorifying self, and boasting of her deeds. Would those around* you describe you as *humble*? Ask the Holy Spirit to expose areas in your life where pride has gotten in the way. List ways you can show humility before your spouse, your parents, your children, siblings, or friends.

- We are called to be separate from the world and warned not to be unequally yoked with unbelievers, lest we participate in their sins and receive God's judgment. In what areas in your life are you are partnering with the world? What steps do you need to take to separate?

"Back to the Future"
End Times Prophecy, from Genesis to Revelation
Lesson 15 - Tribulation: Last Days

REVIEW:
Yesterday we saw that as the seventh bowl is poured out, the antichrist's capital city, *Babylon*, is given a special drink from *the cup of the wine of God's fierce wrath*. Today we are going to take a closer look at God's judgment poured out on this wicked city at the end of the Tribulation.

We have already seen *mystery Babylon*, the Apostate Church, destroyed by the antichrist and his empire at the close of the first half of the Tribulation. But the judgment described in Rev. 18 refers to a literal, rebuilt city of Babylon which is the political and economic capitol of the world at the close of the Tribulation.

We know that Babylon was the location of man's first rebellion against God, as he defied God's command to spread out over the earth and instead built the tower of Babel. We also know that under Nebuchadnezzar Babylon was a magnificent city, with its beautiful streets and hanging gardens (one of the seven wonders of the ancient world). Since its demise when it fell to the Medo-Persians, several attempts to return Babylon to its original glory have been made. Both Alexander the Great and Napoleon planned to rebuild the city but failed in their attempts. The most recent effort by Saddam Hussein, as he dreamed of ruling the world from a rebuilt Babylon, failed as well.[16]

Isaiah and Jeremiah have much to say concerning the final fate of Babylon. It will stand desolate forever, never to be inhabited again. Not even the tents of the nomadic Arabs will be pitched there, nor will any shepherd lead his flocks there. Instead Babylon will be inhabited by desert creatures, with owls living in its houses, hyenas in its tower, and jackal in it palaces. These prophecies have never been fulfilled.

Although the city of Babylon, in present day Iraq, never returned to its original glory, it has always been inhabited, even if at times only by shepherds and nomads. Therefore many scholars believe that Babylon will be rebuilt and become the political and economic headquarters of the antichrist by the midpoint of the Tribulation. Even today Babylon is being partially rebuilt as a tourist attraction, and historic monuments are being reconstructed.[17]

As we turn to Rev. 18, we see the chapter open with another *angel coming down from heaven* announcing the fall of Babylon. So certain is Babylon's fall that the angel repeats himself twice, "*fallen, fallen.*" This angel has *great authority* and, because of the darkness of the 5th bowl judgment, the earth is *illumined with his glory*. Babylon's judgment, spoken of in Rev. 14:8 and 16:19, is upon her.

Reasons for Babylon's destruction are given: She is the *dwelling place of demons* and *the prison of unclean spirits,* she has seduced the *kings of the earth* and *all the nations* into *acts of immorality with her,* and *the merchants of the earth have become rich* by her corrupt economic system.

But first, like the message brought to Lot and his family, God issues a call to his people to *flee* so as to *not participate in her sins and receive her plagues.* Evoking an image of the first tower built in Babylon, God says *her sins have piled up as high as heaven and God has remembered her iniquities*. Although great pressure is on believers to succumb to the antichrist and his system, they must hold fast and receive God's reward, not His judgment.

The angel's cry now turns to God as he calls for God's vengeance on Babylon. The angel requests that God give Babylon punishment that fits her crimes - in fact, double that punishment. MacArthur states that *double* has the sense of fullness or completeness and references Ex. 22 where wrongdoers often were require to pay double restitution under the Mosaic law.[18]

Babylon's sins include proudly glorifying herself instead of God and living sensuously. In her self-sufficiency, she boasts that she doesn't need God (*I am a queen and not a widow*). However in one day her mind will be changed. Because of her sins, those in Babylon will experience the plagues of *pestilence and mourning and famine* – all *in one day*. Then the city will *be burned up with fire*, completing her judgment by our *strong*, all-powerful God.

As the empire of the antichrist is judged and destroyed, we see the wicked mourn, not repent but selfishly mourn. In Rev. 18:9-20 we see three different groups of mourners. The first group mentioned

"Back to the Future"
End Times Prophecy, from Genesis to Revelation
Lesson 15 - Tribulation: Last Days

is made up of the kings of the earth. This group includes more than the 10 kings under the antichrist which earlier participated in the destruction of spiritual Babylon, the Apostate Church. Now it is *all the kings of the earth* that mourn, since they all have *committed acts of immorality* with the antichrist and his evil empire (v. 9). They *weep and lament* as they see their source of power destroyed. We are told in vv. 8, 17, and 19 that this judgment of fire happens quickly, *in one hour*.

The second mourners we see are the *merchants of the earth*. They are mourning not because of the torment Babylon is receiving but because the source of their income, the world's economic capital, is being destroyed – *no one buys their cargoes any more*. A list of their cargoes follows. This list is only representative of the great wealth of the antichrist's empire. Interestingly this list includes *slaves and human lives*. Stephen Davey writes, "*Life was cheap - life only mattered as it advanced the kingdom of Babylon That is the way Babylon has always operated. Life is cheap.*"[19] The merchants like the kings of the earth, can only *stand at a distance* and watch, fearful that they too may share her torment. Little do they know that, unlike the destruction of the city which occurs in *one hour*, their torment will last for eternity.

The final group of mourners is made up of *every shipmaster and every passenger and every sailor ...all who make their living by the sea.* Like the kings and the merchants they do not mourn over Babylon or over their sins, but because their source of business is gone. Some question how Babylon could be a seaport. Perhaps the Euphrates will be made navigable in the last days so that trading vessels and barges, even cruise ships, can reach Babylon, where the wealth of the world is centered. These mariners, like the kings and merchants, marvel at the swiftness of Babylon's destruction.

In Rev. 18:20 we see a different response to this destruction occur in heaven. All the redeemed in heaven, the OT saints, the Church, and the Tribulation Saints, who have been waiting for this moment, are called to rejoice. No doubt all of heaven will rejoice, not at the fate of sinners, but because God's righteousness and judgment has prevailed.

For those of us who are visual learners, we are now given a visual aid. In Rev. 18:21 John sees *a strong angel* take up *a stone like a great millstone* and throw it *into the sea*. Jeremiah also used this illustration in Jer. 51:61-64 as he wrote of Babylon's final judgment. Just as the stone disappeared into the sea, never to be seen again, Babylon too will disappear forever, never to be inhabited again. Normal activities of life – music, work, food preparation, and marriage – will never again be found here.

This chapter closes with the three reasons for Babylon's judgment reiterated. First, her wicked merchants controlled the world. Second, her sorceries deceived the nations. And finally, this city (the capital city of the antichrist and his empire) was responsible for *the blood of the prophets and of the saints and of all who have been slain on earth*.

We will see next week that this final destruction of Babylon signals the end of the Tribulation and causes a great victory celebration to erupt in heaven. The time for Christ's return is at hand!

---

16. Stephen Davey, <u>Armageddon and the Fall of Babylon - Part IV:</u> *The Cradle is the Grave*, Sermon
17. John Walvoord, <u>Major Bible Prophecies</u>, p. 137.
18. MacArthur, op. cit., p. 184.
19. Davey, op. cit.

"Back to the Future"
End Times Prophecy, from Genesis to Revelation
Lesson 16 - The Return of Christ

*** DAY 1: Concurrent Scenes on Earth and Heaven

Nations Gather for Battle
1. Let's review Rev. 16:12-16 which describes the 6th Bowl.
    a. Who is sent to gather the kings (*and their armies*) of the whole world?

    b. What is Satan's purpose for gathering the armies of the world together?

    c. What is God's purpose for this gathering according to Joel 3:2, 12?

    d. How does God supernaturally aid the armies of the East?

    e. What is the Hebrew word for the place the kings gathered? Referencing any commentary you may have, where is this place actually located?

    f. What is the battle which ensues commonly called today?

2. To what areas will this campaign extend?
    a. Zech. 12:1-3, 14:1-2; Micah 4:11-13

    b. Joel 3:2, 9-12

    c. Jer. 49:13-16

3. Psalm 2, while referring to King David, also refers to King Jesus in a prophetic sense. From verses 1-5, what is the Lord's reaction to this "vain" gathering at Armageddon?

Celebration Occurs in Heaven
4. In Rev. 19:1-10 a great celebration in heaven erupts as the Tribulation comes to a close.
    a. What is God being praised for in vv, 1-4?

    b. What is God praised for in vv. 6-8?

    c. In vv. 6-10 we see *the marriage of the Lamb has come* and it is now time for the *marriage supper of the Lamb*. Who is the bride? Who do you think the wedding guests are at this feast?

ON A PERSONAL NOTE . . .
- Today's study reminds me of Gen. 50:20 when Joseph tells his brothers, "As for you, you meant evil against me, but God meant it for good in order to bring about this present result." Sometimes Satan's work unwittingly advances God's plans. Describe a time that God has used (not caused) something bad in your life to advance His kingdom by drawing you or others closer to Him.

- Several reasons for us to praise God are given in Rev. 19:1-10. We can also thank God that we will be in heaven during the horrific Tribulation period, after which we will return with Christ as His bride. Before we continue further, I think we need a celebration of our own. Spend time today in prayer worshiping God as we contemplate our future with Christ. Write your specific praises and thanks in the space below.

"Back to the Future"
End Times Prophecy, from Genesis to Revelation
Lesson 16 - The Return of Christ

REVIEW:
On Earth
Let's review the battles involving the antichrist that we have already studied. During the first part of the Tribulation, we saw the second seal broken and wars erupt as the antichrist expands his empire. Then, just prior to the midpoint of the Tribulation, the king of the North (Syria) and the king of the South (Egypt), apparently in alliance, simultaneously invade Palestine (Dan. 11:40). The antichrist (the Western Ruler) moves in to protect Israel, conquering nations first in the north and then to the south in Egypt (Dan. 11:42). Edom, Moab, and Ammon (Daniel 11:41-42) are spared from conquest. It is probably at this time that Russia and her allies move toward Palestine from the north and the east, making it seemingly hopeless for both Israel and the antichrist, but God intercedes and supernaturally destroys these armies (Eze. 39, Zech. 12:4). With the southern armies defeated and the northern coalition out of the way, the antichrist feels free to break his covenant with Israel and set himself up as the political and religious leader of the world. As the believing remnant of Israel flees to Petra, the antichrist moves his armies into Palestine.

Now as the Tribulation draws to a close, Rev. 16:12-16 tells us that all the armies of the world will come together for battle. We see in Rev. 16:13-14 that it is demonic spirits coming from the mouth of the dragon, the beast, and the false prophet that incite this gathering of these kings of the world for the war. Some see this as a gathering of the armies of the world, disillusioned by the dismal state of world conditions, coming together to challenge the antichrist and his ten kings. In what seems to be a more plausible position, other scholars believe that the antichrist is bringing all the armies together for one last anti-Semitic war against Israel, the people of God. In Rev. 6:14, however, we see Satan's true motive - the armies are being gathered to fight against the armies from heaven.

Our Sovereign God, however, has another plan in mind. He allows this gathering for His own purposes. Ultimately God will sit in judgment on the antichrist, the false prophet, and the armies of the world as they are destroyed at Christ's Return. It is to this end that God Himself dries up the Euphrates River at the sixth bowl judgment, preparing the way for the kings of the east to march west into Palestine (Rev. 16:12).

The battle of Armageddon is often seen as an isolated battle happening just prior to Christ's Second Advent. However the Greek word *polemos*, translated *battle* in Rev. 16:14, indicates a war or a campaign. Just as WWII was a campaign consisting of many different battles, it must be realized that the "battle of that great day of God Almighty" in Rev. 16:14 is actually a campaign.[1]

No one scripture gives us the exact chronology of the battles which happen at Christ's return. In fact there are at least six or seven basic theories among scholars that try to explain the movement of armies and the sequence of battles of Armageddon. Pentecost includes the prior battles of Dan. 11 and Eze. 39 with the battles that now occur just prior to Christ's return, viewing it all as one single campaign.[2]

The final stage of the campaign of Armageddon is set, as the armies of the world are brought toward the plains of Esdraelon, the area around the hill of Megiddo (Rev. 16:13-16). "This hill of Megiddo is located near the Mediterranean with a broad valley stretching out to the east. This valley, around 15x20 miles, is way too small for all the people that will be gathered for this final war. It will however be the central marshaling place, with armies roaming to the south and to the north of this location and from the Mediterranean Sea to the Euphrates River.[3]

Fighting will be underway for several months before Christ returns. Although there is no mention of actual conflict occurring at the Mediggo Valley, scripture does record fighting throughout the land of Israel. We are told in Zech. 12:1-3 that in Jerusalem, a horrific battle occurs and the city is captured by these Satanically-driven armies. Jerusalem does not fall without a fight; and as a result of stiff Jewish resistance, there will be enormous losses on both sides. Zechariah 14:1-2 reveals that houses are plundered, women are raped, and half of the city is exiled. This is an unprecedented time of distress for those in Jerusalem. Remember, however, that most of the believing Jews are in Petra, having fled there at the midpoint of the Tribulation.

"Back to the Future"
End Times Prophecy, from Genesis to Revelation
Lesson 16 - The Return of Christ

In Joel 3 we see the armies of the nations encamped outside of Jerusalem in the Valley of Jehoshaphat. Known as the Kidron Valley today, this valley runs between eastern Jerusalem and the Mount of Olives, then continues east through the Judean Desert, towards the Dead Sea.

Having captured Jerusalem, the antichrist next sets his sights on the faithful remnant in Edom (Bozrah), some 80 miles to the southeast. Jeremiah 49:13-16 describes the gathering of armies there for attack, although in actuality they are being summoned by the Lord for judgment.

The stage is set for the Second Coming of Christ, when Jesus will return with all power and glory to destroy all Gentile world powers and to rule the nations Himself. When the armies of the world see the sign of the Son of man appear in the heavens (Matt. 24:30), they will unite to fight against the Lord Himself. We will look at the results on Day 4.

In Heaven

As we leave our study on the Tribulation period and turn to Christ's return, I feel like celebrating. Heaven obviously does too! While on earth the armies are gathering and things are looking hopeless for Israel, those in heaven are singing a different tune – literally! In anticipation of Christ's victorious return and reign on earth, a Hallelujah chorus erupts (Rev. 19:1-10). The exclamation *"Hallelujah!"* means *Praise the Lord.* In his study Bible, MacArthur says it is probably angels who begin the song (v. 1) with the saints joining in later (vv. 5-6). In this chorus, several of the many reasons to praise the Lord are given. In vv. 1-4 God's deliverance or *salvation* of His people is praised, as is His *true and righteous judgment* of Babylon (and all His enemies). Next in vv. 6-8 it is for His *sovereignty* and for the *marriage of the Lamb* (vv. 7-8) that God is being praised.

In Rev. 19:7-8 we are told that *the marriage of the Lamb has come and His bride has made herself ready*. Hebrew tradition tells us that there were three phases to a Hebrew wedding. The preliminary stage began when a husband and wife were betrothed by their parents. This engagement period lasted around a year. Then at a time signaled by the groom's father, the groom would return for his bride and take her to his Father's house. The second stage was the presentation, a time of festivities leading up to the presentation of the bride to the groom. The third and final stage of the marriage was the ceremony itself. Following the ceremony, a great celebratory supper, or feast, was given by the father of the groom.

The church was betrothed to Christ in eternity past (II Cor. 11:2) and presented to Christ at the Rapture (John 14:3). The bride is dressed in *bright and clean linen* at the Judgment Seat of Christ (Eph. 5:25-27) and will proceed with her groom to heaven for the presentation festivities which take place during the time of the Tribulation. Many scholars believe that the ceremony itself will also occur in heaven, as the verb "has come" used in Rev. 19:7-8 indicates that the ceremony has occurred prior to Christ's return. As the Bride of Christ, the Church will then accompany her groom in His descent to earth, where the wedding supper of the Lamb will begin the Millennial Kingdom (some see it as lasting the entire 1000 years).

The fourth of seven beatitudes in Revelation is given in Rev. 19:9: *Blessed are those who are invited to the marriage supper of the Lamb*. The invited guests are the glorified Old Testament and Tribulation saints, along with believers who survive the Tribulation and enter the Millennial Kingdom in natural bodies. Just as God in His sovereignty chose the Israelites to be His chosen people, he also chose the Church to be the bride of Christ. In the new heavens and earth, the "bride" will be expanded to encompass all the redeemed from all the ages (Rev. 21:1-2).[4]

---

1. J. Dwight Pentecost, Things to Come, p. 340.
2. Ibid., pp. 342-343.
3. John F. Walvoord, Major Bible Prophecies, p. 356.
4. John MacArthur, MacArthur New Testament Commentary: Revelation 12-22, p. 204.

"Back to the Future"
End Times Prophecy, from Genesis to Revelation
Lesson 16 - The Return of Christ

*** DAY 2: National Salvation of Israel

1. What was John the Baptist's message to the Israelites at Christ's first coming? Matt. 3:2

2. How did the nation of Israel respond to their Messiah at His first coming? Acts 2:22-23

3. According to God's pre-determined plan, what was the result of Israel's rejection of the Messiah at His first coming? Romans 11:15, 25

4. In Matt. 23:37-39 Jesus laments over Jerusalem during at the end of His public ministry. What does He say must happen before He will come to Jerusalem again?

5. Old Testament conditions for entering the Millennial Kingdom
   a. In Lev. 26:39-42 what condition must any scattered generation of Israel meet before God would return them to their land promised in the Abrahamic covenant?

   b. Read Jer. 3:11-18. What does God say Israel must do before they can enter the Millennial Kingdom? vv.13-14

   c. What does Hosea 5:15 state must happen before Christ will return to them?

6. Return of Israel to her Messiah (Zech. 12:10-14; Zech. 13)
   a. What does the house of Israel do as they see Christ return? Also Matt. 24:30

   b. What enables them to turn to the Lord?

   c. Describes what happens in Zech. 13:1-2. Read also Ezekiel 36:24-28.

   d. What else does Zech. 13:9 say that those of Israel do?

   e. Which Old Testament covenant, that we earlier studied, will be fulfilled at this time?

7. Paul writes of this time in Romans 11:25-27. What does he say of Israel? v. 26

ON A PERSONAL NOTE . . .
- Isaiah 53 has been seen as Israel's prayer of confession for rejecting their Messiah, the Suffering Servant. Read over the entire chapter but take particular notice of verse 6 which talks of straying sheep that turn to their own way. Ask God to show you an area of your life where you are straying – doing things your own way, based on your own understanding, according to what you think is right. Will you confess your sin in prayer, asking God to forgive you and supernaturally enable you to do things according to His Word and His will? While your salvation is sure, God's umbrella of protection and blessing is conditional on obedience to His commands.

"Back to the Future"
End Times Prophecy, from Genesis to Revelation
Lesson 16 - The Return of Christ

REVIEW:
John the Baptist's message to the nation of Israel was not only that they should repent, but also that with the Messiah in their midst, the kingdom was at hand for their taking. However we saw that by the time of Matthew 13, the nation as a whole had rejected both the Messiah and the Kingdom He was offering. After the coming of the Holy Spirit at Pentecost, Peter reminded his fellow Israelites of this fact. Peter also indicated that this was according to God's predetermined plan and foreknowledge. Later in Romans 11, Paul explains that as result of Israel's rejection of their Messiah, the reconciliation of the world was made possible. Israel's rejection will continue until the complete number of elect Gentiles have been saved. From the time of the Rapture until Christ's Second Coming, God will again turn His attention to the salvation of the Jews. At that time, those natural branches who do not continue in their unbelief will be grafted into the kingdom (Rom. 11:23-24).

Jesus foresaw the time when the nation of Israel would turn to their Messiah when He issued his lament over Jerusalem in Matthew 23:37-39. As He comes to the end of his public ministry and is withdrawing from Jerusalem, Jesus issued this prophetic statement: "For I say to you, from now on you will not see Me until you say, '*Blessed is He who comes in the name of the Lord!*'"

Old Testament scriptures also point to this time. We saw in the Abrahamic Covenant that the promise of their land was an unconditional promise. Israel holds the title to the land eternally. However, the enjoyment of the land by a given generation is dependent on their obedience. In Leviticus 23:33, God promises to scatter any disobedient generation from the land and to desolate the land. Later in Leviticus 23:39-42, God tells Israel that when a generation later confesses both their iniquity and the iniquity of their forefathers, He will remember His covenant with Abraham, Isaac, and Jacob and restore them to the land. We see this cycle occur over and over in the book of Judges.

In Jeremiah 3:13-18, the Lord makes it clear that Israel must acknowledge her iniquity and return to Him before entering the Kingdom. Hosea 5:15 reiterates this thought saying that Israel must acknowledge her guilt and seek His face. In particular, Israel must confess her rejection and crucifixion of the Messiah at His first coming. The nation must turn to the risen Christ as their Lord and Savior before they can enter into His kingdom.

Today we see Israel partially restored to the land, but they are as Ezekiel describes – dead, dry bones. It will not be until the return of Christ that the nation as a whole will recognize Christ as their Messiah and receive God's breath of life (Eze. 37:9). It is then that a regenerated Israel will be gathered and brought into the land (Eze. 37:12) for the Millennial Kingdom.

We know that during the Tribulation many will come to their Messiah as a result of the judgments, the evangelism of the 144,000, the ministry of the two prophets, and the proclamations of angels flying in midair. However, it is at Christ's Second Coming that the greatest revival in the history of the mankind will occur. We saw yesterday that as the nations see the sign of the Son of Man appear in the sky, all the nations mourn. Unbelievers will mourn as they realize the certainty of their fate, but Israel will mourn out of repentance. At Christ's return, not only is the nation of Israel saved from her enemies, but she is saved from her sins as well.

Just as with anyone's salvation, Israel's salvation is a supernatural work of God. Zechariah 12:10 tells us that God will pour out His Spirit of grace and supplication, removing their spiritual blindness as they see Christ for Who He is – their promised Messiah. As they see Him returning as King of Kings and Lord of Lords, *all* the families of Israel will grieve and bitterly weep as one would mourn over a firstborn child. Zechariah 13:1-2 tells us that it is then that the Lord opens a fountain of forgiveness for Israel, cleansing and purifying both the people and their land. It is to this time that Paul points when he writes in Romans 11:26-27, "All Israel will be saved."

We must remember that God is saving Israel, not because of anything they have done, but because of the promises He made to Abraham and his descendants. It is the New Covenant of Jeremiah 31:34-35, based on the death of Christ, which specifically promises the salvation of

"Back to the Future"
End Times Prophecy, from Genesis to Revelation
Lesson 16 - The Return of Christ

national Israel. The judgments and the persecution of the Tribulation will have caused many of God's people to repent, but it is now at the Second Coming of Christ that many, many more have their spiritual eyes opened and gladly turn to their Messiah as Lord and Savior. The 1/3 of Israel who survive the Tribulation (Joel 3:12-13) will enter the Millennial Kingdom under the New Covenant.

"Back to the Future"
End Times Prophecy, from Genesis to Revelation
Lesson 16 - The Return of Christ

*** DAY 3: Christ's Glorious Appearing, Return to Earth

1. In Acts 1:9-11, what do the two angels say about Christ's return?

2. What do we also learn about Christ's Second Coming from Matthew 24:27 and Rev. 1:7?

3. Matthew 24:29-31 records Jesus' words concerning His return.
   a. What cataclysmic things occur at the end of the Tribulation? v. 29

   b. What causes the tribes of the earth to mourn? Why do you think they mourn? v. 30

   c. How is the Coming of Christ described? v. 30

   d. What does Jesus send the angels to do? v. 31

4. Read Rev. 19:11-16.
   a. On what is Christ riding?

   b. What is He called?

   c. What is His first order of business?

   d. Describe His appearance.

   e. What is His title?

   f. Who is accompanying Christ; how are they described?

   g. What is coming from His mouth?

   h. What name is written on His robe and on His thigh?

ON A PERSONAL NOTE . . .
- What emotions does talk of Christ's return strike in your heart – fear and mourning or joy and anticipation? Why? If it is the first set of emotions, please read Appendix One. Share your thoughts on Christ's return with a friend this week.

- What strikes you most about the description of Christ at His return? Worship Christ your King today.

"Back to the Future"
End Times Prophecy, from Genesis to Revelation
Lesson 16 - The Return of Christ

REVIEW:
Today we looked at several passages that describe the return of Christ. First we see in Acts 1:9-11 that after Jesus' ascension the angels told the disciples that Jesus would return in the same way that He had gone. He will return bodily and in the clouds with all power and glory (Matt. 24:30; 25:31; 26:64; Acts 1:9-11). Unlike the time of the Rapture however, we are told in Matthew 24:27 and Rev. 1:7 *every eye* will see His return.

In Matthew 24:29-31 Christ describes signs of His return. IMMEDIATELY after the Tribulation, the sun and moon will be completely darkened, and other cataclysmic events will occur in the heavens. The sign of the Son of Man will appear in the sky, and all the nations will mourn. Israel will realize that it was truly their Messiah that they have crucified and rejected, while unbelievers of all nations will realize that that they face immediate judgment. Christ will then come on the clouds of the sky with great power and glory, sending His angels to gather *His elect* from heaven and earth.

Revelation 19:11-16 gives us the most dramatic description of Christ at His return. The following insights on this passage are taken from the notes in The MacArthur Study Bible and from The Bible Knowledge Commentary by Walvoord and Zuck.

In Revelation 19:11-16 John records prophetically the Second Coming of Christ, as seen in his vision. What a sight it will be! As heaven was opened, John saw Christ sitting on a white horse. In John's day, it was customary for a victorious Roman general to parade on the Via Sacra, a main thoroughfare of Rome. The white horse was a symbol of Christ's triumph over the world's forces of evil, the antichrist, and Satan himself. How different this picture is from Jesus' humble entry into Jerusalem on a colt at His first coming.

Jesus is rightly called "Faithful and True," and true to His Word, He will return to earth in righteousness to judge and wage war. His eyes are "a flame of fire," indicating His piercing judgment of sin; and "on His head are many diadems," representing His supreme right to rule. John sees a name written on Him but is unable to comprehend it, suggesting that even to glorified saints Christ is unable to fully be described or explained. Christ is "clothed with a robe dipped in blood." The blood represents the battles Christ has already won against sin, death, and Satan and is the blood of His enemies. And Christ's title is the "Word of God" (John also uses this title for Jesus in John 1:1). Jesus is the image of the invisible God and the full revelation from God.

Accompanying Christ are the armies of heaven, "clothed in fine linen, white and clean," which consist of the Church (Rev. 19:8), tribulation saints (Rev. 7:13), OT believers (Jude 14, Daniel 12:1,2), and angels (Matt. 25:31). The "armies" do not return to fight, but to reign with Christ during the Millennial Kingdom. Out of Christ's mouth comes a sharp sword with which He will strike down the nations. The word for sword, *rhomphaia,* references an unusually long sword sometimes used as a spear and indicates a piercing action. That the sword comes out of Christ's mouth shows that Christ will win His battles with the power of His Word. He will rule with a "rod of iron," indicating that Christ will rule with swift, righteous judgment. Christ is seen as "treading the wine press of the fierce wrath of God," pointing toward the awfulness of the coming judgments. And the title on His robe and thigh, "KING OF KINGS AND LORD OF LORDS," underscores Christ's absolute sovereignty over all human rulers.

Concerning the significance of this passage in Revelation, John Walvoord writes in Major Bible Prophecies, p. 373, "The main theme of Revelation is the revelation of the glory of Christ at His second coming. The high point of the book is chapter 19. All preceding chapters lead up to it; all the following chapters indicate the events that will follow His revelation. Accordingly, the display of His glory, as revealed in Rev. 19, is in keeping with all the other information we have concerning the Second Coming of Christ."

"Back to the Future"
End Times Prophecy, from Genesis to Revelation
Lesson 16 - The Return of Christ

*** DAY 4: Earth's Armies Destroyed by Christ

Judgment on the Beast, His False Prophet, and His Armies: (Rev. 19:17-21)
1. Why does the angel in the sun summon the birds?

2. Who does John next see? (We studied this on Day 2.)

3. Who is seized and where are they thrown?

4. What happens to the armies of the beast?

A Closer Look
5. Slaughter at Bozrah
   a. Read Jeremiah 49:14-17; 20-22. What phrase in v. 14 associates this with Armageddon? What happens in vv. 20-22?

   b. Turn to Micah 2:12-13 which describes the Lord's rescue of His remnant. What do we see the Lord doing in this passage?

   c. What does Is. 34:6 say about Christ's victory here?

   d. In Is. 63:1-3 Christ is approaching the area of Jerusalem from Bozrah. Describe His garments; how did they get that way? (Compare to imagery in Rev. 14:20, 19:15.)

6. The Winepress in the Valley of Jehoshaphat: (Joel 3:11-14)
   a. What phrase connects this passage with the Battle of Armageddon? v. 12

   b. In v. 13 what imagery again describes the results of the fighting? Compare with Rev 14:14-20.

   c. Describe the Lord's victory over Jerusalem's enemies. Zech 14:12-15

7. Ascent to the Mount of Olives: (Zech. 14)
   a. As Christ stands victoriously on the Mount of Olives, what happens? v. 4

   b. What will the remnant of God's people then do? v. 5

   c. What happens to the light of the sun, moon, and stars in v. 6? So where do you suppose the light in v. 7b originates? (See Is. 60:19-20.)

   d. Describe the waters flowing out of Jerusalem. v. 8

   e. Describe the resulting topography. v. 10

"Back to the Future"
End Times Prophecy, from Genesis to Revelation
Lesson 16 - The Return of Christ

ON A PERSONAL NOTE . . .

- Rev. 19:15, 21 tells us that Jesus slew His enemies with the sword coming from His mouth – His powerful Word. We too have power to overcome temptation and evil by the power of Christ's Word. What other weapons do we try to use – to no avail? What are some specific ways that you use to store God's Word in your heart? How can renew your efforts in this area.

- Christ's presence resulted in physical changes to the earth. What changes have resulted from His presence in your life?

"Back to the Future"
End Times Prophecy, from Genesis to Revelation
Lesson 16 - The Return of Christ

REVIEW:
Revelation 19:17-21 summarizes Christ's victory over His enemies at His return. In this passage John first sees and hears an angel in the sun calling for all the birds of the air to gather for the great supper of God – to eat the flesh of all who are slain by the Lord. God proclaims victory before the battle even begins. Note that the *great supper of God* is distinct from the *marriage supper of the Lamb* referred to in Rev. 19:9.

The beast and the armies of the world are no match for Christ. The beast and the false prophet are first seized and thrown alive into the lake of fire (Rev. 19:20). Then the armies themselves will all be killed by Christ's sword – His piercing, spoken Word (Rev. 19:21).

We saw earlier that the Battle of Armageddon will not be a single battle, but a campaign. On the very day of Christ's return there will be forces gathered in Bozrah in Edom (where Petra is located), twenty miles southeast of the southern tip of the Dead Sea (Jeremiah 49:13-16) and in the valley of Jehoshaphat (Joel 3:2,9-11). Jerusalem will be under siege (Zech. 12:1-3, 14:1-2; Micah 4:11-13). Viewing these three areas of the war together, we see a gruesome picture of unbelievable carnage encompassing the entire land from Mediggo in the north, Jerusalem in the center, and Edom in the southeast (about 140 miles).[5]

Many believe Christ initially returns to the Mount of Olives and proceeds from there. Others see Christ first returning to Bozrah to free the believing remnant at Petra, then making his way from Bozrah to the Valley of Jehoshaphat outside of Jerusalem, and finally ascending victoriously upon the Mount of Olives. Although both viewpoints are plausible, our discussion will follow the latter.

Scriptures gives us vivid imagery of Christ's judgment on the armies at Bozrah in Edom (Jeremiah 49:20-22). Bozrah is the Hebrew name for the city today known by its Greek name of Petra. After capturing Jerusalem, we can imagine that the antichrist's armies have turned their animosity on the remnant of believers in Petra (Bozrah) and there have assembled troops in preparation for attack. It only makes sense to me that Christ would first return to Bozrah, swooping in like an eagle (Jeremiah 40:20-22), to rescue His faithful remnant, the sheep of His flock.

Interestingly, the Hebrew word Bozrah means "sheepfold." An ancient sheepfold had a narrow entrance which opened into a larger circular area. The sheep would be counted as they entered the narrow entrance and then have the freedom to move around within the sheepfold.

Arnold Fruchtenbaum writes, "That is exactly what Bozrah looks like. The only way into this city is by a very narrow passageway which extends for about 1 ¼ miles in length. Once you are through this narrow passageway, which can be defended by only two men against a whole army, you are inside a huge, circular area. It is a place that is 'easily defended'; it is within the wilderness of the area of Jordan; it is also in the mountain ranges of Mount Seir. It is part of the ancient territory known as Edom or modern-day, southern Jordan."[6]

Micah 2:12-13 records the rescue of the believing remnant in Petra from their sheepfold. Christ is the *breaker* who goes before them breaking out of the gate and their *king . . . the LORD at their head.* Isaiah 34:6 refers to this victory as *a sacrifice in Bozra, a slaughter in the land of Edom.*

From Bozrah Christ will victoriously lead His remnant back towards Jerusalem and the Valley of Jehoshaphat, overthrowing His enemies throughout the land. Isaiah 63:1-3 graphically describes Christ's apparel as he approaches from Bozrah. They are *majestic* garments of *glowing colors*, stained *red, like the one who treads in a wine trough*. We also see that Jesus has tread *the wine trough alone*, trampling His enemies *in His wrath* and staining His garments with their *lifeblood*.

Remember that Jerusalem has been captured, with half of the people exiled. Armies are encamped outside in the Valley of Jehoshaphat. Rev. 14:20 tells us that *the wine press was trodden outside the city*, indicating that there is no fighting within Jerusalem itself. By now the Jews left in Jerusalem have repented, mourning at Christ's return. The Lord now spares His children from further carnage. Joel 3:13 describes Christ's victory over the armies of the nations

"Back to the Future"
End Times Prophecy, from Genesis to Revelation
Lesson 16 - The Return of Christ

in the Valley of Jehoshaphat using two familiar images. There Christ will *put in the sickle, for the harvest is ripe* and also *tread, for the wine press is full; the vats overflow for their wickedness is great.* This valley is appropriately named as the Hebrew name Jehoshaphat means "Yahweh judges." It is probably at this time that the antichrist himself is slain (Hab. 3:13; II Thess. 2:8).

Zechariah 14:12-15 also describes the Lord's victory at Jerusalem. The Lord will strike the peoples who have gone to war against Jerusalem with a great plague. The plague will also strike all the animals in their camps. The resulting confusion and panic of the world's armies causes them to turn on each other. God's people, supernaturally empowered, will gather the wealth of all the surrounding nations - all their gold, silver, and garments.

After the Lord's victory over the nations (Zech. 14:3) in the Valley of Jehoshaphat, Zechariah 14:4-11 depicts Christ standing on the Mount of Olives in victory. At this time the Mount of Olives will split in the middle, with half of the mountain moving north and half of the mountain moving south. This no doubt is in connection with the great earthquake of the 7th and final bowl judgment that splits Jerusalem into three parts (Rev. 16:16-19). The newly created valley, running from Jerusalem in the west to an unknown location called Azel in the east, will provide the Israelites in Jerusalem a route of escape from the earthquake (Zech. 14:5a). It is there that the Lord himself with all His holy ones will come to them (Zech. 14:5b).

Zechariah 14:6-8 reveals cataclysmic changes that occur at that time. As the Jews are fleeing through this valley, light will dwindle to complete darkness. But by evening, there will be light, provided by the glory of Christ (Is. 60:19-20).

A spring of living water will open up in Jerusalem and will flow eastward to the Dead Sea and westward to the Mediterranean. It will not dry up in the summer as many streams do in that area, but will flow all year and promote profuse fertility and vegetation (Isaiah 35:1-3, 6-7). Currently Jerusalem is not higher than some of its surrounding areas, but Zechariah 14:10 tells us that topographical changes caused by the great earthquake will result in the whole land of Judah being miraculously leveled to a low plain, except for the city of Jerusalem which will rise above all.

Whew! We have looked at a lot today. And, as mentioned earlier, the sequence of these events is up for debate. But the bottom line is that in His good and perfect timing our Sovereign, Omnipotent Lord, as from eternity past to eternity future, *always* prevails against evil.

Let's sum up the events we have studied so far this week.
- Christ returns to earth with the angels, the glorified New Testament saints, and the souls of the Old Testament and Tribulation saints.
- The Jewish nation repents and turns to the Lord as He appears.
- Satan and his puppets prove no match for our Mighty Warrior (Ex. 15:3). The beast and the false prophet are cast alive into the lake of fire, and their evil armies killed.
- God's people at Bozrah, Jerusalem, and in Judah are physically delivered, and the Lord is in their midst.
- The topography of Jerusalem and Judah is greatly changed.

Tomorrow we will conclude our study of Christ's Coming by looking at other events that occur at this time. I hope you are as excited as I am as we as we transition from Christ's return to His rule during the Millennial Kingdom!

---

5. Charles C. Ryrie, Basic Theology, p. 555.
6. Dr. Arnold G. Fruchtenbaum, "The Campaign of Armageddon," http://www.raptureready.com/rr-armageddon.html.

"Back to the Future"
End Times Prophecy, from Genesis to Revelation
Lesson 16 - The Return of Christ

*** DAY 5: Events Associated with Christ's Return

1. Interval of 45 days: (Dan. 12:11-12)
   An interval of time is given between the end of the Tribulation and the beginning of the Millennial Kingdom.
   a. In v. 11 how many days are specified following the midpoint of the Tribulation?

   b. How many days will the blessed wait?

2. Judgment on Satan: (Rev. 20:1-3)
   a. Who comes down from heaven and what is he holding?

   b. What two things does the angel first do?

   c. After Satan is thrown in the Abyss, what does the angel do? Why?

3. Resurrection of Tribulation Martyrs: (Rev. 20:4)
   a. What phrases describes the Tribulation saints?

   b. What happens to them at this point?

4. Resurrection of the OT Saints: (Dan. 12:1-2, Isaiah 26:19-21)
   a. To whom is the term "your people" referring?

   b. In addition to the Tribulation saints, who else must be raised at this time?

   c. What phrase in Isaiah 26:19 indicates it will be a bodily resurrection?

5. Judgment of Living Israelites: (Eze. 20:33-38)
   a. From vv. 33-34, when can we deduce this judgment will take place?

   b. How does the Lord describe this judgment? v. 35

   c. Can you guess what "pass under the rod" would mean to an Israelite?

   d. To what covenant is the Lord referring?

   e. Who is purged at this time?

   f. Looking again at Romans 11:26a, what is the result?

6. Judgment of Living Gentiles – Sheep / Goat Judgment: (Matt. 25:31-46)
   a. Where do we find Christ in this passage; who is gathered before Him? vv. 31-32

   b. Into what two groups does Christ separate them? v. 33

   c. What determines which group one is put? vv. 35-40, 42-45

   d. What does Christ invite the sheep, those on His right, to do? What does He call them? v. 34

   e. What does Christ say to the goats, those on His left? What does He call them? v. 41

   f. How long will their punishment last? v. 46

"Back to the Future"
End Times Prophecy, from Genesis to Revelation
Lesson 16 - The Return of Christ

ON A PERSONAL NOTE . . .

- As always, one's works during the Tribulation will not earn one's salvation but will give evidence of one's salvation. In the sheep / goat judgment of the Gentiles at the end of the Tribulation, it is one's treatment of God's people that is evaluated. If God were to evaluate your life today, what evidences would He see of your salvation? What evidences would be found of your love and care for *God's people*?

- We must be careful not to judge others but to leave all judgment to God. Read James 4:11-12. Confess any judgmental thoughts or attitudes that the Lord brings to mind and then spend time worshiping Him as the Righteous Judge of all.

"Back to the Future"
End Times Prophecy, from Genesis to Revelation
Lesson 16 - The Return of Christ

REVIEW:
We have seen that each half of the Tribulation will last *1260 days*, with the return of Christ marking the end of the second half. Interestingly enough, we find an interval of days specified in Daniel 12:11-12 which occur between Christ's return and the beginning of the Millennial Kingdom. In v. 11 we see that a time of *1290 days* (30 extra days) is given from the time that the antichrist abolishes regular sacrifices and sets up the abomination of desolation in the temple. Furthermore, he who waits till the end of *1335 days* (45 more days) is considered *blessed*.

What is this all about? Evidently this 75 day interval is a time of preparation for the Millennial Kingdom, when all who enter will be *blessed* beyond our comprehension. This could include the rewarding of resurrected OT and Tribulation saints, judgment of the living, preparation for the Millennial Temple and those who will serve in it, assignments of rule in the Kingdom, and renovation of the earth that has been destroyed. As the first 30 days seem to relate to the temple, some see this as the time that the Millennial Temple is set up and prepared for use.[7] MacArthur sees the first 30 days possibly allowing for the judgment of the living with the 45 days allowing for transition between "Israel's time of being shattered and God's setting up of His kingdom."[8]

Revelation 20:1-6 describes some of the events that occur after Christ's Return and before the Kingdom begins. First we see Satan (and no doubt his demonic hosts as well) removed from the sphere of Christ's earthly reign. In vv. 1-3 we first see that Satan will be bound during Christ's 1000 year reign. We are not given the identity of the angel that binds Satan, though some speculate that it is Michael the archangel. In any event, he seizes and secures Satan without a struggle and casts him into the *abyss.* We have seen that the abyss is a place of temporary incarceration for the most evil of all demons. It is a place where demons fear to be sent (Luke 8:31). The angel then seals the abyss, ensuring that Satan cannot influence the world in any way during Christ's reign.

Dwight Pentecost comments that the Millennial Kingdom is not only the age in which divine righteousness is displayed, but it is also the time of God's final test of humanity under the most ideal circumstances (we will see the results of this test later). Both the full manifestation of righteousness and the test of humanity require Satan to be removed from the sphere.[9]

Accompanying Christ at His return are the angels, glorified New Testament saints (the Bride of Christ), and the spirits of the Old Testament and Tribulation saints. At this time the Old Testament and Tribulation saints are resurrected and receive their glorified bodies. Daniel 12:2 describes the resurrection of the Old Testament saints while Rev. 20:4 describes the resurrection of the Tribulation saints.

This marks the completion of the *first resurrection,* or resurrection of the righteous, saved individuals from the beginning of time till now. Rev. 20:5-6 tells us that those of the first resurrection (the glorified NT, OT, and Trib saints) will be *priests of God and of Christ* and *will reign with Him* during the Millennial Kingdom. The interaction between glorified saints and those living in natural bodies during the Millennial Kingdom is not described in scripture, but it does not pose a problem – our resurrected Lord interacted with his disciples before ascending to heaven.

According to Rev. 20:5, *the rest of the dead,* unbelievers of all times whose spirits are in Hades and bodies are still in the grave at this time, will not be resurrected until the end of the Millennial Kingdom. At their resurrection, known as the *second resurrection*, unbelievers will be judged at the Great White Throne before being sent to their eternal destruction in the Lake of Fire.

So, who will enter the Millennial Kingdom in their natural bodies? At this time all who have survived the Tribulation and Christ's return will individually appear before Christ. Those judged righteous will enter the Millennial Kingdom in their natural bodies, while the unrighteous will be purged or killed.

We saw Israel, as a nation, repent and turn to the Lord at His return - the political and religious leaders and the majority of the people. However personal salvation is always an individual

"Back to the Future"
End Times Prophecy, from Genesis to Revelation
Lesson 16 - The Return of Christ

decision. There will still be those of Israel who refuse to turn from their rebellion. We find a prophetic description of the *judgment of living Israelites* in Ezekiel 20:36-38. Living Israelites will all be gathered to a face to face judgment with the LORD. God, their Great Shepherd, uses the picture of sheep passing under their Shepherd's rod as they are allowed into the fold. Sheep in ancient days would pass under their shepherd rod to be inspected and checked for injury. Passing under the LORD's rod each individual Israelite will be judged to determine if he is worthy to enter the Millennial Kingdom. Those who have not trusted Christ will be put to death and will await in torment their judgment at Great White Throne. Therefore, at the start of the Millennial Kingdom, *all of Israel will be saved"* (Romans 11:26). Note that the parable of the Ten Virgins and the Parable of the Talents, both in Matthew 25, also illustrate this judgment.

I must point out at this time, however, that there are those who see the verses of Ezekiel 20:36-38 as referring to the entire Tribulation itself. They maintain that in contrast to national Israel, it is *every* living Israelite (the 1/3 left at the end of the Tribulation) who is saved at the Lord's Coming. Therefore, no further judgment is necessary as *all of Israel will be saved* (Romans 11:26).

Gentiles who have survived the Tribulation will also be gathered to face individual judgment (Matthew 25:31-46). Often referred to as the Sheep and Goat Judgment, Christ will separate the righteous from the unrighteous, putting the sheep (saved) on His right and the goats (unsaved) on His left. While salvation is a gift from God and not earned by works, one's good deeds are evidence of God's grace in one's life. Here, each living Gentile will be judged based on his treatment of the Israelites during the Tribulation. Those who have been kind to the Jews are saved "sheep," while those who did not come to the aid of the Jewish people are the unsaved "goats." The saved are invited to enter the kingdom. Unsaved Gentiles are also put to death, destined for the Lake of Fire.

Therefore all living believers, whether Jew or Gentile, deemed righteous at Christ's return will enter the Millennial Kingdom in their natural bodies. We can only assume that children who have not reached the age of responsibility will also enter this period and, as they grow up, face the question of whether to trust Christ.

As we leave this week's lesson, let's recap and look at who is where:

- The antichrist and the false prophet are in the Lake of Fire.
- Satan is in the abyss with his evil demons.
- The holy angels have returned with Christ.
- New Testament saints in resurrected bodies have returned with Christ to reign and serve.
- Old Testament and Tribulation saints have been resurrected to also reign and serve.
- Living believers who have survived the Tribulation and Christ's judgment enter Christ's Millennial Kingdom on earth in their natural bodies.
- The spirits of unbelievers of all time are in Hades.

Just as the first coming of Christ accomplished the major purpose of God to provide salvation, so the Second Coming of Christ will accomplish the major purpose of God to place everything in subjection to Jesus Christ as King of Kings and Lord of Lords (I Cor. 15:27). Hallelujah, Amen!

---

7. Tim Lahaye & Thomas Ice, Charting The End Times, pp. 66-67.
8. John MacArthur, The MacArthur Study Bible, NAS, pp. 1223-1224.
9. Pentecost, op. cit., p. 477.

Back to the Future"
End Times Prophecy, from Genesis to Revelation
Lesson 17 - The Millennial Kingdom: Christ's Reign on Earth

*** DAY 1: Introduction to the Kingdom

Length of Millennial Kingdom: Rev. 20:1-7
1. What does the prefix "mille" mean?

2. How many times is the number "one thousand" used in these verses? Why do you think "1000 years" is mentioned so many times in this passage?

Purposes of Kingdom
3. Theocratic Kingdom reestablished:
    a. Who was originally given dominion over the world? Gen. 1:26

    b. Since the fall of man in Eden who has had dominion over the earth? Lk. 4:6; John 12:31

    c. The theocracy of God is now reestablished through Christ (Is. 9:6-7). What will be accomplished during Christ's 1000 year reign? I Cor. 15:24-25

4. Fulfill covenant promises to Israel: Remembering the Davidic, Land, and New Covenant (all sub-covenants of the Abrahamic Covenant) draw a line from each description of the Millennial Kingdom to the sub-covenant that will be fulfilled.

    Jer. 23:5-6; 33:14-17   New Covenant
    Ezekiel 47:13-23   Davidic Covenant
    Ezekiel 11:19-20   Land Covenant

5. Show man's sinfulness and need for Christ, even with Satan bound and the world ruled by Christ:
    a. What is the spiritual condition of all who enter the kingdom in their physical bodies?

    b. However, there will be children who grow up during this period. What will be true of them? Rom. 3:23, 6:23, Rom. 10:9, 12

    c. How is the number of those who rebel at the end of the 1000 years described? Rev. 20:8-9

Heavenly Participants in the Kingdom
6. When Christ returned, who was following with Him? Rev. 19:14

7. Who is included in these armies?
    Rev. 19:7-8

    Rev. 7:13

    Dan. 12:1-2

    Matt. 25:1

8. In John 14:2-3, Jesus said He was going to prepare a place for us. Therefore, what are we as Christians seeking? Heb. 13:14

Back to the Future"
End Times Prophecy, from Genesis to Revelation
Lesson 17 - The Millennial Kingdom: Christ's Reign on Earth

9. What comforting words does Paul give us in I Thess. 4:17 concerning our eternal future?

10. What was the hope of Abraham and the OT saints as well? Hebrews 11:10, 16

11. What is the place, the eternal abode of all *overcomers* called in Rev. 3:12?

ON A PERSONAL NOTE . . .
- Satan will be bound during the Millennial Kingdom to keep from deceiving the nations. Satan knows his time is short; that is why he sends his fiery darts of deception at us. Ephesians 6:10-18 describes the armor of God. We must make it a daily habit to "put on" this strong armor every day (Remember that big, wet, Roman shield that put out the flaming darts of the enemy?). What other scriptures can you find referring to our spiritual warfare?

- This is where memorized scripture comes to our aid. Begin to add a few to memory for when you need a verse to stand on for power against the enemy. Start with the following verses to assure you of *victory over Satan and sin through Christ Jesus our Lord*.

    1 John 5:4   *For whatever is born of God overcomes the world: and this is the victory that has overcome the world—our faith.*
    1 John 4:4   *... greater is He who is in you than he who is in the world.*
    Rom. 8:37   *But in all these things we overwhelmingly conquer through Him who loved us.*

- Write a prayer of protection and victory for you and your family.

Back to the Future"
End Times Prophecy, from Genesis to Revelation
Lesson 17 - The Millennial Kingdom: Christ's Reign on Earth

REVIEW:
I know we have a difficult time realizing the fact that one day Jesus Christ will rule on planet Earth. What a great and glorious day that will be! The physical presence of Christ will bring about major changes as His rule and authority extend over the entire earth. To be a part of the whole earth worshipping Jesus as King of Kings and Lord of Lords will be magnificent indeed! I can't wait, can you!

The 1000 year reign of Christ, most commonly known as the Millennial Kingdom, is the subject of many Old and New Testament passages. The kingdom is the goal toward which all of history has been progressing since man's original fall in the garden. The phrase "thousand years" is used six times in Revelation 20:1-7. This repetition emphasizes that we must interpret this passage literally and that Christ will indeed return before the Millennium and rule over a literal kingdom here on earth for a thousand years. This view is referred to as the *premillennial* view of eschatology. During the Millennial Kingdom all authority is given to Jesus, King of Kings and Lord of Lords, and the whole world will worship God.

The majority of what we know about the Millennial Kingdom is from the Old Testament. Scriptures abound which look forward to this time, a time of fulfillment and completion. Many reasons may be given why a literal, earthly theocratic kingdom is a necessity. We will discuss three of them.

First of all, God's original intention was that the earth would be a theocratic kingdom, under His rule through Adam (Gen. 1:26-28). However when Adam sinned he became disqualified to rule. At that time, ruling authority was turned over to Satan and he has since operated as prince, or ruler, of the world. During the Millennial Kingdom, God will reestablish a theocratic rule over the earth, reigning through the King Jesus - the only one who has ever lived and died in complete obedience to His Father and is now exalted above all names.

A *second* reason for the Millennial Kingdom is that the eternal covenants of God with Israel must be fulfilled. Isaiah 55:11 says, "So will My word be which goes forth from My mouth; It will not return to Me empty, without accomplishing what I desire." During the Millennium, all of the *land*, *seed*, and *blessing* promises of the Abrahamic Covenant and its subcovenants will be fulfilled.

The promises in the *Land* covenant concerning Israel's possession of the land are fulfilled in the Millennial Age. Israel will be re-gathered from worldwide dispersion and living in her land. Having seen the judgment of all her enemies, she will be living in peace and prosperity. The boundaries and the division of the land during the kingdom are found in Eze. 47:13-48:9. The land will stretch north from near Damascus south to the River of Egypt, with the Jordan River as its eastern border and the Mediterranean as its western border. For the first time in the history of mankind, the Israelites will have *full* possession of the land given to them by God in Genesis.

The promises of the Davidic covenant concerning the *seed* will be fulfilled by Messiah in the Millennial Age (Jer. 23:5-6; 33:14-17). As David's legal and physical heir, Jesus will reign as king on David's Throne over the nation of Israel. Remember that in II Samuel 7:16 God promised David that his *house*, his *kingdom*, and his *throne* would last forever.

Last, but certainly not the least, Israel will experience all the *blessings* of the New Covenant. They will be converted and regenerated, receiving both forgiveness and a new heart (Eze. 11:19-20). God will "tabernacle with them," Christ will rule over them, and they will be taught by the indwelling Holy Spirit. As with Christians now, all of this is made possible only through the blood of Christ. In addition to the spiritual blessings Israel will receive, they will also be the recipient of many material blessings. As the glorious center of Christ's reign, Israel will be elevated above the nations, with God's chosen people receiving a double portion of God's blessings. We learn from Isaiah 61:5-7 that the Israelites, known as priests and ministers of the Lord, will have abundant wealth and be served by other peoples of the world. (See Is. 60:5.)

The *third* purpose for the Millennial Kingdom is that it will serve as the final test of fallen man. Although initially all who enter the Millennial Kingdom are saved, many generations will be born

Back to the Future"
End Times Prophecy, from Genesis to Revelation
Lesson 17 - The Millennial Kingdom: Christ's Reign on Earth

who need the saving grace of Christ. During this time Christ will be ruling and providing for one's every need and Satan will be bound in the Abyss. Man will be free from the temptations of the world and of the devil. Yet the rebellion of man at the end of the 1000 years demonstrates that fallen man is corrupt (sins of the flesh) and worthy of all judgment. Man is without excuse and helpless to save himself. Salvation is *always* a gift of God received through faith in Christ alone (Eph. 2:8-9).

There are varying opinions about where Christ, the angels, and the glorified saints will reside during the Millennial Kingdom. While some see the Old Testament and Tribulation saints living on earth during this time, many scholars see the glorified Old Testament, New Testament, and Tribulation saints all living together with Christ and the angels in the New Jerusalem described in Rev. 21. In this second camp, some see the New Jerusalem still in heaven, some see it hovering over the earth during the Millennial Kingdom, and some see it actually on the earth during the 1000 years. Regardless of which view is correct, we are assured in I Thess. 4:17 that from the time we go to be with the Lord at the time of the Rapture we will *always be with the Lord*. That's all the information I need to know!

As we continue this week's lesson we will see that Jesus' 1000 year reign brings righteousness to a sinful world, peace to a war-torn world, and prosperity to an economically-failed world. The Millennial Kingdom will see new spiritual and social life among God's people. And the earth, much devastated by the judgments of the Tribulation, will be renovated for God's glory.

Back to the Future"
End Times Prophecy, from Genesis to Revelation
Lesson 17 - The Millennial Kingdom: Christ's Reign on Earth

*** DAY 2: Government during the Kingdom

1. Look back at Dan. 7:13-14. What promise to Christ is made in Daniel's vision?

2. Is. 9:6-7
   a. By what names will Christ be called?

   b. Although only on this present earth for 1000 years, how long will His kingdom last?

   c. Christ will rule from whose throne? Where? (See Jer. 3:17.)

3. Jer. 23:5-8; 33:14-17 shows Christ ruling over Israel from the throne of David.
   a. What title is given to Christ?

   b. What characteristic of Christ's reign goes hand in hand with justice?

   c. What two kingdoms will be reunited? (See also Eze. 37:15-22.)

4. Read Is. 2:3-4 and the verses in parentheses which describe Christ's universal rule.
   a. From what city and what mountain will Christ rule? (Is. 24:23; Micah 4:1-2)

   b. What is the extent of His kingdom? (Zech. 9:10)

   c. What phrases indicate that Christ' reign will be one of justice? (Is. 42:1-4; Micah 4:3)

   d. What phrases indicate that Christ's reign will be one of peace? (Zech. 9:10; Micah 4:3-4)

5. Read Is. 11:1-4.
   a. We see all parts of the Trinity ruling as the *Spirit* of the *Lord* will rest upon *Christ*. List the facets of God's Spirit which will enable Christ to rule righteously and fairly.

   b. We also see that Christ will rule in complete sovereignty and power. Verse 4 refers to the rod of His mouth - His Word. How is this rod described in Ps. 2:9 and Rev. 19:15?

   c. What does Is. 11:4 say will happen to the wicked – those who outwardly rebel against Christ, His rule, and His law?

6. Glorified Saints will rule with Christ.
   a. What resurrected OT saint may have rule under Christ over all of Israel? Eze. 34:22-24; 37:24-25; and Jer. 30:9

   b. Who will have authority over the twelve tribes of Israel? Matthew 19:28; Luke 22:30

   c. Who else will reign with Christ in His Kingdom? 1 Cor. 6:2-3; II Tim. 2:12; Rev. 2:26

ON A PERSONAL NOTE . . .
- Visualize yourself reigning with Christ over the world and angels? What will it be like?

- Although Satan is *ruler of this world* (John 12:31) for now, Christians are called in Col. 3:15 to *let the peace of Christ rule in our hearts*. Reflect on some of God's attributes that allow us to do this? Thank Him for His peace that passes all understanding.

Back to the Future"
End Times Prophecy, from Genesis to Revelation
Lesson 17 - The Millennial Kingdom: Christ's Reign on Earth

REVIEW:
In Daniel 7, Daniel is first given a vision of four beasts representing the four Gentile empires that would dominate the world from his time onward throughout history: Babylon, Medo-Persia, Greece, and Rome (including the revived Roman empire ruled by the antichrist). Daniel's vision then transfers to heaven where he sees the Ancient of Days on his throne. As Daniel watches, the final beast, the kingdom of the antichrist, is slain and Jesus, the Son of Man, is presented with dominion and reign over the entire world. This prophecy is now fulfilled as Christ begins His rule from the throne of David, not only over Israel but over the entire world. His kingdom on earth will prevail 1000 years before merging into His eternal kingdom in the new heavens and earth. As supreme and sovereign ruler, He will be called *Wonderful Counselor, Mighty God, Eternal Father, Prince of Peace* (Is. 9:6-7).

As the Righteous Branch of David, Christ will rule from Mt. Zion and Jerusalem. Isaiah 2:3 says, *"For the law will go forth from Zion and the word of the Lord from Jerusalem."* He will rule over a reunited Israel (the northern and the southern kingdoms) and over all the nations of the earth with righteousness, justice and peace. As there will be no more war, instruments of war will be used as agricultural tools. King Jesus will reign with the fullness of God's Spirit -*wisdom, understanding, counsel, strength, knowledge, and fear of the Lord.* And he will rule with absolute power and authority (rod of iron). Any rebellion against Him or His word will lead to death.

Now, let's look at the phrase, "King of kings and Lord of lords" (Rev. 19:16). The plural of kings and lords indicates that there will be subordinate rulers. Isaiah 32:1 states, *"Behold a king shall reign in righteousness, and princes shall rule in judgment."* Ezekiel 45:8-9 shares, *"My princes shall no longer oppress My people, but they shall give the rest of the land to the house of Israel according to their tribes."* Zech. 3:7 states, *"thou shall also judge my house (Israel)"* and Is.1:26 says, *"And I will restore thy judges as at the first, and thy counselors as at the beginning . . . ."*

It is interesting to note that some interpret verses in Ezekiel and Jeremiah to say that resurrected King David will be ruling under Christ's authority as prince over the entire nation of Israel. Others see the references to *David* ruling as simply referring to Christ, the *Son of David*.[1]

Scripture is clear that the resurrected saints of all times will also rule under Christ's authority during the Millennial Kingdom. Revelation 2:26 says that *all who overcome and remain faithful to the end* will be given authority over the nations. I Corinthians 6:2-3 indicates that we will not only have authority over the world but over angels as well. The parable in Luke 19:11-27, which says some may rule over ten cities and others over five, indicates that the scope of our authority will be in proportion to our faithfulness during this life. In Matt. 19:28, Jesus reveals to Peter that the twelve disciples will specifically have authority over the twelve tribes of Israel. Perhaps it will be New Testament saints who will have rule over Gentile nations of the earth.

The interaction between glorified saints and those living in natural bodies is not described in scripture, but it does not pose a problem as our resurrected Lord interacted with his disciples before ascending to heaven.

William R. Newell offers the following summary in his writing, The Book of the Revelation, p318:
> "The thousand year reign is the direct administration of divine government on earth for one thousand years by our Lord and His saints. Its earthly center will be Jerusalem and the nation Israel, though Christ and His saints will rule in heavenly resurrection bodies in the New Jerusalem and will take the place now occupied by angels (Hebrews 2:5-8) . . . ."

II Timothy encourages us by saying, "If we endure with him we will also reign with him. It is an overwhelming thought to be ruling with Christ! I don't think our human minds can fully comprehend it. In our natural bodies, we seem so inadequate. But that is part of our glorious inheritance in Christ. What a privilege it will be to rule with Christ during this unprecedented time of righteousness, peace, and joy.

---

1. J. Dwight Pentecost, Things to Come, pp. 498- 501.

Back to the Future"
End Times Prophecy, from Genesis to Revelation
Lesson 17 - The Millennial Kingdom: Christ's Reign on Earth

*** DAY 3: Changes during the Kingdom

1. Removal of the curse for both animal and plant life: Read these verses and record how nature will cooperate with man.
   a. Is. 11:6-9

   b. Is. 30:23-26

   c. Jer. 31:12

2. Removal of sickness and deformity: Discover what these verses teach,
   a. Is. 33:24

   b. Is. 35:5-6

   c. Is. 65:20

   d. Jer. 30:17

3. Removal of mourning and sorrow: Read and summarize the following passages.
   a. Is. 9:3-4

   b. Is .14:7-8

   c. Jer. 31:13-14

4. Physical changes in land of Israel.
   a. What will happen to the land around and under Jerusalem? Zech. 14:10-11

   b. Read Ez. 47:6-9. What all do you learn about the river flowing from under the Lord's temple east to the Dead Sea and west to the Mediterranean?

   c. What do we learn about the trees on each side of this river in Eze. 47:12

5. Political changes – Israel exalted over the nations. Is. 61:3-7
   a. What will the Israelites be called? Why will God exalt the Israelites? v. 3

   b. What will happen to Jerusalem and other cities devastated during the Tribulation?

   c. What do we learn in v. 4?

   d. The nation of Israel will be ministers of God. What two terms will they be known by? v. 6

   e. What does v. 6 say about Israel's material prosperity? (See also Is. 60:5, 11.)

   f. With what will the nation's shame and humiliation be replaced? v. 7

ON A PERSONAL NOTE . . .
- How wonderful it will be for those living during the Millennial Kingdom, with the curse on creation removed. Although we now live in a fallen world, those in Christ have the assurance of eternal life, can enjoy the spiritual blessings of the Lord, and experience everlasting joy. With whom do you need to share this wonderful news? Ask God to give you the both the opportunity and the words to be His witness.

Back to the Future"
End Times Prophecy, from Genesis to Revelation
Lesson 17 - The Millennial Kingdom: Christ's Reign on Earth

REVIEW:
Christ's physical presence will bring about everlasting changes as His rule and authority extend over the whole earth as King of Kings and Lord of Lords. Life for those on earth will be drastically different and improved.

First of all, the curse that was placed on creation at the time of man's fall will be removed. Romans 8:19-21 tells us that creation is now waiting eagerly for the return of Christ, when it will be set free from its slavery to corruption. During the Millennial Kingdom the animal kingdom will once again be at peace with each other and with man. Animals will no longer be carnivorous but will once again be plant eaters. Isaiah 11:6-9 is probably the most well-known passage describing the relationship of animals and man during the kingdom: the wolf will dwell with the lamb, the leopard will lie down with the goat . . . the nursing child will play by the hole of the cobra and the weaned child will put his hand on the viper's den . . . they will not hurt or destroy . . . Amazing, simply amazing!

The removal of the curse will also result in abundance and plenty on the earth. Abundant rainfall and streams of water will water the earth. Free of thorns and thistles, the ground will produce an bountiful harvest, aided also by the increase of light. The Lord's people will be *radiant over the bounty of the Lord* (Jer. 31:12).

Next we see that there will be a removal of sickness and deformity. Isaiah 33:24 tells us that no one will say they are sick. And Isaiah 35:5-6 says that the blind will see, the deaf will hear, the lame will leap, and the mute will shout. Life spans will greatly increase. In fact there is no mention in the Bible of death for the righteous during the Millennial Kingdom. However, we have seen that Christ will slay those who outwardly rebel, and Isaiah 65:20 says that anyone who dies before the *young age* of 100 will be thought to be accursed.

When bad things happen to good people, others ask, "Why?" or "How can God let this happen?" As Christians, we need to learn to ask other types of questions like: "What do you want me to learn about you, Lord, through this situation?" or "How can this situation bring glory to you?" and "How can my faith grow?" This is difficult to do when the situation may be the inability to conceive, the death of a loved one, a wayward teenager, or the loss of a job. Life is full of tears, hurts, disappointments, sickness and death, failed dreams, loneliness, and emptiness. The list of the hurts of life is long. However we are told that those living in the Millennial Kingdom will experience the fullness of joy. With Christ physically present and ruling the world in peace, the curse on creation removed, and no sickness or deformity, the needs of all will be abundantly met. Mourning and sorrow will turn to joy and comfort (Jer. 31:13-14) and great rejoicing will be heard all through the world (Is. 14:7).

There will be great restoration to the Earth after the devastation caused by the judgments and the worldwide wars. In particular, there will be physical changes in and around Jerusalem. At Christ's return, the whole land around Jerusalem will become a plain, with Jerusalem rising above it like a precious diamond in the middle.

In Ezekiel we find that there will be a great river flowing from the temple to the east and then to the south, so deep that no one will be able to wade across (47:3-6). The river banks will be covered with trees (47:7-9), and the river will have fish and other living creatures in it. This is the river formed when the Mount of Olives split at Christ's return. In Zechariah 14:4, 8 we are told that it will flow westward to the Mediterranean Sea and eastward to the Dead Sea.

As a result, the Dead Sea will become fresh water, instead of the twenty-five percent salty water it has been for 1000s of years! (It is today the saltiest body of water in the world.) This river flowing from the Temple of God will provide healing to the land of Israel. God will bless the land of Israel with freshness and greenness. On both sides of the river there will be all kinds of trees which will bear fruit every month. The trees will have leaves year-round which will be used for healing (both corrective and preventative).

Back to the Future"
End Times Prophecy, from Genesis to Revelation
Lesson 17 - The Millennial Kingdom: Christ's Reign on Earth

Not only will Israel experience physical changes in their land, but they will experience political changes in their world. As the city of Jerusalem is elevated over the land around it, so the nation of Israel will be elevated above the nations. Restored and regenerated, the Israelites will again become witnesses of God's goodness, faithfulness, and love – to the glory of His name. God's chosen people will be called "Oaks of Righteousness." With Jesus ruling on the throne of David, Jerusalem will become the center of the millennial earth politically, economically, and spiritually. The cities of Israel will be beautifully rebuilt and the land will prosper. The Israelites will be served by the nations, with Gentiles pasturing their flocks, farming their land, and tending to their vines. Israel will be considered a nation of priests and will be a nation of great wealth. They will receive a double portion of all that God has to give. Gentile nations will be blessed according to their relationship with Israel, as specified in the Abrahamic covenant: "And I will bless those who bless you, and the one who curses you I will curse" (Gen. 12:3). Israel will never again experience the shame of God's discipline but will experience the everlasting joy of His blessing.

Back to the Future"
End Times Prophecy, from Genesis to Revelation
Lesson 17 - The Millennial Kingdom: Christ's Reign on Earth

*** DAY 4: Spiritual Life during the Kingdom

1. Trinity is Present: We have already seen that God the Son will be ruling in Jerusalem from the throne of David. Where do we see God the Father and God the Holy Spirit in the following scriptures?
   a. Eze. 37:27-28

   b. Zech. 2:5

   c. Eze. 36:26-27; Joel 2:28-29

2. Holiness is Pervasive: What is described as "holy" in the following verses?
   a. Zech. 2:12

   b. Is. 52:1

   c. Zeph. 3:11

   d. Is. 4:3-4; Eze. 37:23

   e. Is. 35:8

   f. Zech. 14:20-21

3. Worship is Prevalent: Use the verses given to support that –
   a. All will *know* God.
      Is. 11:9

      Jer. 31:34

   b. All will *worship* God.
      Zeph. 3:9-10

      Is. 45:23-24

      Mal. 1:11

4. Temple is Pinnacle: Skim Ezekiel 40-46 answering the following questions.
   a. The temple will be much larger than any historic temple of Israel. Use Eze. 42:15-20 to give the dimensions of the outer walls. Use Bible footnotes to translate into today's terms.

   b. What will fill the Temple during the Millennial Age? How did Ezekiel respond when he observed the phenomenon? Eze. 43:1-7

Back to the Future"
End Times Prophecy, from Genesis to Revelation
Lesson 17 - The Millennial Kingdom: Christ's Reign on Earth

    c. Read Eze. 40:39; 45:15; and 45:17 and list the millennial sacrifices mentioned. If Jesus has died once for the sins of the world, why do you think animal sacrifices are required?

    d. Zech. 14:16-17

ON A PERSONAL NOTE . . .

- Re-read Is. 9:6-7. I'm sure you recognize these verses as part of Handel's *Messiah,* often performed at Christmas. Perhaps you know the melody and can sing and worship our LORD with this verse. God loves to hear His word spoken back to Him in praise. If not, create your own melody and sing right now!!!

- Through the centuries there have been good emperors, rulers, dictators, kings, presidents, prime ministers, and czars. Jesus will be like no other. He will rule with perfection and justice. Give thanks to Jesus for His perfect rule to come and ask Him to rule supreme in your life today. Write 2 or 3 situations that needs His supremacy and kingship.

Back to the Future"
End Times Prophecy, from Genesis to Revelation
Lesson 17 - The Millennial Kingdom: Christ's Reign on Earth

REVIEW:
As the Millennium begins, all people will be believers. Can you imagine what it will be like for everyone to be believers? Wow! It's going to be glorious! People behaving themselves! No crime! Love will overflow for Jesus and for each other as never before!

This will be a time of unparalleled spirituality. All persons of the Trinity will be manifested in the kingdom. The risen and gloried Christ Himself will be present, ruling in Jerusalem from the throne of David over the entire world. God will be dwelling in their midst with His glory filling the temple. In Zech. 2:5, God says He will be a wall of fire around Jerusalem, as well as the glory in her midst. The Holy Spirit will indwell all believers in the Millennial Kingdom, as in the present age, but in the completeness that we long for now.

The kingdom will be characterized by righteousness, obedience, holiness, truth, and fullness of the Spirit. All who enter the Millennium will be believers, and as the 1000 years unfold, many more will be added. There will more believers on earth during the Millennial Kingdom than ever before.

Holiness will pervade the earth during the Kingdom. It will be a distinguishing trait among the Jewish people in particular during the Kingdom. Israel will be a *holy* land; Jerusalem, a *holy* city; Mt Zion, a *holy* mountain; and God's people, a *holy* people. There will even be a roadway leading to Jerusalem and the throne of the Messiah called the *Highway of Holiness.* During the Kingdom of Christ, everything will be set apart to the service of the Lord. There will be no division between secular and sacred. The pots and bowls in the temple will be the same as the pots and bowls in the people's houses - *holy.* Even the bells on horses will be inscribed, "*Holy to the Lord.*"

Not only will holiness be pervasive, but worship will be prevalent throughout the world. Along with the rulership of Christ, the glory of God dwelling in the temple, and the Spirit indwelling all believers, the Word of God will be widespread knowledge. In Isaiah 11:9, we find that "The earth will be full of the knowledge of the LORD as the waters cover the sea." Jeremiah 31:34 says there will be no need for teachers because all will know God, from the greatest to the smallest. Evidently the Holy Spirit will have a teaching ministry like never before. As a result we are told in Zeph. 3:9-10 that all peoples will call on the name of the Lord. There will be universal worship as every knee will bow and every tongue will swear allegiance to the Lord (Is. 45:23-24). Remember that outward rebellion will not be tolerated. Malachi 2:1 informs us that the Lord will receive offerings of incense and grain in all parts of the world.

According to Ezekiel, the Millennial Kingdom will feature a magnificent temple that will serve as the center for the priestly rituals and offerings. The description of this temple (Eze. 41:1-43:12) is totally different from that of Solomon's Temple (1 Kings 6 and 2 Chron. 3) and that of Zerubbabel's Temple (Ezra 6:3-4). The Millennial Temple will be much larger, with the outside walls spanning approximately 1 mile wide and 1 mile long.

In Ezekiel 43:1-5, Ezekiel sees the glory of the God of Israel enter and fill the temple. In Old Testament times, God's glory had dwelt with the Israelites first in the tabernacle and then in Solomon's temple, but departed in judgment at the time of Israel's captivity in Babylon (Eze. 11:22-23). Just as His glory had departed to the east (Mount. of Olives) so it now returns from the east and enters the temple through the eastern gate. Later in Eze. 44:1-3, we see that this gate is shut, never again to be opened, signaling that God will dwell with man forevermore.

Information is given in Eze. 43:13-46:24 concerning temple worship during the Millennial Kingdom. It is interesting to note that animal sacrifices will be reinstituted. This passage mentions the burnt, grain, peace, sin, guilt, and drink offerings that were present in the outdated Levitical system of worship. In Eze. 45, instructions are given for the Millennial Feasts to be observed. Annual pilgrimages to the temple will again be required of all families, with those who disobey experiencing a plague of drought.

Animal sacrifices in the Old Testament were never a means of removing sin, but pointed ahead to the atoning work of Jesus on the cross. His death was the sufficient sacrifice which paid for the penalty of sin for people past, present, and future. His resurrection from the grave was proof that He had satisfied the Father's requirement. Therefore, why is there a need for a return for these sacrifices now in the Millennial Temple? In the Millennial Kingdom these sacrifices will serve as a memorial of Christ's sacrifice, reminding people of their inability to save themselves and thus their need for Christ.

Back to the Future"
End Times Prophecy, from Genesis to Revelation
Lesson 17 - The Millennial Kingdom: Christ's Reign on Earth

*** DAY 5: King of the Kingdom

1. Fill in the following table giving some of the names and titles by which scripture refers to Christ in the Millennial Kingdom. Identify the one that means the most to you today.

Is. 4:2	
Is. 9:6	
Is. 24:33; 44:6	
Jer. 23:5; 33:15	
Dan. 7:13	
Is. 42:1	
Is. 33:17; John 12:13; Zech. 14:9	
Rev. 19:16	
Is. 33:22	
Is. 11:3-4	
Is. 59:20	
Micah 2:13	
Is. 40:10-11	
Is. 60:30	
Mal. 4:2	

ON A PERSONAL NOTE . . .
- Whom do you know that needs to recognize Christ as both the Son of God and the Son of Man, and, trusting Him as their Savior and Lord, let Him reign in his or her heart? Put a note in your kitchen window at your sink to pray for him/her every day. Pray that Jesus will drop the scales from the eyes of her/his heart and that the Spirit will make the huge hole in his/her heart long for the love of Christ alone. Pray for the opportunity and obedience to share Jesus with him/her. Pray against Satan's efforts to keep this person from hearing the Good News. It is God's will that none perish. God is touching hearts, and we must join Him at His work

Back to the Future"
End Times Prophecy, from Genesis to Revelation
Lesson 17 - The Millennial Kingdom: Christ's Reign on Earth

REVIEW:
We looked today at some names and titles referring to our Lord and Savior Jesus Christ during His 1000 year reign. Each suggests a different facet of His work and His person in the Kingdom. The titles *The Branch of the LORD, the Son of God,* and the *Lord of Hosts* emphasize Christ's deity, while the titles *Branch of David, Son of Man,* and *My Servant* emphasize His humanity. Christ is designated as *King*, not only over Israel, but over the world and over all creation. The titles *King of Kings and Lord of Lords, Lawgiver* and *Judge* further reference His supreme authority. The rest of the Messiah's names that we looked at today, *Redeemer, Wall Breaker, Shepherd, Light,* and *Sun of Righteousness* all speak of Christ's glorious work in bringing salvation to the world.[2]

During the Millennial Kingdom Christ's glory will be fully manifested. Pentecost has summarized the glory of Christ during this time when He reigns as both the *Son of Man* and the *Son of God*.

1. There will be glory associated with the humanity of Christ:

Glorious dominion	Christ is given universal dominion by virtue of his obedience unto death. (Rom. 5:12-21)
Glorious government	As David's son, Christ is given absolute power to govern. (Is. 9:6)
Glorious inheritance	The land and the seed promised to Abraham are realized through Christ. (Gen.17:8)
Glorious judiciary	Christ administers God's will and law. (Deut. 18:18)
Glorious house / throne	Christ shall fulfill all promises to David. (2 Sam. 7:12-16)
Glorious kingdom	Christ will reign over all. (Is.11:10)

2. There will also be glory associated with the deity of Christ:

His omniscience	Is. 66:15-18
His omnipotence	Is. 41:10
Christ will receive worship as God	Ps. 45:6, Is. 66:23, Ps. 86:9, Zech. 14:16-19
Full display of righteousness	Dan. 9:24
Full display of mercy	Is. 63:7-19
Full display of divine goodness	Jer. 33:9
Will of God fully revealed, accomplished through Christ	Matt. 6:10
Holiness of God manifested through Christ	Is. 6:1-3, Rev. 15:4
Manifestation of divine truth through the King	Mic. 7:20, Is. 25:1[3]

As we come to the close of our study on the Millennial Kingdom, let us remember the hymn, "Joy to the World," written by Isaac Watts. This hymn, based on Psalm 98, was written over 250 years ago. We sing it at Christmas to celebrate Christ's First Coming. However, when one reads the words in the second and third stanzas, one realizes that the words are about Christ's Second Coming and Kingdom rule. Sing or read the lyrics below with this in mind.

Joy to the World! The Lord is come!
Let earth receive her King.
Let every heart prepare him room,
And heaven and nature sing . . . .

No more let sins and sorrows grow,
Nor thorns infest the ground;
He comes to make his blessings flow
Far as the curse is found . . . .

He rules the world with truth and grace;
And makes the nations prove
The glories of his righteousness,
And the wonder of His love . . . .

Back to the Future"
End Times Prophecy, from Genesis to Revelation
Lesson 17 - The Millennial Kingdom: Christ's Reign on Earth

Now, before we stop singing, let us join in the song being sung by all creation in Rev. 5:13:
"To Him who sits on the throne, and to the Lamb, be blessing and honor and glory and dominion forever and ever."

2. Ibid., pp. 478-479.
3. Ibid., pp. 480-481.

"Back to the Future"
End Times Prophecy, from Genesis to Revelation
Lesson 18 - Eternity

*** DAY 1: At the Close of the Millennium

1. **Satan's Final Rebellion: Rev. 20:3, 7-10**
   a. Although the sovereignty, power and glory of Christ are clearly revealed during the Millennial Kingdom, what happens at the end of the 1000 years?

   b. What does the devil do upon being released?

   c. Where does Satan lead the armies?

   d. What is the outcome for these armies, for Satan?

   e. Who else is still in the lake of fire?

   f. What does the future hold for them, for how long?

2. **Great White Throne Judgment: Rev. 20:11-15**
   a. Read John 5:22-30. Based on John 5:22, who is sitting on the great white throne that John sees?

   b. What happens as a result of the Lord's presence? How is this event described in II Peter 3:10-12?

   c. Who must those standing before the throne be? What kind of bodies do they have? (See John 5:29.)

   d. What books are also opened at this time? (See also Daniel 7:9-10.)

   e. On what basis are the dead judged?

   f. What two things are first thrown into the lake of fire; then who?

   g. What is "being thrown in the lake of fire" called?

ON A PERSONAL NOTE . . .
- Here is one last appeal. If you are not certain that your name is written in the Lamb's Book of Life, please turn to Appendix One and make "The Best Decision of Your Life." Is there anyone that you need to share the gospel with before it is too late? Give someone the best gift of all - the good news of Jesus Christ!

"Back to the Future"
End Times Prophecy, from Genesis to Revelation
Lesson 18 - Eternity

REVIEW:

Against the backdrop of Christ's glory during the Millennial Kingdom, we see the depravity of man. At the end of the Millennial Kingdom, Satan is let loose from the abyss, where he has been held prisoner for 1000 years. Satan will go out to deceive the nations, incredibly gathering a large number of people from the four corners of earth to rebel against Christ. Some believe that during this 1000 years, those who are not saved will not live past age 100 (Isaiah 65:20) and that Satan's followers will be a rebellious youth movement.

In the beginning of the Millennial Reign, there will be only adult Gentiles and Jews who are saved, as both unsaved Gentiles and unsaved Jews will have been removed before the kingdom started. The children of these adults will be allowed to enter the Millennial Kingdom; it will be necessary for these children to make a decision regarding their salvation. Likewise, children who are born in the kingdom will also face the need for salvation. There will be a number of people who outwardly conform but never make a decision for Christ – *professors* but not *possessors*.

This rebellion demonstrates the wickedness of human hearts. They are rebellious in spite of living in a Satan-free environment full of the knowledge of God and under the rule of our glorious Lord. It is final proof that environment alone cannot change one's fallen human nature. This change can only occur when one experiences new birth, a supernatural act of God in which one receives a new heart, mind, and spirit and becomes a child of God.

Pentecost says it this way: During the Millennial Kingdom, "the release of Satan is viewed in Scripture as the final test that demonstrates the corruption of the human heart . . . . Man has failed under every test. He has been tried and tested under every possible condition, in every possible way. The purpose, for which Satan was released, then was to demonstrate that, even when tested under the reign of the King and the revelation of His holiness, man is a failure."[1]

Satan and his armies surround Jerusalem, attempting to capture both the city and its saints. But fire comes from heaven and devours the armies. The devil is thrown into the lake of fire, joining the beast and the false prophet. There "they will be tormented day and night forever and ever" (Rev. 20:10). This verse contradicts the belief that those in the lake of fire will "burn up" and exist no more.

John next sees God in the person of Jesus Christ on His Great White Throne of judgment. At this time, the present heavens and earth are dissolved in judgment. The time pointed to by II Peter 3:7 has arrived: "But by His word the present heavens and earth are being reserved for fire, kept for the day of judgment and destruction of ungodly men."

We have discussed before that there are three heavens mentioned in Scripture: 1) the earth's atmosphere; 2) the heaven where the planets and stars are; and 3) the dwelling place of God. It is our present created universe, the first two heavens along with our present earth, which is now incinerated. Foretold many times in Scripture, II Peter 3:10-12 describes this catastrophic event: ". . . the heavens will pass away with a roar and the elements will be destroyed with intense heat, and the earth and its works will be burned up."

Although by splitting the atom man has demonstrated the power to destroy the earth, this "uncreation" is a meltdown of universal proportions. Not only is our universe filled with burning stars, comets, and asteroids but we know that the core of our earth itself is a fireball, its core being a flaming, boiling, liquid lake of fire. In final judgment of sinful creation, our universe is instantly incinerated in fiery judgment, bringing to an end what is known in Scripture as "The Great Day of The Lord."

At this time, John also sees the unsaved from all ages standing before the Great White Throne. These wicked spirits who have been kept in Hades are resurrected to appear before God the Son for judgment (Rev. 20:13). They too are given an eternal body (John 5:29) – one that can never be destroyed but will endure eternal punishment, as they for eternity remain wicked and in rebellion against God.

"Back to the Future"
End Times Prophecy, from Genesis to Revelation
Lesson 18 - Eternity

Each unsaved individual is judged according to his deeds (thoughts, words, and actions) which have all been recorded divinely in the "books." This is not a judgment of salvation - that has already been determined. Just as believers will be judged and rewarded for their good works, so the wicked will be judged and punished according to wicked works. Instead, this is a final judgment of "works" (not unlike the judgment of Christians at the Judgment Seat of Christ). This indicates that there will be different degrees of punishment on the unsaved. The idea that there will be different degrees of punishment is supported by Matt. 10:14-15, 11:22; Mk. 12:38-40; Lk. 12:47-48; and Hebrews 10:29.

The Book of Life, containing names of all genuinely saved, is opened as the final check. Their names not being found in the book, all are cast into lake of fire (*gehenna*); this eternal separation from God is called the "second death." The wicked will spend eternity in Hell, in conscious awareness of their punishment (Matt. 8:12; 26:20).

At the conclusion of this judgment, God's creation will be purged of all evil, His holiness, righteousness, and justice vindicated for all eternity.

Note: Scripture is silent concerning the saints of the Millennial Kingdom at this time. We can assume that the Millennial Kingdom saints have been glorified to join the saints of all the ages. If there are saints who died in the Millennium, they would have been resurrected. Those living at the end of the 1000 years would also have been glorified, similar to living Church Age saints who were translated at the Rapture.

---

1. J. Dwight Pentecost, Things to Come, p. 548.

"Back to the Future"
End Times Prophecy, from Genesis to Revelation
Lesson 18 - Eternity

*** DAY 2: New Heavens and Earth: Rev. 21:1-8

1. What does John now see at the beginning of Rev. 21?

2. What has happened to our present heaven and earth? (also II Peter 3:10; Rev. 20:11)

3. What does II Peter 3:13 say about this new universe? What does Isaiah 66:22 add?

4. Describe the differences in this new universe that are found in the following passages.
    a. Rev. 21:1
    b. Rev. 21:23
    c. Rev. 22:3a

5. What will be the focal city of this new earth? Where has the city been up to now? v. 2

6. Who is its architect, how is it described? v. 2

7. Where does God *tabernacle,* or dwell, in this new universe? v. 3

8. What will we no longer experience in the new earth? v. 4

9. In Rev 21:6 John hears Him on the throne say, "It is done." What do you think Jesus means? (See I Cor. 15:24-27.)

10. Who will inherit the new earth and all *these things*? v. 7 (Refer also to I John 5:4-5.)

11. Where will everything unclean or sinful be? v. 8

ON A PERSONAL NOTE . . .
- In the letters to the seven churches in Rev. 2-3, list the awesome promises Christ made concerning the *overcomer's* inheritance, filling in your name. For example, Patti will eat of the tree of life in the Paradise of God (Rev. 2:7). Worshipfully meditate on these truths.

"Back to the Future"
End Times Prophecy, from Genesis to Revelation
Lesson 18 - Eternity

REVIEW:
Yesterday's study of Revelation 20 closed with the entire created universe being destroyed by God. In addition, the unsaved of all ages were judged and cast into the lake of fire to be tormented forever, joining Satan and his demons, the Beast, and the false prophet.

Now in Revelation 21 John sees a new heaven and earth. This new universe was prophesied in both the Old and New Testaments (Ps. 102:25-26; Is. 65:17, 66:22; Luke 21:33; and Heb. 12:22-24). We are told in II Peter 3:13 that this new universe is one in which righteousness will dwell and Isaiah 65:22 adds that this universe will endure before the Lord forever.

Since the old heaven and earth has passed away, this has to be a new, and not a renovated, heaven and earth. The word *new* indicates that it is completely different in quality. The first difference mentioned is that the earth will have no sea. Today nearly ¾ of the earth is covered by water, which all life depends on for survival. Unlike our human bodies, our glorified bodies will not require water. Our new environment "will no longer be water-based and will have completely different climatic conditions" (The MacArthur Study Bible, p.1993). Some take "*no more sea*" as a metaphor meaning that there will be no national boundaries. Still others say that since the sea symbolized fear (with its shipwrecking storms and dangerous sea creatures) to the ancient world, the absence of a sea means that there will be no more fear.

In this new universe the earth will no longer be dependent upon the light of the sun and moon (Rev. 21:23). Instead the glory of God will illumine the universe, the Lamb being its lamp. We know also that there will be no curse on this new and perfect creation of God.

Coming down out of heaven (the third heaven) from God is the New Jerusalem. The fact that the city is *coming down from heaven* indicates that it has been in existence prior to this time. It has, in fact, been where the Church has dwelled with Christ since its rapture. This is the same city that Jesus told his disciples about in John 14:2. We will discuss this city further tomorrow.

This city is a holy city, created by our Holy God and inhabited by those who have shared in the resurrection of the holy. The New Jerusalem is pictured as a bride since the city is the home of Christ's bride, at this point including not just the Church but the saints of all time.

Next we are told exciting news – in the new heavens and earth, God will tabernacle or dwell among His people! In the New Jerusalem on the new earth, we will fellowship with God, see Him as He is, worship Him, and serve Him. Living in the presence of God and His Son, with the curse removed, we will experience life as we cannot imagine. Every tear will be wiped away and there will be no more death, mourning, crying, or pain.

In Revelation 21:5-8, John hears Jesus speak from the throne. The words "It is done" are reminiscent of Jesus' words from the cross. Christ broke the power of Satan and sin at the cross, But only now has Satan and death been conquered and brought into subjection under Christ's feet. Christ can now deliver the Kingdom to His Father (I Cor. 15:24-27) and the eternal glory of Rev. 21, 22 can begin.[2]

What a wonderful inheritance we have been promised. As part of the redeemed, believers from all ages, we will inherit God's new unblemished creation and inhabit New Jerusalem on the new Earth. No unclean or sinful person will live among us, as they will all be in the lake of fire. God will forever dwell among us, and there will no longer be any death, mourning, crying, or pain. He will be our God, and we will be His "sons." We will drink from the spring of the water of life, availing ourselves of all of His spiritual blessings throughout all eternity.

---

2. John MacArthur, The MacArthur Study Bible, p. 1724.

"Back to the Future"
End Times Prophecy, from Genesis to Revelation
Lesson 18 - Eternity

*** DAY 3: Descent of the New Jerusalem: Rev. 21:9-22:7

1. What causes the city to shine like a very costly stone?

2. From verses 12-14, describe the city's great wall.

3. Give the dimensions of the city.

4. Looking at the wall, how thick was it, and of what was it made?

5. List the stones which make up the wall and the foundation stones.

6. Of what was each gate made? What would this bring to mind?

7. How is the city itself described; its street? Rev. 21:18,21

8. Why will there be no physical temple in the city?

9. What other things will the city not have?
   v. 23
   v. 25
   v. 27

10. Why will there also be no darkness? Rev. 21:23; 22:5

11. Describe the river in the city.

12. Describe the Tree of Life.

13. Who will rule from the throne in the city?

14. From Rev. 22:3-5 what four privileges will we have? How long?

ON A PERSONAL NOTE . . .
- The Tree of Life was barred from Adam and Eve in their fallen nature. Why was this is their best interest as well as in ours?

- The glory of God and Jesus illumines the New Jerusalem, the New Earth, and the New Heavens forever. What dark situation in your life must you allow God's glory (His Word, His will, His ways) to illumine? Will you take this situation to God in prayer? "Shine, Jesus, shine!"

"Back to the Future"
End Times Prophecy, from Genesis to Revelation
Lesson 18 - Eternity

REVIEW:

As we saw yesterday, the New Jerusalem is pictured as coming down out of heaven from God. This New Jerusalem is the heavenly city especially prepared by God for the saints. Believers glorified at the Rapture were taken by Christ to heaven and have been living in the New Jerusalem with Christ since that time.

Many writers think that at Christ's 2nd coming, when He returns to earth with His Bride to reign, the New Jerusalem is transferred from heaven to a place in the air over the land of Palestine. The Church age saints are joined by the Old Testament and the Tribulation saints, who are resurrected and take up residence in this "satellite city" during the Millennial Kingdom. These saints are in their eternal state possessing their eternal inheritance, and they are in an eternal relationship with the Lord. Also occupying the New Jerusalem will be the holy angels.[3]

At the end of the 1000 years, the city is removed during the destruction of the present heavens and earth, and then descends to its permanent location on the new earth. With the addition of the Millennial Kingdom glorified saints, it will be the home of the angels, the Church, and the saints of all times for eternity. It will be the location of God's throne and the center of the new earth.

The center of the new earth, the New Jerusalem, is 1500 miles long, wide, and high. Some think that the city is a pyramid, but it is probably cubic in shape. In Solomon's temple, the Holy of Holies was a cube (I Kings 6:20). "The city is a gigantic jeweled city with streets of gold. From a study of the various materials used, it seems that all the materials in the New Jerusalem are translucent and, as such, have no dark shadows. The light of God will penetrate every corner."[4] Aglow with the glory of God, its beauty is indescribable.

The wall surrounding the New Jerusalem is 72 yards thick and is made of jasper. There are twelve gates in the wall, three on each side, with an angel standing at each gate. A single pearl makes up each gate. Representing Israel, the gates have the names of the twelve tribes written on them –similar to the gates of Jerusalem's wall during the Millennial Kingdom (Eze. 48:31-34).

The twelve foundation stones of the city wall are "adorned with every kind of precious stone" (Rev. 21:19). Though the exact color of each stone described cannot be ascertained, every brilliant color of the rainbow is represented and enhanced by the glory of GOD. Representing the Church, the foundation stones have written on them the names of the twelve apostles of Christ.

There is no temple in the New Jerusalem, for God Almighty and the Lamb are its temple. We saw yesterday that there is no sun or moon; God's glory lightens the city continuously. There is no night and the city gates are never closed.

Flowing from the throne of God and of the Lamb is the river of the water of life, symbolizing the continual flow of eternal life to the inhabitants.[5] This river flows down the middle of the great street of the great city. On each side of the river, the tree of life bears a different fruit each month. Either trees are on both sides of the river or the tree is so large that its branches reach both sides.

The leaves of the tree are for *healing*. But in the new heavens and earth, there will be no sickness or death. The actual word in Greek is *therapeian*, from which we get our word *therapeutic*. These leaves are better understood to be health-giving, promoting the enjoyment of life.[6]

The throne of God and of the Lamb will be in the city. The redeemed will serve Him with immense satisfaction. It will be a time of unparalleled blessing. Believers will experience intimacy with God. We will see His face, His name will be on our foreheads, and we will reign with the Lord forever. Hallelujah!

3. Pentecost, op. cit., pp. 577-580.
4. John Walvoord, Major Bible Prophecies, p. 421.
5. John MacArthur, op. cit., p. 1995.
6. Walvoord, op. cit., p. 424.

"Back to the Future"
End Times Prophecy, from Genesis to Revelation
Lesson 18 - Eternity

*** DAY 4: Life in the Eternal City

Using phrases from the given verses support the following descriptions of life in the eternal city. (Taken from J. Dwight Pentecost, <u>Things to Come</u>, p. 580-583)

1. A life of fellowship with Him
   I Cor. 13:12; I John 3:2; John 14:3, Rev. 22:4

2. A life of rest
   Rev. 14:13

3. A life of full knowledge
   I Cor. 13:12

4. A life of holiness
   Rev. 21:27

5. A life of joy
   Rev. 21:4

6. A life of service
   Rev. 22:3

7. A life of abundance
   Rev. 21:6

8. A life of glory
   II Cor. 4:17, Col. 3:4

9. A life of worship
   Rev. 7:9-12, Rev. 19:1

ON A PERSONAL NOTE . . .
- Although we do not currently enjoy this kind of physical life here on earth, we have been blessed with every spiritual blessing (Eph. 1:3, II Peter 1:3). How is Satan currently stealing and killing the abundant life Jesus offers (John 10:10)? List practical ways you can take to reclaim your joy in Christ.

- Which of the above passages is most meaningful to you? Spend time in prayer today worshipping God for who He is and thanking Him for the inheritance He has promised us.

"Back to the Future"
End Times Prophecy, from Genesis to Revelation
Lesson 18 - Eternity

REVIEW:
Many books have been written on what Heaven will be like. However Scripture does not give us many details concerning life in God's eternal kingdom. You have looked up many verses today, which I will let speak for themselves. Hopefully, these verses have given you hope, encouragement, and joy.

In his book, The Glory of Heaven, John MacArthur points out that in Heaven we will have perfect bodies, perfect souls, perfect pleasures, perfect knowledge, perfect relationships, and perfect love. However, he goes on to say that the most marvelous thing about heaven will be unbroken fellowship with God Himself. One of my favorite quotes from his book is the following:

> *"Simply put, we're going to be with a Person as much as we are going to live in a place. The presence of Christ is what makes heaven heaven. 'The Lamb is the light thereof' (Rev 21:23). And perfect fellowship with God is the very essence of heaven."* [7]

I John 3:2 says "we know that when he appears, we will be like him." We shall be transformed into His likeness. While we are enamored by that thought here on earth, our occupation in the eternal state will not be with our position or glory, but with God, Himself. In Things to Come, J. Dwight Pentecost sums up this thought by writing,

> *"We shall be fully occupied with the One 'that loved us, and washed us from our sins in his own blood, And hath made us kings and priests unto God and his Father' (Rev.1:5-6), ascribing 'Blessing and honour, and glory, and power, ... unto him that sitteth on the throne, and unto the Lamb forever and ever' (Rev. 5:13), saying, 'Blessing, and glory, and wisdom, and thanksgiving, and honour, and power, and might, be unto our God for ever and ever. Amen' (Rev. 7:12), for 'Worthy is the Lamb that was slain to receive power, and riches, and wisdom, and strength, and honour, and glory and blessing' (Rev. 5:12)."* [8]

---

7. John MacArthur, The Glory of Heaven, p. 142.
8. Pentecost, op. cit., pp. 582-583.

"Back to the Future"
End Times Prophecy, from Genesis to Revelation
Lesson 18 - Eternity

*** DAY 5: We've Come Full Circle - Now What?

1. *What began in Genesis is brought to completion in Revelation.*
   Mark Hitchcock, in <u>The Second Coming of Babylon</u>, points out several contrasts between God's original creation in Genesis and the new creation of Revelation. List the differences found in the following pairs of verses.

<u>Genesis</u>	<u>Revelation</u>
1:1	21:1
1:16	21:23
1:5	22:5
1:10	21:1
2:10-14	22:1
3:19	21:4
3:24	22:2, 14
3:17	21:4

2. In Rev. 22:6, what is said about all John has seen and heard in his vision?

3. What is John to do as a result of these words he has been given?
   a. Rev. 22:7

   b. Rev. 22:9

   c. Rev. 22:10

   d. Rev. 22:12 (implied)

4. At the close of Rev. 22, Jesus issues one last invitation:
   a. With what warning and promise does Jesus make in v.12 and close with in v. 20?

   b. By what titles does Jesus identify Himself? vv. 13, 16

   c. What blessing and curse does He issue? vv. 14-15

   d. What does Jesus invite unbelievers to do? vv. 16-17

"Back to the Future"
End Times Prophecy, from Genesis to Revelation
Lesson 18 - Eternity

5. What final warning does Jesus give concerning the words of prophecy given in Revelation? vv. 18-19

ON A PERSONAL NOTE . . .
- Read II Tim. 4:8 and Rev. 1:3. In what ways have you been blessed during this study of God's Word? What has God taught you this semester? How has your perspective on life changed? Write down your answers as a testimony and memorial to God.

- Write down the name of someone with whom you wish to share what you have learned?

"Back to the Future"
End Times Prophecy, from Genesis to Revelation
Lesson 18 - Eternity

REVIEW:
The Bible opens with the promise of Christ's first coming (Gen. 3:15). It now closes with the promise of Christ's Second Coming (Rev. 22:12, 20). As previously noted, Jesus' words, "*I am coming quickly*," underscore that His return is imminent (it could happen at any time).

As John's vision comes to an end, the angel with him reminds John that the words concerning all he has seen and heard are *faithful and true*, repeating Jesus' words of Rev. 21:5. Because of the certainty of these words and the imminence of Christ's return (Rev. 22:7), John is instructed to do four things.

First John is told he must **heed** (or obey) the words of this book (vv. 7, 9). As we studied in the first chapter of our study, knowledge of end times should cause us to lead holy lives.

Second John is told he must **worship** God (v. 9). Seeing our Lord exalted in prophecy – His regal majesty, power, and glory – gives us a proper understanding of Who He is and should cause us to fall to our knees in worship.

Third John is told, *"Do not seal up the words of the prophecy of this book."* In other words, "Do not keep these words secret, but proclaim them to all generations." Knowing what the future holds should cause us to urgently **share** the gospel with those we know, in hopes that they will share our inheritance with us for eternity.

In Revelation 22:12 Jesus says that He is coming quickly to render reward to every man, according to what he has done. Implied in this verse is the fourth command – **serve** the Lord. The knowledge that Jesus is returning soon should cause us to serve Him vigorously, that we may receive a *full reward* (II John 8).

There is no support in the Bible for a lazy, procrastinating, self-serving, self-centered Christian. On the contrary, our time is short and we must be about our Master's business!

Because Christ's return is imminent and because God's desire is that no man perish (II Peter 3:9), our Lord issues one final invitation to unbelievers (Rev 22:12-18).

The titles Christ uses for himself in this passage bear witness to His Person. The three terms found in verse 13, *the Alpha and Omega, the first and the last, and the beginning and the end*, describe Christ's completeness, timelessness, and sovereignty. The title Christ uses for Himself in verse 16, *the root and the descendant of David*, expresses both His deity (root) and His humanity (descendant). And finally, the title also found in verse 16, *bright morning star*, confirms that Jesus, the Son of God and the Son of Man, is Israel's Messiah. (See Numbers 24:17, II Peter 1:9; 2:28.)[9]

Jesus also reiterates the fate of those who do not respond to His invitation. Heaven is exclusively for believers – those who have come to Christ (*washed their robes*). All others (*the dogs*) will be outside, eternally tormented in the Lake of Fire.

Because of Whom He is and because of what He has said, Jesus urges unbelievers to join the Spirit and the bride in urging for His Return (*say, "Come"*). One who is *thirsty* must *come* to Christ, drinking of *the water of life*, before he can truly long for Christ's Return. If you have come this far in our study without *taking the water of life without cost*, I plead with you to do so now before it is too late! (Turn to Appendix One if you need help.)

As we come to the close of our study, we must be careful that we heed the warning of our Lord and Savior given in Rev. 22:18-19. We must be careful that we do not add or take away from the words written in the book of Revelation. We find this same warning relating to the entire cannon of Scripture throughout the Bible. As we continue to study prophecy and share what we know about end-times, we must be careful that we do not misrepresent what the Bible says in any way.

"Back to the Future"
End Times Prophecy, from Genesis to Revelation
Lesson 18 - Eternity

Let me say it has been a blessing to study end time prophecy, journeying through the Bible, together with you. Let me also encourage you to not be discouraged if you don't remember or understand everything we have studied. You have established a base upon which to build. Every time I teach this class or look at the material, the Holy Spirit reveals something new.

Take comfort in knowing that as you have obediently studied God's Word, you have learned what the Spirit has desired you to learn. And take joy in the promise of Rev. 1:3, "Blessed is he who reads and those who hear the words of the prophecy, and heed the things which are written in it, for the time is near."

> **May God bless each one of you as we finish this study praying,**
> ***"Come, Lord Jesus!"***

---

9. John MacArthur, <u>MacArthur New Testament Commentary</u>, Vol. 2, pp. 306-307

Chart 1: An Overview of the End Time

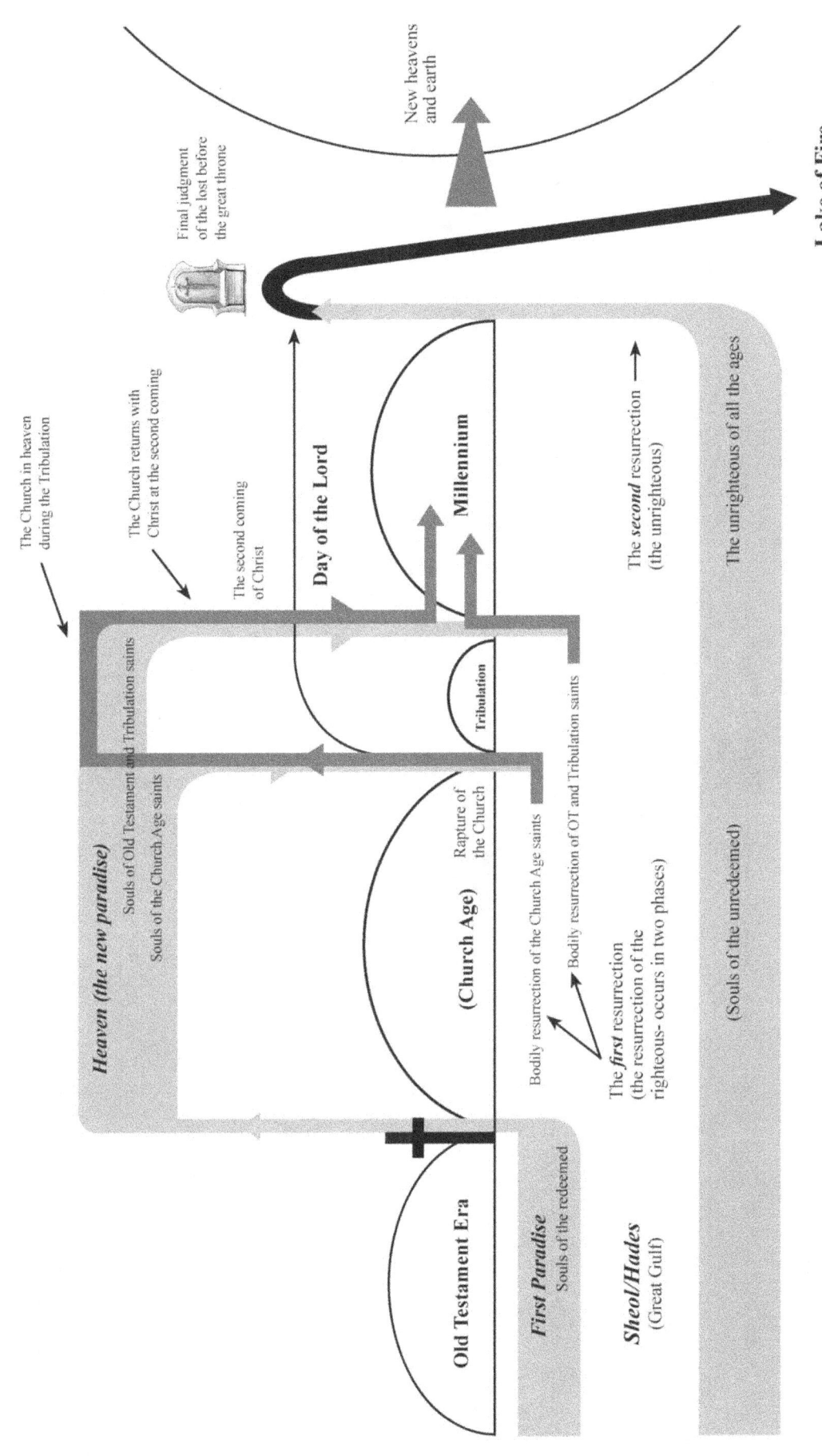

*Adaptation of chart on page 247 of *What the Bible Says About the Future*, Sam A. Smith.

Chart 2: Who? Where? When?

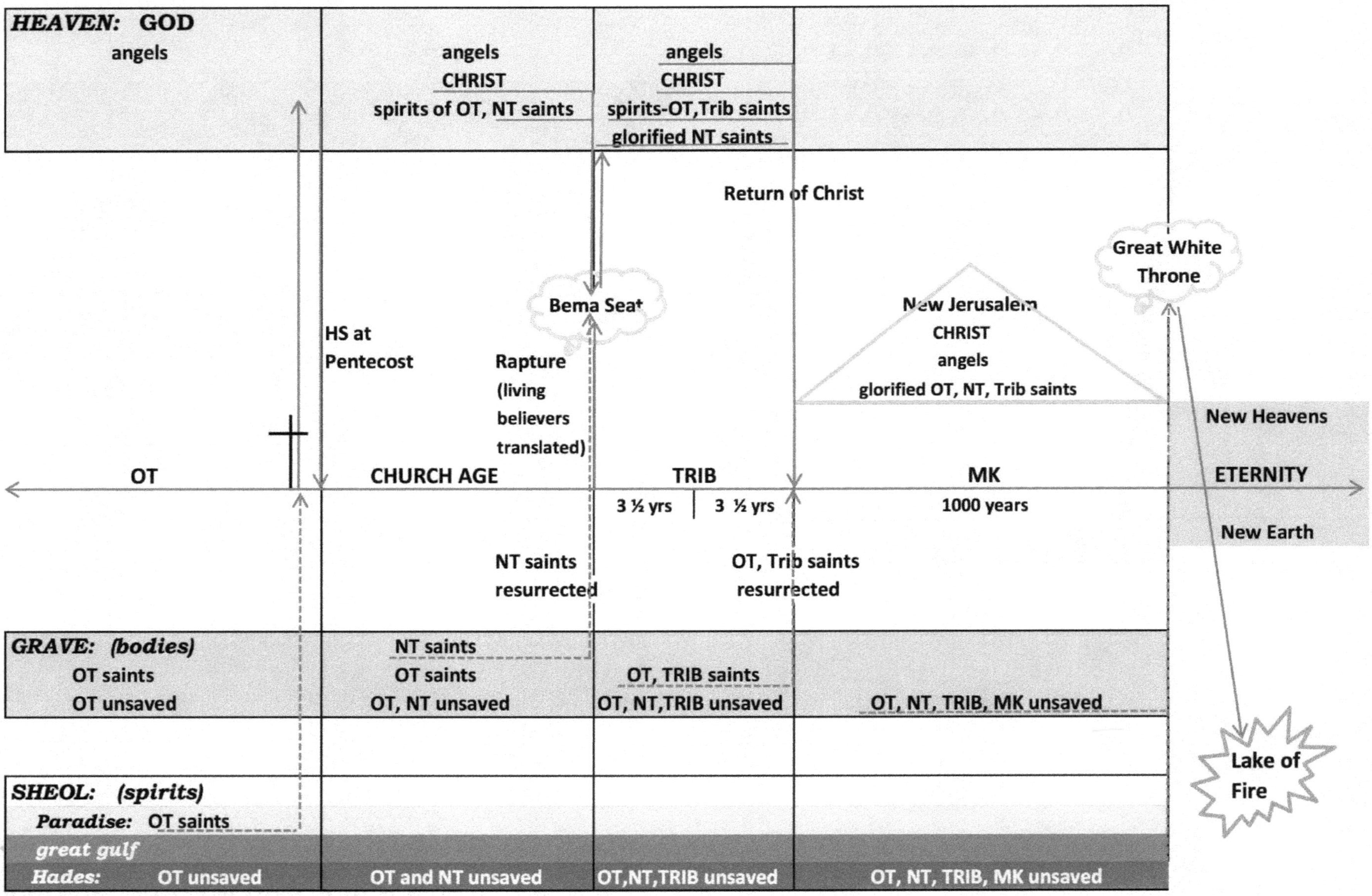

HEAVEN: GOD
angels

	angels	angels	New Jerusalem
	CHRIST	CHRIST	CHRIST
	spirits of OT, NT saints	spirits-OT, Trib saints	angels
		glorified NT saints	glorified OT, NT, Trib saints

- HS at Pentecost
- Rapture (living believers translated)
- Bema Seat
- Return of Christ
- Great White Throne
- New Heavens
- **ETERNITY**
- New Earth
- Lake of Fire

OT	CHURCH AGE	TRIB	MK
		3 ½ yrs | 3 ½ yrs	1000 years

- NT saints resurrected
- OT, Trib saints resurrected

GRAVE: (bodies)
OT saints
OT unsaved

	NT saints		
	OT saints	OT, TRIB saints	
	OT, NT unsaved	OT, NT, TRIB unsaved	OT, NT, TRIB, MK unsaved

SHEOL: (spirits)
Paradise: OT saints
great gulf
Hades: OT unsaved

	OT and NT unsaved	OT, NT, TRIB unsaved	OT, NT, TRIB, MK unsaved

"Back to the Future"
End Times Prophecy, from Genesis to Revelation
Appendix One: The Best Decision of Your Life

Today, there is a lot of confusion regarding what the Bible is all about. This page is intended to help us clear up that confusion. Take your Bible and read the Scripture passages listed below. Let God speak to you through these verses. The central message of the Bible can be summarized in the following five points:

GRACE (undeserved favor)
According to the Bible, heaven is a gift (Romans 6:23). God offers to everyone the wonderful gift of eternal life. And since it's free, we can do nothing to deserve it or even try to earn it. The Bible says this is impossible (Ephesians 2:8-9).

MANKIND
However, the Bible also says we are unable to receive the gift of eternal life because of one problem: our sin (Romans 3:23). Sin is universal—everyone sins. Even if we were striving hard to limit our sinning each day, the Bible declares that it is not enough to earn a place in heaven with God. We cannot save ourselves because God's standard—perfection—is too high (Matthew 5:48).

GOD
The Bible reveals the unique attributes of God. He is both loving and merciful (1 John 4:8). Therefore, He does not want to punish us for our sins. However, the Bible also reveals that God is holy and just. According to His character, God cannot have sin in His heaven and must punish sin (Exodus 34:7).

JESUS CHRIST
Yet, God solved our dilemma by sending His only Son, Jesus Christ, to earth. He lived a perfect, sinless life. He also declared He was God in the flesh (John 1:1-4, 14). His life was miraculous, but Christ's death and resurrection is even more amazing. Jesus Christ took our sins in His own body so that our debt of sin would be paid in full (Isaiah 53:6). Jesus Christ made the way for everyone to receive the gift of eternal life. It's free to us because Christ paid for it.

FAITH
So how do you receive the free gift of eternal life? By faith! By placing your trust in Jesus Christ alone and not any good thing you can do, the Bible says you will have eternal life (Acts 16:31).

So if heaven is your desired destination, recognize you cannot get there on your own good works, moral life, or belief that God exists. The Bible clearly states that "God so loved the world that He sent his only begotten Son so that whosoever believes in Him will have eternal life and not perish" (John 3:16).

If you want to transfer trust from yourself to the only One who can give you eternal life, then pray to God the following words:
> *"Dear God, Thank you that heaven is a free gift. I admit that I have sinned and that I cannot save myself. I know that You love me, but I also realize You are just and must punish my sins. Thank You for Jesus who is God and who died to pay the penalty for my sins. And now by faith, I place my full trust in Jesus Christ alone for eternal life. I now receive the gift of eternal life. Come into my life, forgive me of my sins, and help me become the person You want me to be. In Jesus' name, Amen."*

Now read John 6:47. **Jesus says that in believing, you have eternal life!**

"Back to the Future"
End Times Prophecy, from Genesis to Revelation
Appendix Two: Destination of the Dead

Definition of Death
Eph. 2:1 — spiritual death - separation of a created being from God
Gen. 35:18, James 2:26 — physical death - separation of spirit from body
Rev. 20:14 — eternal death - final and permanent separation from God in the Lake of Fire

Destinations of the Dead
To help us understand the Rapture, we must first look at the different destinations of the dead that are found in Scripture.

I. Intermediate Destinations
  A. In the Old Testament - "sheol"
   1. Sometimes interpreted "grave," "hell," or "pit" - Num. 16:30, 33
   2. Sometimes means "a place of conscious existence after death"- Gen 37:35
      - **For wicked**, a place of judgment, punishment, shame, and suffering
        Num 16:30, Deut.32:22, Job 24:19, Ps. 9:17, 31:17; Prov. 9:18
      - **For righteous**, a place of refuge and reward
        Job 14:13, Hosea 13:14,
   3. Ryrie (Basic Theology, p.605) says that "when an unredeemed person died, his soul, spirit, or immaterial nature went to sheol to wait for the resurrection of the body at the end of the Millennium"

  B. In the New Testament - "hades", sometimes translated as "hell"
   1. Refers to the General place of the dead - Matt. 11:23, 16:18; Luke 10:15; 16:23
   2. Hades / Sheol - Luke 16:19-31
      - place of comfort (Abraham's bosom)
      - great gulf fixed
      - place of torment

  C. Believers after the Cross*
   1. Heaven - "Paradise" Luke 23:43; II Cor. 5:8, 12:4
   2. In Rom. 8:38-39, we are given the guarantee that nothing, including death will ever separate us from Christ.
   3. Psalm 23:4 assures us that we need not fear death because Jesus is with us.
   4. II Cor 5:6-8 and Phil 1:21-23 promises us that death brings us immediately into the presence of the Lord.

  Scholars are divided as to the two-compartment theory of Hades before Christ's death. Walvoord and others cite Eph. 4:8-10 and I Peter 3:18 to support this theory. Ryrie and others think that Paradise has always been in the presence of the Lord.

II. Eternal Destinations
  A. The Unsaved - *"gehenna"* = Hell
     Gehenna" refers to Valley of Hinnom, just outside Jerusalem. This was the city dump where a fire was continually burning.
     This is the same place referred to as the "Lake of Fire" - Rev. 20:14

  B. The Saved - New Jerusalem, New Heaven, New Earth
     Rev. 21 & 22

"Back to the Future"
End Times Prophecy, from Genesis to Revelation
Appendix Three: Progression of the Book of Revelation

Progressive Revelations

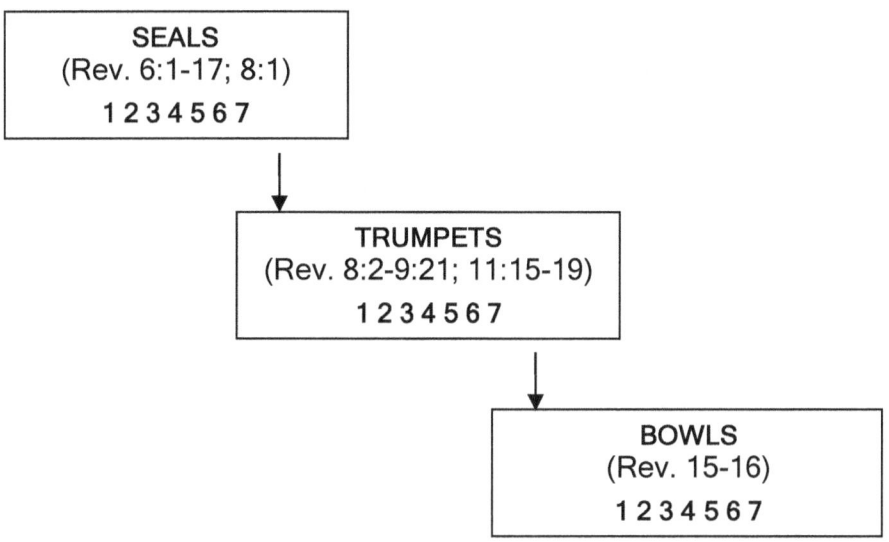

Parenthetical Revelations
view a subject without advancing the order of events in the Tribulation.

#1: Rev. 7	144,000	
	Martyrs	
#2: Rev. 10:1-11:14	Angelic Announcement – 7 peals of thunder	
	Two Witnesses – killed and resurrected	
#3: Rev. 12-14	Seven Important Personages of end-times	

                                                            1. *Woman with child - Israel*
                                                          2. *Dragon - Satan*
                                                          3. *Man-child - Christ*
                                                          4. *Michael, representing angels*
                                                          5. *Remnant of Israel (144,000)*
                                                          6. *Beast out of the Sea - coming world dictator*
                                                          7. *Beast out of the land - false prophet*

                              Fall of Babylon Predicted
                              Judgment on Worshipers of the Beast
                              Martyred Dead of Great Tribulation Blessed
                              Judgment at Second Coming

        #4: Rev. 17-19:10   Destruction of Babylon as a Religion
                                         Destruction of Political Babylon (as a city & an empire)

"Back to the Future"
End Times Prophecy, from Genesis to Revelation
Appendix Four: The Holy Trinity and the Unholy Counterfeit

Jesus	**Antichrist**
Performs, miracles, signs and wonders	Performs miracles, signs, and wonders (II Thess 2:9)
Appears in the Millennial temple	Appears in the Tribulation temple (II Thess 2:4)
Is God incarnate	Claims to God incarnate (II Thess 2:4)
The Lion from Judah	Has a mouth like a lion (Rev 13:2)
Makes peace covenant with Israel (Eze 37)	Makes peace covenant with Israel (Dan 9:27)
Inspires worship of God the Father	Inspires worship of Satan
Followers sealed on the forehead (Rev 7:4)	Followers sealed on forehead/hand (Rev 13:16-18)
Worthy name (Rev 19:16)	Blasphemous names (Rev 13:1)
Married to virtuous bride	Married to harlot (Rev 17:3-5)
Crowned with many crowns	Crowned with 10 crowns (Rev 13:1)
King of Kings	Called a King (Dan 11:36)
Sits on a throne	Sits on a throne (Rev 16:10)
Rides a white horse (Rev 19:11)	Rides a white horse (Rev 6:2)
Has an army	Has an army (Rev 19:19)
Violently died	Violently died (Rev 13:3)
Resurrected	Resurrected (Rev 13:3)
Comes again to reign	Comes again to reign (Rev 13:3)
1,000 year reign	3 ½ year reign (Rev 13:5-8)
Holy Trinity: Father, Son, Holy Spirit	Unholy Trinity: Satan, antichrist, false prophet

taken from Stephen Davey's sermon, <u>The Many Faces of Evil: – Part V Counterfeit.</u>

Holy Spirit	**False Prophet**
Exalts Christ (John 15:26)	Exalts the antichrist (Rev 13:12)
Reveals divine revelation (John 16:13)	Reveals satanic revelation (Rev 13:11)
Seals believers to God forever	Seals unbelievers with the number of the antichrist (Rev 13:16)
Builds up the body of Christ	Builds up followers of the antichrist
Enlightens mankind with God's truth (John 14:17)	Deceives mankind with Satan's lie (Rev. 13:14)

adapted from Stephen Davey's sermon, <u>The Many Faces of Evil – Part VII: The Fifth Column</u>

"Back to the Future"
End Times Prophecy, from Genesis to Revelation
Appendix Five: Resources

BOOKS:

Basic Theology. Charles C. Ryrie.

The Bible Knowledge Commentary - Old Testament. John Walvoord & Roy B. Zuck.

The Bible Knowledge Commentary - New Testament. John Walvoord & Roy B. Zuck.

Escape the Coming Night. David Jeremiah.

Exploring Revelation. John Philips.

The Glory of Heaven. John F. MacArthur.

Living Hope for the End of Days. John S. Barnett

The MacArthur New Testament Commentary Revelation 1-11. John F. MacArthur

The MacArthur New Testament Commentary Revelation 12-22. John F. MacArthur

Major Bible Prophecies. John F. Walvoord.

The Prophecy Knowledge Handbook. John F. Walvoord.

The Revelation. John F. Walvoord.

Revelation: Worthy is the Lamb. Sam Gordon.

The Second Coming. John F. MacArthur.

The Second Coming of Babylon. Mark Hitchcock.

Things to Come - A Study in Biblical Eschatology. J. Dwight Pentecost.

Understanding End Times Prophecy. Paul N. Benware.

What the Bible Says about the Future. Sam A. Smith.

ALSO:

Stephen Davey's Sermon Series on Revelation, www.wisdomonline.org.

"The Campaign of Armageddon," Dr. Arnold G. Fruchtenbaum, http://www.raptureready.com/rr-armageddon.html.

"The Character and Military Career of the Antichrist," Friends of Israel's 2007 Bible Prophecy Conference, www.foigm.org/thecharacterandmilitarycareerofantichrist.

www.ingramcontent.com/pod-product-compliance
Lightning Source LLC
Chambersburg PA
CBHW081219170426
43198CB00017B/2664